Making Twenty-First-Century Strategy

An Introduction to Modern National Security Processes and Problems

Dennis M. Drew
Donald M. Snow

Air University Press
Maxwell Air Force Base, Alabama

November 2006

Air University Library Cataloging Data

Drew, Dennis M.
   Making twenty-first-century strategy : an introduction to modern national security processes and problems / Dennis M. Drew, Donald M. Snow.
      p. ; cm.
   Includes bibliographical references and index.
   ISBN 1-58566-160-0
   1. Strategy. 2. National security—United States. 3. United States—Military policy. I. Title. II. Snow, Donald M.

   355.03—dc22

Disclaimer

Air University Press
131 West Shumacher Avenue
Maxwell AFB, AL 36112-6615
http://aupress.maxwell.af.mil

Contents

Chapter   *Page*

DISCLAIMER . . . .   *ii*

FOREWORD . . . .   *vii*

ABOUT THE AUTHORS . . . .   *ix*

INTRODUCTION . . . .   *xi*
    Notes . . . .   *xviii*

SECTION I
FRAMING THE PROBLEM

1   STRATEGY IN PERSPECTIVE   3
    Warfare in the Eighteenth Century   4
    Foundations of Modern Warfare   7
    Contrasts in the Cold War   10
    Conclusions   12

2   THE STRATEGY PROCESS—AN OVERVIEW . . .   13
    Determining National Security Objectives . . .   14
    Formulating Grand National Strategy   17
    Developing Military Strategy   19
    Composing Operational Strategy   22
    Formulating Battlefield Strategy (Tactics) . . .   23
    Influences on the Strategy Process   25
    Conclusions   26

SECTION II
THE POLITICAL DIMENSION

3   GRAND NATIONAL STRATEGY   31
    Vital National Interests   31
    Instruments of National Power   42
    Conclusions   50
    Notes   51

4   THE POLITICAL ENVIRONMENT OF
   GRAND STRATEGY   53
    Influences on Grand Strategy   55
    Strategic Culture 69

Chapter		*Page*

Summary and Conclusions 74
Notes 75

5   GRAND STRATEGY ACTORS AND
     INSTITUTIONS 77
     Executive Branch 78
     Legislative Branch 90
     Other Actors 92
     Conclusions 98
     Notes 99

SECTION III
THE MILITARY DIMENSION

6   MILITARY STRATEGY 103
     Force Employment Strategy 103
     Force Development Strategy 108
     Force Deployment Strategy 110
     Coordination of Military Strategy 112
     Conclusions 113
     Note 113

7   OPERATIONAL STRATEGY 115
     Orchestrating Campaigns 116
     Operational Strategy: Design Choices 122
     The Essence of Operational Strategy:
        Orchestrating Theater Campaigns 125
     Conclusions 130
     Notes 130

8   ASYMMETRICAL WARFARE STRATEGIES 131
     Insurgent Warfare 132
     Counterinsurgency Concepts 142
     New Internal War 143
     Fourth Generation Warfare 150
     Terrorism 154
     Conclusions 162
     Notes 164

Chapter   *Page*

9   NUCLEAR STRATEGY 165
      Dynamics of Nuclear Evolution 167
      Basic Concepts and Relationships 172
      Nuclear Stability 177
      Current Strategic Issues 179
      Proliferation of Weapons of Mass
         Destruction 180
      Missile Defenses 184
      Conclusions 186
      Notes 187

SECTION IV
INFLUENCES ON THE PROCESS

10   FOG, FRICTION, CHANCE, MONEY, POLITICS,
     AND GADGETS 191
      The Clausewitzian Trio 191
      Strategy and the Clausewitzian Trio 195
      Economic Influences on Strategy 196
      Political Influences on Strategy 199
      Impact of Technology on Strategy 201
      Conclusions 203
      Notes 203

11   WORLDVIEWS AND DOCTRINE 205
      The Ground Force Worldview 206
      The Naval Worldview 207
      The Airman's Worldview 208
      Worldviews and Military Doctrine 209
      Evolving Worldviews 213
      Conclusions 216
      Notes 217

SECTION V
CONTINUING DILEMMAS

12   THE DILEMMAS OF CONVENTIONAL WAR 221
      For Whom and What Do We Prepare? 221

Chapter   *Page*

      Operations Tempo and the All-Volunteer
        Force 224
      What Roles for Allies? 226
      Dealing with 24-Hour News 228
      Conclusions 229
      Notes 230

13   ASYMMETRICAL WARFARE DILEMMAS 231
      Nature of the Problem 235
      Countering Asymmetrical Wars 239
      Conclusions 246
      Notes 248

14   THREATS, INTERESTS, AND RISKS 249
      Strategy during the Cold War 251
      Contemporary Strategy 254
      Conclusions 256

      BIBLIOGRAPHY AND SUGGESTED
      READINGS 259

      INDEX 263

Illustrations

Figure

1   The strategy process 25

2   National interest matrix 33

Foreword

National security strategy in the post–Cold War world has proven to be far more difficult and contentious than in the era of superpowers and their allies facing each other in a nuclear standoff. Today the world is not so neatly divided, and the issues involved seem much more complex and intractable. Serious issues involving nuclear weapons remain and are now accompanied by a host of equally complex issues, some of which involve—or perhaps are driven by—matters of religious faith. The result is that understanding national security strategy and the process that develops that strategy remain subjects of overwhelming importance.

The gestation period for this volume has lasted more than a quarter of a century. It began in 1980 when Dennis Drew published "Strategy: Process and Principles" in the *Air University Review*. The strategy process model described in the article became the organizing scheme for Drew and Donald Snow to produce an in-house textbook designed to introduce students at Air University's Air Command and Staff College to some of the basic notions of national security strategy. Although *Introduction to Strategy* was a very rudimentary text, it remained in steady use in both the resident and nonresident curricula until 1988. Over that period, it introduced tens of thousands of mid-career military officers to the vagaries of strategy making.

In 1988 Snow and Drew produced *Making Strategy*—a new, expanded, and more sophisticated version of their original text. The new text remained organized around the strategy process model first published in 1980. Demand for *Making Strategy* was remarkable considering that although it was written during the Cold War, it was reprinted by Air University Press for the seventh time in 2001.

Snow's and Drew's newest version has been slightly retitled and almost totally rewritten to reflect radically changed political-military realities. *Making Twenty-First-Century Strategy* addresses not only traditional strategy concerns but also the chaotic nature of the post–Cold War world and the stark realities of terrorism, nuclear proliferation, and military conflicts along religious fault lines. Although the authors have changed a great deal in this edition, the original strategy process model, first published in 1980, remains the constant organizing scheme.

I have no doubt that *Making Twenty-First-Century Strategy*, like its predecessors, will have a long, useful, and influential life. The nexus of global terrorism, weapons of mass destruction, and militant radical religious beliefs has produced a dangerous and complex conundrum for strategists. The potential for a flawed strategy to bring about dire political, military, economic, and social consequences makes analytical clarity a priority issue. In this volume, Donald Snow and Dennis Drew continue their long tradition of offering a framework for analysis that provides a significant degree of clarity and insight.

STEPHEN R. LORENZ
Lieutenant General, USAF
Commander, Air University

About the Authors

Col Dennis M. Drew, USAF, retired, is professor of military strategy, theory, and doctrine and associate dean of the School of Advanced Air and Space Studies at Air University, Maxwell AFB, Alabama. While at Air University he has also served as the director of the Airpower Research Institute and on the faculty of the Air Command and Staff College. He holds a BA degree from Willamette University, an MS degree from the University of Wyoming, and an MA degree from the University of Alabama. Colonel Drew has authored or coauthored several books, many book chapters and monographs, and numerous articles concerning military affairs for professional journals.

Dr. Donald M. Snow recently retired as professor of political science at the University of Alabama. He is a past chairman of the section on Military Studies of the International Studies Association and is a Fellow of the Inter-University Seminar on Armed Forces and Society. He has also taught at the professional schools of the US Air Force, the US Army, and the US Navy. He holds BA and MA degrees from the University of Colorado and a PhD from Indiana University. Dr. Snow is the author of several books and numerous journal articles on defense issues ranging from nuclear strategy to counterinsurgency warfare and terrorism.

Introduction

This book is about national security strategy: what it is, what its objectives are, what problems it seeks to solve or at least manage, and what kinds of influences constrain and create opportunities for the development and implementation of strategies. The heart of the problem with which national security strategy deals is the series of threats—normally military, but increasingly semi- or nonmilitary in character—that the country must confront and somehow overcome or contain.

When the original version of this book[1] was published in 1988, the set of threats facing the United States was reasonably static—those problems associated with the Cold War confrontation with a communist world led by the Soviet Union—even if there were signs of change on the horizon. In the ensuing decade and a half, that configuration of problems largely dissolved, along with the concrete parameters within which we operated. In its place is a much more diffuse, shifting, and controversial set of problems that is simultaneously simple, compelling, and arguable. Making strategy is no longer a simple, straightforward process, if it ever were.

The making and implementation of strategy at the national level is largely an exercise in risk management and risk reduction. Risk, at that level, is the difference between the threats posed to our security by our adversaries and our capabilities to counter or negate those threats. Assessing risk and resolving it has two primary dimensions. The first is the assessment of risk itself: what conditions represent threats to our security, and how serious are those threats relative to one another and to our safety? The answers to these questions are not mechanical and obvious but are the result of subjective human assessments based on different political and philosophical judgments about the world and our place in it. The other dimension is the adequacy of resources to counter the threats that we identify. In circumstances of plenty, where there are adequate resources (manpower, materiel, perceived will, etc.) to counter all threats, this is not a problem. In the real world, each of these dimensions presents a real set of issues, which we must acknowledge up front.

In the real world it is impossible to remove risk altogether for each of the reasons suggested. There is indeed honest disagreement about what threatens us and how great different threats are relative to one another and to our safety. During the Cold War, the threat was direct—the avoidance of a Soviet attack, possibly nuclear, on the United States and its allies. Virtually everyone agreed such a threat represented the greatest risk facing the United States and that reducing that risk was the major priority. The only question was how best to allocate resources to achieve that end. Since the end of the Cold War, the United States no longer faces an equivalent threat (even terrorists do not threaten the *existence* of the United States, as Soviet nuclear missiles once did). Much of the current policy debate, which manifests itself in strategic choices, is about what the threatening conditions are today and hence what to do about them.

The other dimension, particularly evident in the military area, is resource availability to counter threats. The collapse of the communist world was accompanied by a worldwide reduction in military spending that included the United States, if at lesser levels in this country than elsewhere. These reductions were especially evident between the demise of the Soviet Union and the 11 September 2001 (9/11) terrorist attacks and were supposed to represent a "peace dividend" at the same time federal deficit spending declined and disappeared. Stimulated (or at least justified) by the "war" on terrorism, additional resources have again become available and formed part of the reason for the return of deficits. The national security argument has been that additional resources are needed to reduce the risk posed by international terrorism.

At least three factors have altered the security environment and thus the problem of formulating and implementing national strategy. The first and most obvious is the impact of crucial events, notably the end of the Cold War and the 9/11 attacks. In fundamental strategic terms, the end of the Cold War is structurally more important because it disrupted the entire strategic environment and required a fundamental rethinking about the structure of the threat, the risks it entailed, and how we should respond. Debate about this "post–Cold World" continued inconclusively for the decade between the demise of the Soviet Union at the end of 1991 and September 2001, although most observers agreed it was an environment of reduced threats and greater opportunities internationally. In this environment American strategic policy was overwhelmingly internationalist (seeing problems and their solutions in international terms) and multilateralist (seeking collective solutions to those problems). Economic globalization was the symbol of the decade.

The other crucial event, the New York City and Washington, DC, bombings, altered the focus of concern, although the change itself was less fundamental than it was shocking and eye-opening. International terrorism, after all, represents a narrower threat to the United States than a potential Armageddon with the Soviets, but it did serve to refocus attention around an intellectually tangible if operationally more elusive opponent. Either stimulated or empowered by the reaction to the 9/11 events, the response was a return to the more geopolitical military thinking of the Cold War rather than the less geopolitical emphasis on economics that emerged as the dynamic of international relations during the 1990s. American policy, with strategy following in its wake, turned toward a new grounding in an evangelical form of internationalism (the neoconservative vision of promoting a democratic order through the application of American power, including force) and unilateralism (carrying out policy without the participation and approval of the international community when deemed necessary). Unilateralism and evangelism are hardly unique aspects of American policy across time, but their combination in its present form is. The Bush Doctrine has become the blueprint of the early 2000s.

The second factor has been the emergence of the United States as overwhelmingly the most powerful state in the world in economic, political, and especially in military terms. During the post–Cold War period (1991–2001), it became fashionable to refer to the United States as the "sole remaining superpower" or, in Secretary of State Madeleine Albright's memorable phrase, "the indispensable nation."[2] A French journalist even coined the term *hyperpower* to suggest the great and accelerating power gap between the United States and the rest of the world.[3]

The distinction was not deemed of overwhelmingly great importance during the 1990s, when some observers suggested the United States might be a hegemonic (supreme or paramount) power but was also viewed as a benign, internationalist power, which consulted its friends and allies before exercising its power and thus not a great cause of international concern. However, the gap has widened significantly, especially in military matters. Further, the growing gap was accompanied by a shift in emphasis away from a multilateralist to a unilateralist predilection that its neoconservative champions liked to refer to as "benign hegemony," but which international critics have viewed as less altruistic.

The third factor altering the environment has been the broadening of the content and nature of national security problems. Although the primary emphasis in this book is on military strategy and problems, one must acknowledge and accommodate the semi- and non-military aspects of policy formulation and execution. International terrorism, for instance, has some military aspects, as in the campaign to deny al-Qaeda a sanctuary in Afghanistan, but it is also significantly an intelligence and law enforcement problem and thus ranks as a semimilitary problem that requires devising military plans that accommodate that reality. Homeland security, which will be a recurring issue in the pages that follow, is similar in nature. As the unfolding situations (at this writing) in Iraq and Afghanistan illustrate, important parts of implementing strategy, such as nation building, have little military content at all, but these nonmilitary aspects of strategy must be successful for the military components to have any chance of relevance in terms of overall goals.

This brief discussion seeks to outline in broad terms the changing environment. It is relevant, even early in the overall argument, because it affects the strategy process at all levels. Strategy making is about devising plans and gains its meaning when applied to a concrete international environment that can and does change. As an example, planning for the use of force in the 1990s assumed multilateral solutions to relatively minor threats to the United States. Most of the new problems posed by that decade were in the general area of "military operations other than war" or "peacekeeping operations." In the twenty-first century, however, the emphasis has shifted to the essentially unilateral use of American force (under the umbrella of a "coalition of the willing") to effect "regime change" against an antidemocratic opponent. The implications for the two assessments are starkly different.

Historically, planning for military employment in the United States has centered around three major planning cases or for survival. Greater accuracy at long range meant increased casualties, placing greater emphasis on medical services and increasing the need for an efficient replacement system. More replacements strained the troop training system as well as the logistical system, including the industrial production required to equip new soldiers. Breech-loading weapons were also used during the Civil War (although generally not as standard issue), which increased the average rate of fire and placed greater strain on logistical systems and industrial capacity.

All of these factors, which were the fruits of the Industrial Revolution, led to the establishment of layers of subordinate commands to control mass armies and the proliferation of specialized staff organizations to provide technical expertise. The Prussians first recognized the need for superior staff work and, during the Napoleonic Wars, established a general staff system that—with later modifications—became the envy of the Western world. Other states followed suit, to one degree or another, but few equaled the system of general staff education and training developed by Prussian military reformers such as Gerhard von Scharnhorst, Augustus von Gneisenau, and Carl von Clausewitz and later perfected by Helmuth von Moltke. Not only had the horizons of the strategists expanded, but also with a general staff system in place, the number of those involved in making strategy or influencing strategy decisions expanded exponentially.

The development of the internal combustion engine magnified the changes in the process of making strategy. It led to the development of the tank, which revolutionized land warfare. At sea, the internal combustion engine (combined with the efficient storage battery) was crucial to the development of submarines, which revolutionized war at sea. And, of course, the gasoline engine was the key ingredient needed to take warfare into the air (balloons had been used but only to a limited degree and with limited success). The advent of airpower greatly multiplied complications to the strategists' world by forcing them to think in three dimensions. As it developed and began to mature over time, airpower also meant that the home front—the center of industrial production needed to sustain modern mechanized military forces—could be attacked directly without the need to fight through the adversary's deployed forces and defense systems. Airpower put the home front on the front line, providing strategists with both new opportunities and new concerns.

Contrasts in the Cold War

The development of nuclear weapons at the end of World War II brought the trend toward total war to its logical extreme. The so-called weapons of mass destruction (WMD) were so potent that many believed they would never be used in an all-out war between two nuclear-armed major powers. The costs to both sides in such a struggle would be far greater than the value of any possible objective—or so it seemed. The fact that such weapons existed and could not be "uninvented" meant that their use had to be deterred, and the only deterrent available was a secure arsenal of nuclear weapons ready for devastating retaliation should an enemy strike.

To complicate the matter further, in the age of airpower and intercontinental ballistic missiles (ICBM), the threat of attack was only minutes away. For Americans, the near-instant vulnerability was startling after two centuries of near-isolation behind broad oceans. Unlike any other time in American history, large standing military forces ready for immediate use were required in peacetime. The strategists were now fully engaged in peacetime as well as wartime and were as concerned with preventing war as with waging it. Moreover, they were faced with an overwhelmingly important question that could not be answered with any degree of certainty. Could a major war be prevented from escalating to a full-scale nuclear confrontation?

At least partially due to the uncertainty of escalation, the Cold War era became, for the major powers, another age of limited war, somewhat reminiscent of the eighteenth century. Cold War conflicts were fought by the major powers on a limited scale for limited objectives and were not fought directly against each other for fear of escalation to a nuclear confrontation. However, restraint on the part of the major powers did not necessarily mean restraint on the part of those lesser states that fought the major powers. For example, the North Vietnamese waged a war against the United States and South Vietnam that was limited only by their means, not by their objectives or commitment. The same held true for the Afghans fighting the Soviets.

The Cold War reversal of the 200-year trend toward total war further complicated and frustrated life for the strategists of the major powers. They were forced to contend with the problem of achieving difficult military objectives with self-restrained force against fully committed, albeit militarily lesser foes, while at the same time maintaining the forces needed to deter (or, if required, prosecute) larger and more desperate struggles against major antagonists.

The end of the Cold War and the collapse of the Soviet Union presented a very different set of circumstances with which American strategists had to deal. Most significantly, the Soviet Union no longer posed a survival threat, and the United States emerged from the Cold War as the only remaining superpower. In terms of pure military might, the United States dwarfed all potential rivals and most (if not all) combinations of potential rivals to an extent perhaps never equaled in recorded history. There was no question, particularly after two conflicts against Iraq (1991 and 2003), that attempting to wage war against the United States using conventional forces and strategies was, at best, a dubious proposition.

In the face of such overwhelming conventional military might, strategists of America's opponents have moved to employ some of the classic strategies of the weak against the strong. The terror tactics employed on 11 September 2001 are, as of this writing, the most obvious case in point. Employed by a radical Muslim group with a worldwide organization, this terror campaign presents problems very similar to those posed by the Vietcong in South Vietnam during the early and mid-1960s. In a sense, American strategists face an insurgency on a global scale, fueled by religious rather than political fervor. Whether or not American strategists are more successful in dealing with this global insurgency than were their predecessors in Vietnam remains to be seen.

Modern strategists must also cope with a breathtaking rate of technological change, a rate that gives every indication of continuing to accelerate. Although the struggle to use available technology effectively or to cope effectively with the enemy's technology has become increasingly complex, American strategists have fully embraced modern high technology on the battlefield. The substitution of technological prowess for American blood is the modern equivalent of the more traditional notion of substituting fire and steel in the place of American lives in battle, a notion long embraced by American military leaders. As a result, vast weapons research and development programs have become essential parts of what Pres. Dwight D. Eisenhower once referred to as the military-industrial complex.

The high costs of high-technology weaponry highlight yet another problem with which modern strategists must deal. As the liberal democracies adopted policies promoting social welfare, greater and greater demands have been placed on the financial resources of the state. Military funding requests now compete with compelling requests for resources in other areas of public interest such as public health, education, and the like. This is a particularly vexing problem for American strategists in an era when the United States clearly does not face a survival threat, does not have anything close to a peer military competitor, and must answer to a citizenry that expected some sort of "peace dividend" resulting from victory in the Cold War.

Conclusions

As the twenty-first century begins, modern strategists have a very full plate. Their horizons have expanded from the narrow confines of the battlefield to the limitless expanse of outer space. The spectrum of conflict with which they must cope has expanded in two directions—upward toward nuclear Armageddon and downward to the shadow wars of the guerrilla, the insurgent, and the terrorist. Strategists are beset by competing ideas about how military forces should be used, how to deal with the complexities of technological advancement, and the importance of military forces relative to other national priorities.

The fundamental functions of the military strategists, however, are basically the same as they were in the time of Frederick the Great, as, in fact, they have always been—developing, deploying, and orchestrating the effective employment of military forces. Strategists continue their age-old struggle to overcome the problems involved in marshaling and using military forces in order to achieve a desired objective while coping with myriad influences, many of which are beyond anyone's control. Only the context of the struggle has changed.

returned to Iraq for the specific purpose of regime change, that is, to unseat Saddam Hussein and his Ba'ath Party cronies.

The two Iraqi cases illustrated how clear and constant micro-level objectives could be in the post–Cold War period. But it is worthwhile to note the ironic twists in both cases as policy makers were criticized for being too focused on the stated objective. In the first case, many later regretted not seizing the opportunity to quickly rid the Middle East of a bloody tyrant. In the second, it appears at this writing that a laser-like focus on getting rid of the tyrant precluded sufficient planning for the near chaos that followed his removal.

Whatever the difficulties may be, the point remains that a determination of national objectives at both the macro- and microlevels is the first and, arguably, most crucial step in the strategy process. Success without clear objectives amounts to little more than bumbling good fortune. This subject will be explored in considerable detail in chapters 3, 4, and 5.

Formulating Grand National Strategy

After identifying and assessing national objectives, strategists must determine which instruments of national power are necessary to achieve the objectives and how those instruments are to be used. *Grand national strategy* (grand strategy) can be usefully defined as *the art of coordinating the development and use of the instruments of national power to achieve national security objectives*. Political scientists often refer to grand strategy as national policy. Although policy is an arguably broader term than this definition of grand strategy, the two terms are often used synonymously.

The reader should note that this definition of grand strategy includes both the development and use of all the instruments of national power (e.g., economic, political, informational, military, etc.) *and* the coordination of these instruments in pursuit of an objective. In most cases significant national objectives can be achieved only through the coordinated use of several (if not all) of the instruments of power. It is also important to note that without coordination, the instruments of power can work at cross-purposes. For a nonmilitary example, consider that federal health officials have for many years supported programs to discourage the use of tobacco because it was a health hazard. Paradoxically, several levels of government (particularly state and local levels) came to rely on the revenues produced by so-called sin taxes on tobacco products to finance, among other things, health programs. Obviously, to the degree that health officials succeeded in driving down tobacco use, state and local governments suffered from revenue declines. The final irony in this example was that a third player, the US Department of Agriculture, paid subsidies to tobacco farmers. Such are the vagaries of domestic politics. Government policies working at such cross-purposes may be only mild and somewhat humorous irritants in domestic affairs; but in national security matters, when many lives and perhaps the fate of the country may be at stake, such policy conflicts are deadly serious affairs. To prevent such self-defeating behavior, those charged with making grand strategy decisions must assign what are essentially roles and missions to the various instruments of power, determine methods to make the roles and missions mutually supporting, and identify areas of potential conflict.

Grand strategy is the highest-level connection and primary interface between nonmilitary instruments of power and the military establishment. This is an important point for at least two reasons. First, grand strategy becomes the focal point for arguments about the utility of military force in any given international confrontation. This was particularly important during the Cold War because the commitment of forces to combat could have led to escalation and unintended superpower confrontation. The utility of force function remains important in the post–Cold War world because, for better or for worse, in this new environment the United States has taken on a role befitting its status as the world's only superpower. But even a superpower has limits on its available military forces. The unpleasant reality that military forces tend to remain in the places to which they are deployed long after the end of hostilities—the extreme cases being Germany and Korea, where US troops remain deployed more than 50 years after the end of hostilities—only exacerbates force limits. In the post–Cold War era, American troops remained committed to dealing with Iraq during the entire 12 years between the first and second Gulf Wars in order to enforce UN economic sanctions against the Iraqis. At this writing,

more than 150,000 troops remain in Iraq months after organized combat terminated in the second Gulf War, with no apparent prospect for withdrawal. Thus experience indicates that
any commitment of forces has the long-term potential to make
a commitment of forces to another contingency situation much
more difficult in terms of available forces.

The second reason a robust military-nonmilitary interface
is important at the grand strategy level is the hydra-headed
nature of virtually all international contingencies. It is nearly
impossible to conceive of the military instrument of power being used in isolation to resolve an international dispute. In
1979, for example, after militant Iranian "students" had seized
the American Embassy in Tehran, thus trapping a significant
number of US personnel inside, virtually every instrument of
US power was mobilized to resolve the situation and rescue
the hostages. Allies and many adversaries were convinced to
support the US position, thus isolating Iran politically; very
considerable Iranian assets in the United States were frozen
and made unavailable for their use; and US trade with Iran was
halted. The public was, at best, only vaguely aware of these
diplomatic and economic pressures. Most of the public only
remembers the failed rescue attempt that ended so tragically
at the Desert One site deep in Iran. Few of the general public realized at that time that the rescue attempt mounted by
the military was part of a much larger and more complex effort. This is often the case. The press tends to concentrate on
military actions. This is particularly true of the electronic press
because military maneuvers and the thunder of guns make for
much better television than do diplomatic maneuvers and the
freezing of economic assets. As a result, the general public is
less informed about political and economic pressures, which
may be the decisive factors in favorably resolving a dispute.

Developing Military Strategy

After selecting the appropriate instruments of national power
and assigning their roles and missions, the process becomes
somewhat fragmented as different governmental organizations
focus on their specialized strategies in support of the overall
effort. Of interest in this volume is *military strategy*, which we

19

define as *the art and science of coordinating the development, deployment, and employment of military forces to achieve national security objectives.* Military strategy, in other words, is the application of grand strategy to the military realm.

As mentioned earlier, the decisions in the strategy process must be addressed for both long-term objectives and near-term contingencies. For example, the United States develops military forces and deploys those forces during peacetime to meet the general requirements of grand strategy in meeting the long-term objective of preserving US sovereignty. The nuclear deterrent forces deployed during the Cold War were a case in point. These forces were intended to support the broad policy of deterring a nuclear attack upon the United States. They were not deployed in response to a specific contingency—although nuclear "saber rattling" was used from time to time during situations such as the Cuban missile crisis in 1962.

On the other hand, the United States also develops and deploys forces as required to deal with specific contingencies and unexpected crises. In these cases, "develop" will probably entail tailoring existing forces in terms of size, equipment, and armament and training them for a specific mission. The forces developed and deployed for the attempted rescue of the hostages from the US Embassy in Tehran mentioned earlier are a case in point. They were a patchwork force composed of units from all of the armed services quickly cobbled together for one very dangerous, complex, and ultimately unsuccessful mission.

It is possible in some circumstances that the development and deployment of military forces will achieve the objectives sought without their actual employment. Such was apparently the case with the nuclear deterrent forces which were carefully developed and permanently deployed at a high state of readiness during the Cold War but, thankfully, were never employed. The term *apparently* is used because to do otherwise would commit the "negative proof" fallacy. Prudence, however, requires planning for the employment of developed and deployed forces. At this level such employment plans are quite broad and generally are concerned only with long-term and very general employment possibilities. At the military strategy level, employment plans might address such broad issues as whether a nation's forces should be employed as expeditionary forces or reserved

In the first instance, multiple iterations of decisions between levels may be required to find a satisfactory match of requirements and capabilities. In the latter instance, results on the battlefield feed back to all decision levels and may radically alter the entire process by changing the ultimate objective sought.

Influences on the Strategy Process

Numerous external factors constrict and twist the straight-line flow of decisions that range from national objectives to battlefield strategy. The list of these external influences, most of which are totally beyond the control of strategists, is almost endless and includes, at the very least, such factors as the nature of the threat, domestic and international politics, economics, technology, physical environment and geography, cultural heritage, and military doctrine. Figure 1 graphically portrays the strategy process and the pushing and tugging of outside influences on the process, but it shows only a few of the influences that form the parameters of the situation within which strategists operate. The importance of any particular influence is situational.

Figure 1. The strategy process

For example, economic considerations are highly significant at the grand-strategy step because budget allocations accompany the assignment of roles and missions. In the same manner, economic factors have a heavy impact on military strategy because of the costs involved in developing forces. However, the economic influence on battlefield strategy is only indirect.

Conclusions

This chapter began by noting that strategy is a subject often wrapped in an aura of great mystery. We have attempted to remove much of the mystery by describing strategy as a complex, multilevel, iterative, decision-making process linking broad political ends with specific battlefield ends and means, a process influenced by a host of outside influences. As complex as it is, at least two other factors further complicate the process.

First, the seemingly neat and compartmentalized steps of the process are neither neat nor compartmentalized. They tend to blend and flow from national objectives to tactics. Some writers have coined such intermediate terms as *grand tactics, low-level strategy*, and *high-level tactics* in attempts to provide precise descriptions of certain situations. Use of these exacting terms is unnecessary if one bears in mind that the strategy process is a series of interrelated decisions rather than a group of loosely related planning events.

The second factor that complicates the process revolves around the questions of where and who makes decisions within the process. Who determines national objectives, either in a broad sense or as they pertain to a specific situation? Who determines grand strategy? One might assume grand strategy would be the purview of an organization such as the National Security Council (NSC), but is that true? What role does the Congress play in those decisions, particularly given its role in providing funding? How is military strategy determined? How do the military services, the Office of the Secretary of Defense, and the Joint Chiefs of Staff fit into the process? The same sorts of questions can be asked at the operational strategy level, particularly in relation to joint operations and the integration of allied forces. Many of these issues will be discussed in chapter 5.

The strategy process copes with the complex context of the modern age and accomplishes the same function as that performed almost intuitively by the warrior kings of the eighteenth and early nineteenth centuries. In the chapters that follow, we examine each element of the process (except tactics) and many of the outside influences on the process in much greater detail, beginning with the political dimension of the process.

SECTION II
THE POLITICAL DIMENSION

Chapter 3

Grand National Strategy

The term *strategy* is military in derivation, and the clearest applications of strategy are in the military realm. Other groups and individuals have appropriated the term as part of their lexicons as well. Thus, there are business strategies, strategies for Saturday's football game, and a host of other usages. For our purposes the term is associated with the broad set of goals and policies a country adopts toward the world, usually to refer to the broadest definition and sense of national foreign policy.

Used in this manner, strategy also retains its essential nature as a process relating means to ends, but the means and ends are at a somewhat different level. Grand national strategy is the process by which the country's basic goals are realized in a world of conflicting goals and values held by other states and nonstate actors. The ends of grand strategy are usually framed in terms of achieving national interests. The role of the strategy process is to provide means for achieving those ends. Those means, in turn, are traditionally described in terms of the instruments of national power. They are usually categorized as the political (or diplomatic), economic, and military instruments of power. The result of amalgamating those interests into a coherent set of means is the grand strategy of a country over time. For most of the first 45 years after World War II, that strategy for the United States was containment of communism. With communism not only contained but virtually obliterated, there has been an ongoing debate over a suitable successor strategy.

Grand national strategy thus emerges as *the process by which the appropriate instruments of power are arrayed and employed to accomplish the national interests.* Therefore, the building blocks of grand national strategy are the goals or national interests that are to be served and the instruments that may be used to serve those ends.

Vital National Interests

The idea of a vital national interest is unique to the sphere of international politics, and it is a term that is commonly defined by two characteristics. The first characteristic is that a vital interest is one on which the state will not willingly compromise. By illustration, the territorial integrity of the United States is a matter on which the country would not willingly compromise; we would not, if we have any choice in the matter, cede any part of American soil. The term *willingly* suggests that there are occasions when the state may be forced to concede some of its interests. The second characteristic is related—a vital interest is often viewed as one over which a country would go to war. Thus, if someone claimed a portion of American soil, not only would we refuse to compromise our claim; we also would fight to guarantee our retention. This second usage of the term is objectionable to some because of its circularity. Thus, if vital interests are involved and war is justified, it follows that anytime a country goes to war, vital interests must have been at stake, which is not always the case.

Vital interests normally do not exist within domestic society but only within the relations (international politics) between sovereign states. The international system has no peaceful, authoritative mechanism to resolve matters that are vital to its members, nor does it have mechanisms to enforce community will when vital interests clash. The reason, of course, is that since nations believe that some things are so important that they cannot be compromised, they want neither the mechanisms that might reach compromising decisions nor the mechanisms to enforce compromises that might be unacceptable to them. Instead, in the international realm, states prefer to maintain maximum control over their vital interests, up to and including the use of organized armed force to protect or promote those interests.

Like all other states, the United States has a variety of interests, some of which are more important than others and some of which are amenable to promotion in different manners. Donald Neuchterlein, in a number of works, has provided a useful way of distinguishing between various interests.[1] His framework is shown in figure 2. In this depiction, "Intensity of Interest" refers to how important a given interest is to the United States (or any other country). The highest level of intensity is to the left of the heavy vertical line, and the lowest is to the right. The heavy vertical line between the categories of "Vital" and "Major" indicates the point where the criteria of vital interests come into play. "Basic Interest at Stake" refers to categories of substantive interest, which are arranged in roughly descending order.

		Intensity of Interest			
		Survival	Vital	Major	Peripheral
Basic Interest at Stake	Defense of Homeland				
	Economic Well-being				
	Favorable World Order				
	Promotion of Values				

Figure 2. **National interest matrix** (Adapted from Donald Neuchterlein, "National Interests and National Strategy," in *Understanding U.S. Strategy: A Reader*, ed. Terry L. Heyns [Washington, DC: National Defense University, 1983], 38.)

The notion of intensity of interest is basic here, and its categories require definition. According to Nuechterlein, a *survival interest* exists when the physical existence of a country is in jeopardy due to attack or threat of attack. Clearly, protecting its existence is the most basic interest the state has. If a state cannot survive, no other interest matters. For the United States, this has meant avoiding nuclear devastation by the Soviet Union, in reality the only direct threat to our survival, even in an age of terrorism where the country's territory, but not its physical existence, is threatened. The strategy problem is how to avoid this circumstance (the subject of chap. 9).

The second level of intensity is *vital interests*, which Nuechterlein says are circumstances where serious harm to the nation would result unless strong measures, including the use of force, are employed to protect the interest. The litmus test for vitality is how intolerable a situation would be if not resolved in your favor, and people can and do disagree about what they feel is tolerable and intolerable. The emergence of an aggressive, hostile regime in Mexico (or the collapse of the Mexican political system due to the effects of drug-driven corruption) would clearly violate our interests in a friendly, stable neighbor on our southern border, and we would act forcefully to avoid that intolerable outcome. When the Sandinistas threatened to install an arguably Marxist government in Nicaragua in the 1980s, there was sharp disagreement about whether that would be tolerable.

Before proceeding to the other levels of intensity, note that protection of survival and vital interests is not always compatible and may, indeed, be contradictory on occasion. The clearest example of contradiction occurs when protecting a vital interest jeopardizes survival. For instance, the defense of NATO Europe during the Cold War could have entailed the use of nuclear weapons, which could have escalated to a homeland exchange between the United States and the Soviet Union that would have threatened the existence of both. Conversely, if the Soviets believed that the subjugation of Western Europe was vital to them, they faced the same dilemma since attaining that end would also have involved the risk of a survival-threatening nuclear escalation.

The third level of interest is *major interests*, which are situations where a country's political, economic, or social well-being may be adversely affected but where the use of armed force is deemed excessive to avoid adverse outcomes. The difference between a vital interest and a major interest is thus that an adverse outcome on a major interest may be painful but tolerable.

The fourth level of interest is *peripheral interests*. These are situations where some national interest is involved but where the country as a whole is not particularly affected by any given outcome or the impact is negligible.

The most difficult and contentious determination is between vital and major interests. Since the demarcation line Nuechterlein draws represents the distinction between what the country should and should not be willing to defend with armed force, the location of the line can arguably be the most basic item in the national defense debate. Indeed, in the difficult debates about defense policy, defense spending, and the like, one can get a rather clear understanding of various viewpoints by knowing on which side of the line participants place different situations. There is little real disagreement over which interests are absolutely essential (e.g., deterring nuclear war), but there are matters of honest difference among political actors about how best to achieve goals (in other words, differences over appropriate strategies) and also about what issues do and do not involve vital interests.

It is the junction point between vital and major interests that is the problem, and this is understandable. In these situations, interests are at stake, and, by definition, various outcomes do make a difference to the United States. Policy disagreements tend to be about how much difference the various outcomes make and thus what one should be prepared to do to protect these interests.

The situations in the Persian Gulf and Central America illustrate this tension and difference, if in varying ways. Pres. Jimmy Carter in his 1980 State of the Union Address, only three weeks after the Soviet invasion of Afghanistan, declared free transit through the Persian Gulf and access to Persian Gulf oil to be vital American interests. What became known as the Carter Doctrine declared that the United States would defend its access to the Gulf with armed force if that access were threatened. As a result US naval vessels have routinely patrolled the Gulf and been stationed nearby in the Arabian Sea ever since, and the United States has gone to war once directly to protect that access (the Gulf War of 1990–91) and once indirectly (in Iraq in 2003) in order to protect vital interests stated in the Carter Doctrine. General American interests tied to the region also caused the United States to intervene in Afghanistan to oust al-Qaeda terrorists who were financed in part by oil revenues.

But how vital is the Persian Gulf to the United States? Certainly the Gulf region is important in that much of the oil we depend on is produced there and could not be easily replaced at equivalent cost. Thus, our economic well-being and vision of a favorable world order would be compromised by certain political outcomes in the region—such as the emergence of rabidly anti-American regimes there. But does that constitute reason enough to use US armed force in the region? Part of the rationale for promoting "regime change" in Iraq was to produce a democratic alternative to the Saddam Hussein dictatorship that will serve as a model for other countries there and hopefully lead to a progressively peaceful, democratic Persian Gulf area. Will this happen? If not, how adversely will our interests be affected?

The political situation in Central America, and especially Nicaragua, during the 1980s was similar and even livelier. There was general agreement that US interests in the area would be better served by a Nicaraguan government other than that of the Sandinistas (although there was no universal agreement as to who should constitute that alternative). The questions that divided the political spectrum were, how much of a problem did the Marxist Sandinistas create for their neighbors and for us? and, hence, what should we have been prepared to do about the Nicaraguan situation? Few argued at the time that the situation was so intolerable that the United States should have contemplated direct military intervention, that is, declared the situation a clear and compelling vital interest. Rather, the debate was over whether we should give military support to the United Nicaraguan Opposition (the Contras), thereby placing the situation astride Nuechterlein's line, either in the vital or major interest category.

Because direct defense of territorial assets has not been a major US requirement since World War II, a great concern has been determining which external situations pose threats to basic US interests. In the twentieth century, the existence of a Europe not controlled by a hostile power or powers was identified as an imperative objective. The US military instrument of power has been employed twice in combat to that end, and the quest for European security has led to the grand national strategy of containment since the 1940s. Northeast Asia (Japan and Korea) has also been considered vital to US interests since 1945 (although Korea was not explicitly part of the equation until it was invaded in 1950).

The fact that American security interests are primarily external adds a special character and source of contention in the formulation of US grand national strategy. With the direct (if ultimate) threat to American territory generally limited to the nuclear case and the limited case of terrorism, the primary roles assigned to American forces—the threats to which those forces must prepare to respond—are expeditionary defenses against foreign powers posing an indirect threat to the achievement of basic American goals. Terrorism and the devotion of major assets to homeland security have expanded that priority to US soil, of course. This situation creates an imperative for American forces not required in countries whose military forces are primarily or exclusively concerned with territorial defense (e.g., while Poland has no need for a rapid deployment force for overseas deployment, it does require forces to defend its territory), but it also causes disagreement. Expenditure and sacrifice for direct homeland defense is a far less contentious idea (although people may disagree about the levels of effort needed) than is the less-immediate, more-abstract notion that a situation in some distant land poses a vital threat. For instance, the necessity of American participation in the Vietnam conflict would have been much easier to "sell" if the US government had been able to argue credibly that the North Vietnamese and Vietcong would next head for San Diego Harbor. By contrast, when the 9/11 attacks shockingly demonstrated our physical vulnerability to harm, the country responded strongly and decisively to the idea of homeland security.

The extended, expeditionary nature of US security objectives gives rise to a more significant debate and disagreement over which security objectives should be deemed vital than would otherwise be the case. Isolationism (the conscious attempt to withdraw from international involvement), for instance, is a stronger impulse in American culture than in cultures more directly threatened by foreign aggressors. The degree to which American vital interests are threatened in any given geographical area is the source of considerable division within the United States because of the physical remoteness of our territory from harm's way. The United States is not unique in this regard. British debate over involvement in continental European affairs during the period when the English Channel effectively shielded the British Isles from direct territorial peril provides a parallel example. Just as the twentieth century demonstrated to Britain that being an island does not ensure invulnerability, international terrorism has taught that same lesson to Americans.

The remoteness of many of the areas of interest to the United States makes the debate over whether interests are vital or major/peripheral more lively and has affected the debate over the relative national emphasis on security and nonsecurity goals. By definition, interests deemed vital require military resources if the gap between threat and capability (i.e., risk) is to be narrowed. Providing the required resources usually comes at the expense of other demands, such as social programs. If the same interests are designated as major or peripheral, the pressure to divert resources to military ends disappears because, in risk terms, assaults on major or peripheral interests represent a smaller threat.

The end of the Cold War has somewhat altered this debate. Since the demise of the Soviet Union, the United States is the only superpower. This status, by definition, means we have interests everywhere and the global reach to influence situations in our favor. Arguably, this expands our global responsibilities and means that more situations are major or vital to the United States than when we were not the only global power. There is, of course, disagreement over how much the United States should extend its interests and levels of activity around the world.

This competition is important because of the reciprocal relationship between grand strategy objectives and the means available to achieve them. To some extent, ends must be determined by less-than-abundant available means; thus, risks must be borne where it is determined adequate resources are not available. Since national priorities generally exceed resources available to fulfill them, they are contentious in the sense that various people rank them differently in the competition for resources. Advocacy of competing objectives is always spirited and generally stated in terms of absolute need.

The post-Vietnam debate over defense during the second half of the 1970s can be viewed in these terms. Part of that debate centered on what objectives should be pursued: where and in what situations was American ability to project power necessary and proper? Given the outcome in Vietnam, many Americans wanted to limit that capability to ensure the United States could not physically get into another similar conflict. At the same time, a perceived erosion in defense capabilities—particularly relative to the Soviet Union (e.g., war materiel expended in Vietnam had not been replenished)—raised questions about American ability to meet security objectives.

The administration of Pres. Ronald Reagan entered office committed to the proposition that the then-current spending levels did not provide the wherewithal to meet legitimate objectives. It secured a large military funding increase to reduce what it considered intolerable levels of risk—what it called the Carter "unilateral disarmament" during the 1980 presidential campaign. By the mid-1980s, the resulting buildup had arguably reduced risk considerably, but public and congressional concern about huge budget deficits and their political and economic consequences had fueled yet another debate over relative spending priorities.

The degree of external threat and public willingness to respond to differing levels of threat are additional sources of friction that affect perceptions about vital interests. The two problems are, of course, related and sequential. If people recognize a high degree of threat, their willingness to combat it through defense spending is likely to be higher than if the threat level seems low (as it did during much of the 1990s). But, since the direct threat to basic American values is limited to the nuclear case, the credibility of other threats is often ambiguous and debatable.

It was one thing, for example, to argue the need for a credible deterrent against Soviet nuclear aggression, but it was quite another proposition to argue that basic American values were undercut because of the violence in Kosovo during the late 1990s. In the nuclear case, the threat was to American survival and was unambiguous and easily recognized. Thus, avoiding its consequences was an objective with which grand national strategy had to come to grips (although people can and do argue vehemently about the appropriate military strategies, tactics, and deployments necessary to achieve the objective). In the second case, there was ample room for disagreement. Although it was quite clear that Albanian Kosovars and Serbs were engaged in sometimes gruesome atrocities against one another and that the result was a humanitarian disaster, it was not so clear whether the situation was any of our business. The argument that intervention was justified on the grounds of a "humanitarian vital interest" in ending the slaughter did little to clarify the debate.

The translation of basic national interests into objectives leading to the formulation of grand national strategy and the factors influencing that translation can be exemplified. Beginning in the late 1940s and extending to the end of the Cold War, US grand national strategy was the containment of communism. The core assumption of the strategy is that Soviet-dominated communist states should not be allowed to spread beyond the boundaries established at the end of World War II because further spread would eventually pose a direct threat to the United States. Originally devised for and applied to the power balance in Europe, the basic containment formulation was extended to encompass the Sino-Soviet periphery, although the primary author of the strategy, George F. Kennan, denied that this extension was his intent.[2] The effect of containment was to draw a line on the map and to declare that any forced change outside that line was a threat to American interests. Whether those interests at any specific place were vital—so that the United States would militarily defend them—or merely major, in which case our support would be more limited, was an ongoing source of debate.

Although there was disagreement about the operational implications of containment and the extent to which the United States should enforce the containment line, there was remarkable consensus for containment in the postwar period. Much of this consensus arose from two related factors. The first was the existence of a clear, unambiguous opponent whose threat to us was equally clear and worthy of combating (engaging in risk reduction). Second, that concrete nature meant that applications of the principle of containment were also clear and deductive. The most obvious symbol of the Cold War competition was military; and knowledge of the contours of that threat logically suggested what needed to be done to reduce the risks Soviet military power might represent.

Disillusionment with application of the containment strategy in Southeast Asia and the perception that détente was moderating US-Soviet relations resulted in less-explicit references to containment as basic strategy through the mid-1970s and beyond. Because the strategy was in place for more than 40 years and was the reference point for a whole generation of strategists, it was a difficult construct to abandon, even after the end of the Cold War. The concreteness and worthiness of the problem and its handling became intellectually comfortable. The Cold War and containment were solid and real, unlike the murky ambiguity of the environment since the Cold War ended.

The international environment has undergone two distinct changes since the beginning of the 1990s. The end of the Cold

War in 1991 (when the Soviet Union ceased to exist) ushered in a decade of relative tranquility in national security terms. The major threat to the United States disappeared, and the United States emerged as the only superpower with no foreseeable military competitor. As the first *Quadrennial Defense Review (QDR)* of 1997 put it, the United States lacked a "peer competitor" that could challenge it militarily for the near or midterm. Instead, the focus of grand national strategy moved to the economic realm in the form of an aggressively globalizing economy and the phenomenon known as *globalization*. The Clinton administration, in office for almost all this period, redirected strategy toward a principle it called "engagement and enlargement," wherein the United States would attempt to produce a more stable, peaceful world order by expanding what it called the "circle of market democracies"—countries championing political democracy and private enterprise economics—by engaging the most promising candidates and attempting to draw them into the enlarging network of similar states. The military realm was relegated to the peripheries, largely engaging in efforts to bring order to chaotic situations in countries of marginal interest to the United States such as Somalia, Haiti, Bosnia, and Kosovo.

The terrorist attacks of 9/11 forced another paradigm change, this time back toward the geopolitical focus that had dominated the Cold War period, if with a different focus. The rallying cry became the "war" on terrorism (the term *war* is in quotation marks because the campaign against terrorism bears only tangential resemblance to the normal definition of war in military terms). The United States divided the world into two camps—those who joined in the effort to suppress international terrorism, and the "axis of evil" and its supporters. Although a comprehensive grand strategy has yet to emerge from this complex of activities, operationally the orientation is captured in the three pillars of the Bush Doctrine: the "distinctly American internationalism" (a preference for international action but willingness to act unilaterally); the preservation of American military superiority; and the willingness to engage in preemptive action rather than only reacting to provocations or attacks. The emerging rationale—based largely on the so-called neoconservative worldview—is something called "benign hegemonism," the use of unchallengeable American power toward good ends, like the promotion of democracy.[3] The American action in Iraq in 2003 is the most obvious example of the principle in operation.

Instruments of National Power

Different perceptions of the international environment lead to different strategies about how best to achieve national ends. Because the international system is one of anarchy (the absence of any authoritative mechanism to enforce values), states must, to some extent, rely on their own ability to realize national interests. It is the mark of a significant power that it possesses an appropriate mix of ways either to convince or coerce other states to act in accordance with its interests in different circumstances. Since the Cold War was a heavily military confrontation, military means were often most applicable to solve problems. During the 1990s, economic levers were supreme much of the time. Since 9/11, the pendulum has swung back toward military means.

The array of means a state has available to achieve its interests is generally known as the instruments of power. In conventional terms, these instruments are generally placed in a threefold classification, although some analysts add other categories, such as intelligence. The *military instrument* refers to the extent to which a country's armed forces can be employed (or used as a threat) to achieve national ends. The *economic instrument* refers to the application of a state's material resources in achieving those ends. The *diplomatic* (or *political*) *instrument* refers to the ways the international political position and diplomatic skills of the state can be brought to bear in pursuit of national interests. Each instrument is applied for the same purpose: to achieve outcomes that serve the national interest.

A range of employment strategies accompanies each instrument. The potential use of the military instrument, even when its application is not threatened, always lurks in the background to condition international relationships. The potential for thermonuclear confrontation certainly served as a conditioner in US-Soviet relations, which forced the two superpowers to treat one another more carefully than would otherwise have been the case. In a somewhat similar vein today, overwhelming American military superiority and the apparent will to employ it is argued to increase the effectiveness of American efforts overall, as in adding leverage to US efforts to broker a peace settlement between Israel and the Palestinians. Indeed, perpetuating that advantage is a central reason why maintaining superiority is one of the pillars of the Bush Doctrine.

At the same time, armed forces can be employed in a variety of other ways to influence events. Some employments are relatively mild and more symbolic than substantial, as in the movement of naval forces into waters adjacent to a local conflict to indicate support for a particular regime. Depending on the objectives and the perceived level of threat, more-active strategies include providing arms to combatants, assigning technical or combat advisers, moving forces forward in the area, and intervening in hostilities. The ultimate application, of course, is direct combat in support of (by definition) vital interests.

The economic instrument also takes varied forms, and the extent to which it can be employed depends greatly on the country's economic strengths. In this regard much of the concern over declines in American world power in the 1970s and 1980s was at least implicitly a commentary on the relative strength of the US economy within the global economic system. As the world's leading economic power, the United States can wield considerable economic leverage. Despite concerns about an economics-driven decline in the 1970s and 1980s, by the 1990s the American economy had rebounded, largely on the strength of preeminence in the high-technology or telecommunications revolution. This leadership provided an enormous advantage in assuming the leading role in the globalization phenomenon. The adoption of the "American model" of economic development during the decade formed the foundation for the policy of engagement and enlargement that was the engine for the American-dominated decade.

The economic instrument is more explicitly amenable to the "carrot-and-stick" approach than other instruments. Hence, economic assistance or preferential trade relationships can be used as positive inducements (carrot) to produce desired behavior, and the threat of withholding aid or using quotas or tariffs to disadvantage trade can be a sanction (stick) if another country does not take desired actions. The same strategy can be applied in other economic areas, such as foreign direct-investment policy, to encourage or constrain overseas activities of American corporations, and in policies more closely associated with the military instrument, such as arms transfers. Cumulatively, economic inducements provide one of the strongest forms of "soft power"—the positive attraction and desire to emulate the American system.

The diplomatic/political instrument is somewhat more derivative and amorphous. Because of the United States' position as the political leader of the international system, its proposals automatically receive more attention and scrutiny than the proposals of a less-powerful country. It is not clear whether US political "clout" derives purely from that position or whether its underlying source is American economic and military strength, which provides the real muscle for our political efforts. What is clear is that diplomatic skill can help turn events in a state's favor. During the nineteenth century, for instance, the influence of the comparatively weak Hapsburg monarchy in Austria-Hungary was largely the result of the diplomatic brilliance of foreign minister Count Klemens Wenzel von Metternich. The ability to mediate successfully and to produce unique and mutually acceptable solutions to complex issues without application of military or economic power is the essence of the diplomatic instrument.

These instruments, of course, do not exist and are not applied in a vacuum. The extent to which a country has military might, economic resources, or skilled diplomats is one source of limitation, but democratic societies in particular have other constraints, especially arising from domestic affairs. For constitutional, statutory, and political reasons, the president of the United States cannot exercise the military instrument with complete impunity in support of strategic objectives over which there is political disagreement. Constitutional entrustment of the power to declare war to the Congress is a limit on such a prerogative, and the War Powers Act of 1973 attempts to place statutory limitations on presidential ability to employ American forces in combat in situations where war is not declared. There are clear limits on these constraints, however. The United States has not engaged in a declared war since World War II, having forfeited the right to declare war except in self-defense by signing the United Nations charter. Politically, the need for public support places some constraints on the president, but these are not airtight. Disagreements about how bloody the war might be did not keep George H. W. Bush from gaining a congressional resolution in support of hostilities in 1991, and the Congress granted George W. Bush virtual carte blanche to wage war against Iraq in 2003.

The economic instrument has similar constraints. The degree to which the US government can manipulate economic assistance is limited by the comparatively small and static size of its assistance budget. Foreign aid has been described as a budgetary element with no real domestic constituency. As a result it has not grown with inflation, causing its real value to decline. The United States consistently stands at or near the bottom of aid givers measured as a percentage of gross domestic product (GDP).

Manipulation of trade relationships is also constrained by domestic considerations. For example, providing favorable trade terms for the import of foreign textiles or other consumer goods is likely to hurt domestic industries and cause internal resistance from, among others, trade unions. Restrictions on trade, such as the embargo against Iraq that the Bush administration sought to have lifted after the war, are likely to result in selective domestic sacrifices against the target population and thus be deemed unfair. In the same vein, the US government cannot order private firms to invest in particular countries nor can it completely control their activities if they do invest. In an age of privatization, deregulation, and instant global telecommunications, the ability of any government to monitor, and hence to control, economic activity has been considerably compromised by the rapidly evolving international economic system.

Several other factors complicate the task of developing strategies for particular instruments of power. First, the instruments are highly interrelated and thus cannot be viewed in isolation. In modern warfare, military success or failure depends to a large degree on the national economic, technological, and industrial base and the extent to which that base can be mobilized and applied to the war effort. At the same time, military spending is a significant part of the American economy, and fluctuations can reverberate throughout the economy (the effects of base closings on local economies, for instance). The country's economic health also depends to some degree on diplomatic skill in negotiating favorable trade agreements with foreign governments. To complete the circle, diplomatic success depends on activities that can be backed up by economic and military rewards or sanctions. In other words, treating the various instruments of power in isolation oversimplifies reality.

Second, each of the instruments of power is, in fact, a combination of multiple factors, and any one factor can be crucial in a given situation. It is difficult, for example, to identify any single index of military power that allows prediction of a clash between two reasonably equal, or even not-so-equal, foes because so many factors comprise military prowess. In addition to such obvious factors as the amount of manpower and firepower available to any contestant, numerous other influences may prove critical. Some of these are tangible, such as the length and security of supply lines; others are more difficult to measure precisely, such as morale, leadership, strategic and tactical soundness, compatibility between physical capabilities and political objectives, and sheer luck. To a great extent, military history is a chronicle of calculation and miscalculation in comparing military instruments and their capacities to serve national ends and of constant adaptation to changing realities. A contemporary example of these uncertainties is the impact of asymmetrical warfare and the further impact of the stunning American victory in Iraq against a foe expected to adopt asymmetrical methods but which simply collapsed instead.

Third, one may speak analytically about the individual instruments of power and their use in various strategies; but, in application, some combination of instruments usually must be brought to bear, often in an ad hoc rather than a carefully preplanned manner. This complex intertwining occurs for two related reasons. On one hand, any given situation may involve multiple objectives with political, economic, and military/security dimensions, and different strategies may be necessary for the various aspects. The extent and mix of actions employing one or more instruments of power will vary depending on the situation and the stage it is in at any given time. On the other hand, situations evolve over time; thus, an appropriate strategy at one point may be forced to yield to another strategy at a different point. The situation in Iraq and Afghanistan illustrates the first factor, and the Iranian hostage crisis is a good example of the second factor.

The effort to dislodge and bring to justice the al-Qaeda terrorist network in Afghanistan in 2001 and the military campaign to remove Saddam Hussein illustrate the way attaining an overall goal may require different strategies and different instruments at different points in time. In Afghanistan the refusal of the Taliban government to turn over the al-Qaeda leadership after 9/11 created the need for a military campaign, first to bring down that government and then to find some suitable replacement. The first phase involved conventional military actions by the Northern Alliance of Afghan fighters and American air-power and special forces. It was successful since the combination of forces left the Taliban with no choice but to stand and fight, leaving them vulnerable to destruction from the air. In Iraq the situation was similar. The goal of military action—variously justified as regime change to remove Saddam Hussein, the destruction of alleged Iraqi weapons of mass destruction, or severing of the connection between the Iraqi government and terrorists—clearly dictated a military campaign to physically remove the barriers to Hussein's overthrow. That was accomplished by the coalition of American and British forces (with some minor assistance from other coalition members) within a matter of weeks, but removing the barrier posed by opposition military forces was by no means the only problem that had to be surmounted for ultimate success.

The second and ultimately decisive phase of both campaigns was the reconstruction of the two states after the war, a process known as nation building. The rationale for the efforts was somewhat different in the two cases. In Afghanistan the justification was to create a stable political and economic condition in that extremely poor country that would make it resistant to future penetration by terrorists—what was sometimes called "draining the swamp" of conditions conducive to the recruitment of terrorists. In Iraq the goal was more ambitious—to nurture an Iraqi democracy that would become a regional beacon and begin the movement toward peace and tranquility in the region.

Military force is, of course, much more conducive to bringing down old political structures than to building new ones. While the US military retains some residual responsibility for maintaining order in both countries until indigenous mechanisms can replace them (a process easier said than done), the economic and political instruments of power become paramount as the nation-building process proceeds. Once elementary order is instituted, the emphasis necessarily shifts to economic assistance to repair and replace infrastructure and services interrupted or destroyed by war and then to bring the economy back onto its feet by providing jobs and income to begin restoring economic normalcy. At the same time, political assistance is necessary to help populations lacking democratic traditions adapt democratic forms to their unique cultural and political circumstances. Neither of these tasks is easily accomplished, and both are ongoing processes at this writing.

The Iranian hostage crisis of 1979–81 illustrated both the interrelation of the various instruments and an emphasis on one or the other at different times during the crisis. Diplomatic activities were conducted throughout the period that Americans were held captive, but they were generally muted and highly secret. Initially, the economic instrument of power was applied through levying a trade embargo and freezing Iranian financial assets in the United States. When economic pressure failed to secure the hostages' release, the military instrument was applied in the unsuccessful raid at Desert One in late spring 1980. In the end diplomatic efforts, heavily assisted by Algerian intermediaries, secured the release of the embassy personnel, although the effects of economic sanctions and the Iranian need for money and spare parts to continue prosecuting the war with Iraq had a considerable impact.

The fourth factor that complicates strategy making for particular instruments of power is the fact that different countries are predisposed by culture, history, and circumstance to prefer greater or lesser reliance on different instruments of power. During the heyday of British power in the nineteenth century, the United Kingdom sought to rely primarily on diplomatic skill to maintain a balance of power conducive to British commercial interests on the European continent—a preference influenced by a relatively small population and cultural aversion to maintaining a peacetime standing army. The Soviet Union relied heavily on the military instrument, partly because of its experience with foreign invaders and partly because a weak Soviet economy restricted its economic leverage. The United States has historically emphasized the economic instrument, reflecting a preeminent economic system and an aversion to maintaining a large peacetime military force dating back to the American Revolution.

Fifth and finally, the relative emphasis placed on different instruments of power fluctuates with time. During the latter decades of the twentieth century, it was fashionable in the United States and Western Europe to derogate military power as a means of realizing foreign policy objectives. Partly as a result of the Vietnam experience and partly as a result of the tremors created by the various oil "shocks" and skyrocketing energy costs, emphasis shifted to something called *economic interdependence* and later *globalization*. Advocates of interdependence argue that the world's countries were becoming so inextricably tied to one another through burgeoning trade in energy and mineral resources and in agricultural and industrial goods that no state remained self-sufficient in any meaningful way. Countries have to cooperate to survive since hostilities with virtually any rival risk cutoff of vital goods. States are forced to cooperate from fear of the economic consequences of not being part of the globalizing economy, much as fear of mutual vaporization forced some level of US-Soviet cooperation. The argument for interdependence suggested the relative rise of the economic instrument among the tools of power, and its champions optimistically suggest that once cooperative patterns become widespread, they may become the norm. This line of reasoning became the mantra of the 1990s, along with a diminished role for military force.

There is evidence, however, of a growing awareness that interdependence has a darker, more-Machiavellian side in which the military instrument plays a potentially greater role. Especially in light of international terrorism, this construct suggests that mutual dependence does not always lead to cooperation and prosperity, as the collapse of the East Asian economies in 1997–98, with ripple effects globally, demonstrated at the turn of the millennium. While few observers believe a recessive global economy will continue indefinitely, the economic experience of the last few years suggests that unbridled optimism about the inevitability of globalization is unwarranted.

Conclusions

As the preceding discussion suggests, grand national strategy making is a process of determining what interests the state has, what priorities to place on various interests, and what national instruments of power are available, appropriate, and acceptable for achieving individual interests and the aggregate of those interests. The process is inevitably political because it involves public policy choices about the relative interests that are at stake, their intensity, and the risks each involves—all matters of legitimate political disagreement. This determination is always contentious, especially in the gray areas separating interests that are vital from those of a lower level of intensity, such as major interests. This distinction is especially important for military strategists because the location of the line between vital and lesser interests is supposed to define where the military will and will not ply its trade.

The number of vital interests a state has that are actively opposed by other states influences the extent of its reliance on the military as opposed to other instruments of national power, as does the aggressiveness with which those interests are pursued. At the same time, the availability or absence of certain kinds and amounts of power may place limits on the interests that a nation can pursue. A small, developing state, for instance, cannot define its vital interests in global terms because it lacks the military—and other—means to prosecute them. At the other extreme, the United States possesses such enormous military power that it can pursue a wide range of interests by applying the relevant instrument of power to the particular problem at hand. The possession of a broad and powerful array of instruments of power is, to a large extent, what differentiates the United States from other world powers and earns it the designation as the sole remaining superpower.

Thus, matching the instruments of power to the interests of the state is a primary task of the strategy maker. What those interests are and what instruments will be available in what quantities to pursue those interests are matters of public policy choices. The choices are made in the political realm, where decisions are made about which scarce resources are allocated to what ends. The discussion in the next two chapters looks at the "political dimension" and how it affects strategy, beginning with the political environment and then moving to the actors and institutions in the political realm.

Notes

1. Donald E. Nuechterlein, a former professor at the Federal Executive Institute, has worked in the Departments of State and Defense and in academia. He is the author of several books on US foreign policy, including *A Cold War Odyssey* (Lexington, KY: University Press of Kentucky, 1994). He resides in Charlottesville, Virginia.

2. Diplomat and Pulitzer prize–winning historian George F. Kennan coined the name "containment" to describe postwar foreign policy in a famous but anonymous article in the journal *Foreign Affairs* in 1947 when he was chief of the State Department's policy planning staff. Identified only as "X" in the journal, Kennan also predicted the collapse of Soviet communism decades later.

3. Bush Doctrine, *National Security Strategy of the United States* (Washington, DC: The White House, September 2002), 1, http://www.whitehouse.gov/nsc/nssc1/html.

Chapter 4

The Political Environment
of Grand Strategy

There is a widely held misconception—especially within military circles—that military affairs and, more specifically, the making of military strategy are somehow divorced from politics. Basic to this image is a notion that any association with politics, which is viewed as impure and even tawdry, taints and compromises the professionalism underlying the military art and science. From these assumptions flows the conclusion that military performance, including the making of strategy, should protect itself to the greatest extent possible from the contamination of politics.

This unfortunate misconception reflects an extremely narrow view of politics. A distinction sometimes made between "low" politics and "high" politics may be useful here. Low politics generally refers to the partisan clash over political objects such as "pork barrel" projects, which aid officials for reelection and other self-interested actions. High politics, on the other hand, generally refers to actions and considerations motivated by the kinds of concerns discussed in chapter 3. Objections to politics as tainting are generally aimed at low politics. The kinds of political concerns associated with strategy are generally over political disagreements about higher national interests.

If politics is viewed broadly as the ways in which conflicts of interest over scarce resources are resolved, the relationship between politics and military power is intimate and reciprocal. Obviously, application of military power is one of the ways that conflicts can be resolved. The absence of more-formal means of conflict resolution that marks the anarchic international system often dictates that the military instrument of power is *the* means by which conflicts are resolved. At least the military instrument is always a potential means for resolving differences involving the clashing vital interests of states.

Put a slightly different way, the reasons for using military power are politically determined. Military strategy is very much an ends-means relationship in which the ends are politically mandated and defined. The role of strategists is to determine proper ways to apply military force to achieve those political ends. "War," as the Prussian strategist Carl von Clausewitz clearly put it, "is the continuation of political activity by other means."[1] Its objective, to borrow from the British strategist Sir Basil Liddell Hart, is to create "a better state of the peace" and that better state is invariably defined in terms of maintaining or altering the political relationship between the adversaries.[2]

To cite the most recent example of this dynamic in action, regime change in Iraq (a political preference of the US government about which the Saddam Hussein government disagreed) could only be achieved by the physical, military overthrow of the Iraqi regime. The strategy for militarily overthrowing that regime was thus the means to a political end, a better state of the peace (at least from our perspective) that did not include Saddam Hussein as the ruler of that country.

This construction of the relationship between military activity and politics is essentially noncontroversial and unobjectionable because it leaves the military profession relatively free of association with the day-to-day manifestations of partisan politics and politicians (low politics). It fits well within the historical American tradition of a highly apolitical military establishment. It is when the notion of politics moves from the so-called high road to the low road of partisan politics that a taint begins to appear.

Understanding strategy requires a more sophisticated understanding of the political environment in which strategy is made and carried out. Military affairs are influenced by, as well as have an influence on, the politics of national security. At the most obvious and gross level, the political process determines how much money is available in the defense budget (which is often the partial product of low politics) and thus what military capabilities are available to carry out what strategies. At the same time, the amount and kind of military force available constrain or create opportunities to realize various political purposes, usually defined in terms of various national interests. The two emphases clearly interact. How much money is available influences what capability can be developed and the ends that can be pursued. At the same time, how much capability one wants influences how much money one prefers to spend on defense.

Since strategy is not made in a vacuum but within the political context, that context must be understood if good strategy is to result. To that end, this chapter essentially explores two sets of political factors. The first of these is a series of ongoing influences and limitations from the political realm. Following that, the discussion moves to the influence of the strategic culture and how it is determined by the country's history and geography.

Influences on Grand Strategy

Viewed broadly, grand national strategy formulation occurs in the context of setting American foreign policy objectives. How to apply military force successfully and when or if force will achieve national objectives is the unique province of the strategy maker—the contribution strategists make to the national debate over achieving broad foreign policy goals.

As a political process aimed at resolving differences and achieving ends, grand strategy making resembles other policy areas; that is, the same patterns of legislative-executive interaction and bureaucratic maneuvering are present in agriculture or energy policy as are involved in national security policy. The difference is in how many Americans are affected by different policy areas and how profound that influence may be rather than in the nature of the process. Because national security involves some matters that deal directly or indirectly with fundamental questions for the state such as national survival, however, the nature of grand national strategy involves some unique influences not present in other areas.

At least six characteristics define and influence the grand strategy process in the United States:

- security policy is potentially fundamental in its effects,
- its objectives are external rather than domestic,
- its objectives are generally negative rather than positive,
- it has a basically conservative bias,
- its problems and solutions are often highly technical, and
- it is more vulnerable to the vicissitudes of the budgetary process than other areas of public policy.

Each of these factors affects the design of strategy and its content; collectively, these factors help define the milieu for strategy making. The reason for delineating these characteristics is neither to celebrate nor decry their existence; rather it is to recognize the opportunities and limitations they present to strategists.

Fundamental Nature

The first characteristic is the fundamental nature of grand national strategy. As noted, national security policy has as its primary objective protecting the country from those who would do it harm (national existence or survival interests, as described in chap. 3). Since physical protection from devastation or subjugation is the most basic national interest, the purposes of national security policy are universal in nature in the sense that they affect everyone. If they are tested, every citizen, especially in a nuclear or a terrorist world, has a stake in them. This universality, and the fact that implementation of security policies is inevitably an expensive proposition, injects a breadth of interest and emotional quality into debates about national security that is absent in, for instance, forestry and fisheries policy.

This universality and its life-and-death quality cut both ways in the public debate. At one level, it is difficult for all but a tiny minority to openly oppose a vigorous and robust national security policy and grand strategy because of the stakes. Underestimating the threat and thus failing to reduce risk appropriately has potentially deadly consequences that do not so obviously apply to appropriations for highway construction; it is a matter of priorities. At the same time, the potential expense of modern military engagement, both in blood and treasure, gives pause about where and when employment of the military instrument of power is appropriate. In the contemporary context, the very low American casualty rates since the end of the Cold War may seem to have loosened some of these inhibitions, but the economic expense of casualty-minimizing technologies may prove a counterweight. The resulting contention usually concerns where the boundary between vital and less-than-vital interests should be located.

External Objectives

The second characteristic influencing the grand strategy process is that the national security policy leading to formulation of such strategy is generally directed toward foreign problems rather than domestic priorities. This external dimension creates three sources of complication in the strategy process.

The first source concerns knowledge. Foreign governments and their policy makers are the objects of security policy, and strategists and policy makers are likely to have less knowledge about what motivates and influences them than is the case in domestic politics. Rather than using direct means to acquire knowledge about problems and their solutions, US decision makers usually have to use less-direct means, such as intelligence gathering and analysis, sometimes without a presence on the ground. These sources inevitably are less than perfect in terms of the information collected, and interpretation of imperfect information may be adversely affected by cultural and other biases.

The post–Iraq War dispute over whether Saddam Hussein possessed weapons of mass destruction, and if he did, in what quantities, illustrates this problem. The United States had not had an embassy in Baghdad since the first Persian Gulf War, and thus lacked the critical ability to develop a reliable intelligence network within the country that could definitively answer the questions. Instead, it had to rely on what proved to be less than totally reliable information, some of which proved simply to be false. These failures compromised some postwar analyses of the objectives of the invasion.

The second source of complication is the fact that national security strategies are directed toward adversaries or potential enemies, not friends and allies. This means that policy options are generally delineated and discussed in an atmosphere of suspicion and distrust. As a result, assessments of defense policy are made in a contentious atmosphere of presumed hostile intent, where facts are often beclouded and their interpretation is open to varying analyses. When Saddam Hussein denied that Iraq possessed WMD stores on the eve of the invasion, the virtually automatic response, rightly or wrongly, was to dismiss his demurral out of hand.

The classic debate over capabilities and intentions further illustrates this phenomenon. As a general rule, US intelligence capabilities provide the government with rather precise information on the military capabilities of adversaries but usually provide only a limited idea about why they possess those capabilities (the adversaries' intended use for those capabilities). Since armaments can be, and are, possessed for a variety of reasons, determining an adversary's intention is a logical prerequisite to fashioning policies to deflect threats and to reduce risk. But with complete information regarding only half of the intentions-capabilities tandem, the problem becomes a dilemma: can one infer an adversary's intentions from capabilities alone or must one know the adversary's intentions to make any sense of the capabilities presumably developed to support those purposes? The situation is aggravated by the knowledge that any number of intentions can underlie a given capability and that an adversary is not likely to reveal his intentions to the "enemy." To make matters worse, the suspicions that create an adversarial relationship in the first place can result in a tendency to dismiss as propaganda any enemy statements of intent that are not totally malevolent.

The 2003 debate about why the Democratic People's Republic of Korea (DPRK or North Korea) announced its intention to arm itself with nuclear weapons illustrates this point. Although the United States knew with some precision whether the DPRK could build such weapons and at what rates of production, why they would do so was less clear. Since the DPRK had been an adversary since 1950, the first inclination was to assume they were arming themselves with the intent to use nuclear weapons in a future regional conflict or even against the US homeland. Two alternate explanations were that such weapons might be a deterrent against an Iraq-style US invasion or that the mere threat to build them was designed to reactivate negotiations between North Korea and the West. Which interpretation was correct? In the opaqueness of adversarial relations, the tendency was to accept the most dire, negative explanation.

The third source of difficulty arising from dealing with foreign problems is control. Not only do we not always know the intentions of our adversaries, it is not always possible to anticipate and hence deter actions harmful to our interests. The

United States would have preferred that India and Pakistan not demonstrate their nuclear capabilities by testing weapons in 1998. Due to intelligence failures, the United States had little forewarning of the imminence of the "nuclearization" of the subcontinent; and even if we had, it is not clear what we could have done to prevent the event. One purpose of strategy is to *influence* foreign governments not to do things harmful to our interests, but we do not *control* events outside our borders. Major uncertainties do arise and cannot always be anticipated and deflected.

Negative Objectives

These uncertainties are compounded by the third influence on strategy—grand strategy has a basically negative purpose. Often the purpose of national security policy is not so much to promote positive goals as it is to prevent others from engaging in hostile, harmful actions. There are, of course, situations where policy is intended to promote positive purposes, as in nurturing democratization or economic reform in Third World countries. Even then the reasons underlying positive policies may be preventative, as in making a society less permeable for hostile elements such as terrorists—the current centerpiece of democracy promotion in the Middle East. Thus, security policy often seeks to keep things from happening, and problems exist in demonstrating the success of a negative policy. If the purpose is to deter hostile action against our interests, we can clearly demonstrate that the policy failed if the adversary carries out the action we sought to prevent. Unfortunately, it is logically impossible to conclude that the failure to carry out the action was the result of our strategy. A state may choose not to act for a variety of reasons, only one of which may be our deterrence strategy. To prove the success of a deterrence strategy requires committing what, in formal logic, is known as the fallacy of affirming the consequent. An example from the Cold War may clarify this anomaly.

The Soviets maintained massive conventional and nuclear forces (capabilities) that could have been used for an invasion of Western Europe throughout the Cold War period. The adversarial relationship between the United States and its European allies and the Soviet Union suggested that these forces might have been intended for such an attack. The policy problem for the United States and its allies was to deter the Soviets from carrying out this presumed intent. The policy solution was the containment strategy implemented by the NATO alliance that included a high degree of military readiness in Europe.

The most important question about containment and the military strategies implementing it was, did it work? The Soviets never invaded NATO countries, but can their failure to do so during the 40-plus years of the Cold War be attributed to US deterrent policy and force posture? Perversely enough, the question could have been answered definitively only if the Soviets had invaded Western Europe. In that event, containment policy would obviously have failed.

Since an invasion did not occur, is it possible to conclude that the containment strategy was successful? Unfortunately for analysis and evaluation, the answer is no. Why? The answer is that there are any number of reasons that might explain the Soviets' lack of aggression, and US containment strategy is only one. The most prominent alternative explanation is that the Soviets were simply not interested in conquering and then having to occupy Europe. There is no reliable way to know which explanation was the correct one. The Soviets maintained that they did not harbor such an intention, but it is the perverse nature of adversarial relations that we always assumed they must have been lying. You cannot trust your enemies, and if you can trust them, they must not be the enemy.

Conservative Bias

The first three factors combine to help define a fourth characteristic—a built-in conservative bias in defense strategy making. In the absence of definitive knowledge of what motivates adversaries and in view of the potentially cataclysmic results of guessing wrong, the natural and quite prudent policy is to play it safe—to hedge bets by preparing for the largest number of conceivable contingencies; that is, to reduce as many potential risks as possible. The result may be a higher level of military preparedness than would be the case under more-optimistic planning assumptions. The problem is exacerbated in the current climate of uncertainty about current and future threats.

During the Cold War the adversary was known, including the threats and risks inherent in different courses of action. The result was that strategizing and force planning were *threat-based*, measured and crafted against a concrete object. In the current environment of shifting threats and future uncertainties, there is no standard against which to plan. The result has been to develop strategies and forces based upon technological possibilities for military capacity, or *capability-based* planning. Since the range of potential threats in such an environment is only limited by the imagination, such strategy development is potentially very costly.

The operational manifestation of this conservative bias is the worst-case planning syndrome. In essence the worst case is devised by looking at a scenario combining estimates of adversary capability (constructed by extrapolating somewhat beyond known capability) with the most malevolent intention. Strategies and forces are then developed to counter the worst case. The assumption is that configurations adequate to thwart the worst-possible contingency will also be effective in lesser situations. Lacking a concrete worst case after the implosion of communism in 1991, the Defense Department devised a hypothetical worst case in the early 1990s—simultaneous medium-size wars with Iraq and North Korea.

There are, however, at least four drawbacks to this conservative bias and its manifestation, worst-case planning. First, constructing the worst case risks exaggerating the threat beyond what it may actually be or even have the realistic likelihood of becoming. If the worst case fails to materialize in anything like its predicted form, its proponents are likely to be accused of "crying wolf." This criticism has been raised about the color-coded terrorist alert system devised by the Department of Homeland Security. Second, when worst-case preparations indeed exceed the capability and intent of the actual or potential adversaries, they may seem unduly provocative and may make matters worse by raising warning signals in the minds of those potential adversaries about our intentions. Third, preparing for the most stressful possible contingency is almost always more expensive than preparing for lesser prob-

lems; the longer the worst case does not arise (possibly because of the preparations), the greater the pressure to reduce
costs because of a growing belief the threat is not lively. Fourth
and finally, preparing for the worst case can presume that doing so readies one for lesser cases as well, but this is only if
those cases are analogous to the worst case. If lesser contingencies are not microcosms of the worst case, the results can
be irrelevant preparations that delude us into believing we can
do things we cannot, in fact, do. The most obvious example of
the fallacy of the lesser-included case was in Vietnam, where
it was presumed at the outset that a force prepared to confront a much more formidable, heavily armed Soviet adversary
would have little trouble against an apparently less-fearsome
Vietcong and North Vietnamese opponent.

Technological Nature

The fifth influence is technological. Spurred primarily by
enormous increases in the sophistication and applications
of computer and related telecommunications technologies, a
qualitative revolution has taken place in the lethality of weapon
systems rivaling such earlier innovations as the tank and the
airplane in its impact on warfare thinking. This revolution extends across the spectrum of weaponry and has elevated the
importance of technological processes within the strategy-making
process to the point that, in some instances, technological possibility has become the primary determinant of strategy.

The effect of technology on strategy is paradoxical, complex,
and too extensive for detailed consideration here. It can, however, be exemplified in two contemporary ways: the revolution
in military affairs (RMA) and resultant gap between those who
have undergone the RMA and those who have not, and the
impact on strategic thinking that this imbalance creates for
strategy and counterstrategy.

The current major change in the technological nature of warfare is the result of the so-called RMA. Such quantum changes
occur from time to time in military affairs and give the possessor enormous advantages on the battlefield over the non-
possessor. This was clearly the case in nineteenth- and early
twentieth-century Europe, when a series of technologies deriving

from such inventions as the internal combustion engine (for cars, trucks, tanks, heavier-than-air aircraft, and the like) and batteries (for submarines) removed the advantages that earlier advances in warfare, notably firepower, had conferred on the defender.

The present RMA is proving to be of the same order of magnitude as that which began at the beginning of the last century. Its base is high technology, notably advances in the rapidly unifying areas of computation and telecommunications and their application to warfare. The examples are numerous and familiar: battlefield management through real-time television images recorded and transmitted to remote command posts; advances in munitions range and accuracy that allow the possessors to rain violence on opponents with great precision while outside the adversary's response range and to selectively destroy targets, thus reducing collateral damage; and the ability to coordinate the rapid movement of diverse force elements over large areas in ways that bewilder the opponent. Much of the "shock and awe" of the American attack against Iraq derived from these kinds of technological applications to the modern battlefield.

The genesis of the current RMA is the Vietnam conflict, where computers were first widely introduced into the military. At that time the implications of the new technologies had not been fully realized (for instance, the idea that computers could serve as communications devices was not conceptualized, much less implemented, until the late 1960s), nor had the doctrinal and strategic implications been incorporated into military thinking. In the interim between Vietnam and the Gulf War of 1990–91, there were considerable advances in the uses of computers (especially in telecommunications), a conscious effort to plumb the implications of these technologies for military purposes, and reductions in both the size and cost of increased capabilities related to computerization. The result was a considerably different form of military campaign against which the Iraqis had no adequate conceptual or physical defense. In the following decade-plus, this gap widened even further, as the RMA made American forces progressively more potent and sophisticated, while the Iraqi forces became less sophisticated than before.

There are several direct implications of the RMA. At the most dramatic level, it has created an apparently insurmountable capability gap between not only the United States and developing countries like Iraq, but essentially also between the United States and the rest of the world. While the United States cut back on military expenditures, especially manpower, during the 1990s, it did so to a lesser degree than did other countries in both the developed and developing world. Nor did it decrease its commitment to the application of the RMA to its forces and the strategies for which they are designed and utilized. The United States emerged from the twentieth century with not the largest armed force in the world (which belongs to China), but with by far the most sophisticated force. In addition to having the most technologically advanced weapons, the United States is the only country to have the technological infrastructure to train personnel to use these weapons and to maintain them—yet another part of the technological gap.

The United States' dedication to an RMA-based force has produced the overwhelming superiority in arms with which it faces the twenty-first century. The nature of the high-technology revolution has been, since its beginning, that getting ahead in the race is progressive. Since today's computers design tomorrow's, whoever has the superior devices in this generation will likely arrive at the next generation first and with the best product, and so on. The United States accumulated that advantage in both technology and its military applications in the 1990s, and now it is a matter of choosing to maintain, or even expand, the gap. This physical superiority, combined with the policy intent to maintain it, is of course at the heart of the strategy underlying the Bush Doctrine.

The RMA changes the calculation of military employment. During the 1990s, the official view within the US body politic was that Americans would not tolerate casualties in warfare. At the beginning of the decade, the resolution that Pres. George H. W. Bush requested from the Congress in support of the Gulf War was almost hamstrung by prophecies of very large American battlefield losses (which, of course, turned out to be wildly exaggerated), and the Clinton administration concluded after the ranger massacre in Mogadishu, Somalia, that *any* casualties were unacceptable. The bombing campaign against Yugoslavia over Kosovo, where aerial bombers were required to stay above

15,000 feet to minimize the possibility of being shot down, exemplifies this fixation.

This unwillingness to incur casualties, of course, very greatly limits the kinds of situations into which armed forces can be committed. During the 1990s, that limitation dictated deployment almost exclusively in peacekeeping missions, where active combat was not present. The RMA, however, reduces that problem by creating such an advantage for our forces that relatively few of them become casualties of war. This was first experienced in the Gulf War, where the United States incurred less than 150 losses, and the numbers from the active combat phase of the 2003 war were even smaller.

The reduction in American (if not necessarily adversary) casualty prospects obviously expands the number and kinds of situations for which those forces may be employable in the future. That may, in turn, be something of a double-edged sword. If the fear of casualties inhibited the commitment of forces, the loss of that inhibition may embolden planners and policy makers to insert forces into situations more readily, even too readily. Whether casualty reduction will ultimately prove to be a virtue or a vice remains to be seen.

The highly unorthodox method used by al-Qaeda terrorists in attacking the United States stimulated a strategic debate about the alternate forms that warfare against the nation might take, leading to descriptions such as "fourth generation warfare" and the symmetrical/asymmetrical distinction, a problem briefly raised in the introduction. The imbalance in conventional, European-style warfare capability between the United States and any conceivable opponent is so enormous that any opponent facing the prospect of military conflict with the United States can only conclude that it has no chance whatsoever fighting according to the accepted rules of warfare (fighting symmetrically). The Iraqis learned this lesson so well in 1991 that they mounted essentially no conventional defense in 2003, knowing full well that doing so would ensure their utter defeat and destruction. Given that problem, what is a potential opponent to do?

The shorthand answer is that such an opponent must change the rules of engagement in a way that will remove the American advantage in firepower, logistics, and information gathering and processing, among other things. One way to attempt to negate the American symmetrical advantage is to disperse; avoid direct, head-on engagement; and, instead, pick and choose isolated attacks in places where firepower cannot be concentrated, as the opposition did for the most part in Vietnam. A particularly weak opponent may resort to acts of terrorism as the only way to engage in effective actions, a tactic perfected by Hezbollah in its successful campaign to remove the Israelis from southern Lebanon between 1982 and 2000 and which has been a prominent tactic of the intifada against the Israelis ever since. In changing the rules, it is quite likely that the opponent will violate the accepted Geneva laws of war (e.g., attacking civilians, mistreating prisoners) and will be deemed cowardly, immoral, unethical, and the like. For many advantaged by conformance to linear or conventional rules, asymmetrical warfare will be viewed as less than savory.

The asymmetrical response confronts strategists with a quandary and a dilemma. The quandary is that the United States may have perfected conventional warfare to the point that it has made symmetrical responses so suicidal as to rule them out for opponents. We may, in other words, have gotten so good at European-style warfare as to make it obsolete, much like making nuclear war so deadly as to become unthinkable. There is thus a very real question of whether we shall ever have the meaningful opportunity to engage in the style of warfare we have perfected. In the process, we may well have created an environment where asymmetrical warfare is our opposition's only style of choice.

The dilemma (and irony) is that in creating this situation, we may have put ourselves in the position of fighting a kind and style of warfare *at which we are disadvantaged*. It takes no detailed command of US military history to point out that the only times the United States has fared well in what we now call asymmetrical conditions is when we were the asymmetrical warriors (e.g., the American Revolution). When we have been the conventional warriors facing an asymmetrical foe, we have not fared so well: the Seminole Wars of the 1820s, the Philippines insurgency of 1898–1902, and Vietnam come readily to mind.

The strategic questions that arise from this are twofold. First, is American symmetrical superiority so great that no opponent can fashion an effective counterstrategy? When the invasion of

Iraq was taking place, the Iraqis may have determined that no resistance would be effective or that they could not keep pace with the advance. For instance, they did not mount the predicted asymmetrical urban-guerrilla defense of Baghdad and instead absorbed the invasion and mounted a fifth-column campaign of assassination of American occupation forces. The other question is how the United States adapts to asymmetrical warfare: what is the American *counter*-counterstrategy in the face of asymmetrical attacks? The American ability to adapt to low-level Iraqi opposition to our occupation (e.g., sniper attacks, suicide bombings) is a lesson in countering counterstrategy.

Economic Constraints

The sixth influence on grand strategy is economic. Implementing the American grand strategy, whether containment or some alternative, is an expensive proposition. Although the expense can be moderated somewhat by manipulating the number of places on the list of vital (as opposed to major or peripheral) interests, defending America from a wide range of potential enemies and maintaining military superiority is a costly task. This economic burden runs afoul of the traditional aversion for large-scale, peacetime defense spending. The United States, after all, was founded partially as a reaction to British taxation to pay for forces supposedly guarding the colonies from Indians (a burden—taxation without representation—that many colonists found unnecessary and unacceptable). In addition the American tradition historically was to reduce its forces to a minimum size—and hence, cost—when we were not at war. This, of course, meant that prior to the post–World War II period, the United States regularly entered wars unprepared and unmobilized, but our protection from enemies by wide oceans made this circumstance acceptable. The potential problem created by such a situation was revealed by the near-disaster in Korea.

The current situation seems far removed from that half-century-old era. When the United States moved from its mobilization-demobilization past to a permanent state of readiness—including large active duty forces and sizable reserves—the Cold War was the central reality, and there seemed little choice. It is arguable that 40 years of perpetually high defense spending has caused us to forget our historical aversion to such spending; there is little clamor for

67

great reduction, and the "peace dividend" promised in the 1990s (as a result of the need for less spending with the Cold War over) seems little more than a long-forgotten lament.

In comparative terms, American defense spending is greater now than it was during the Cold War by one measure, less by another. As a percentage of global spending on defense, the United States dwarfs the rest of the world in a way that was not true during the Cold War, when both adversaries and friends spent considerably more than they do now. At the same time, the United States spends less on defense than it used to in terms of the percentage of the federal budget devoted to defense across time or actual buying power adjusted for inflation. Those who argue the country spends more or less (or too much or too little) are thus arguing from different bases.

Large expenditures—including contributions to the deficit and debt—have been justified on both political and more purely military grounds. Politically, the maintenance of military superiority is a pillar of the Bush foreign policy, because it permits the United States an option in pursuing an aggressive policy of both promoting democracy and combating terrorism. In this view potential opponents will pay much more attention to a militarily dominant United States that can back its demands with action than a United States that lacks that ability. Militarily, the more robust the American military is, the better able it is to protect its soldiers on the battlefield, thereby limiting casualties.

The alternatives in this debate over defense spending are thus established. Within the George W. Bush administration, the prevailing preference is for military robustness, with deficits a lower order of priority. The other tradition, expressed first in the post–World War II era by President Eisenhower, is that a balanced budget is the key underpinning to true national security, an assumption at least tacitly accepted by the Clinton budget balancers. But how is this possible? Can the two views be reconciled with one another?

If the primary value is to reduce the deficit, one must decide how; and there are only a limited number of methods. These, of course, include increases in federal revenues by additional taxation (also known euphemistically as revenue enhancement) or reductions in spending. Neither is very appealing because each takes something (income or benefits) away from voters, but reduced spending seems most likely, given the American public's widely recognized distaste for further taxes and the Bush administration's enthusiasm for tax reductions. In the 1990s the situation was enhanced by economic prosperity that brought additional revenues into government coffers and close monitoring of spending.

If the alternatives are increased budget deficits and hence enlarging debt versus reduced defense and/or social spending, which is the priority? As of 2000, about 85 percent of all governmental expenditures were in three categories: entitlement programs (e.g., Medicare), national defense, and servicing (paying the interest on) the national debt. All other government functions comprised only 15 percent of the total. Entitlements are difficult to cut because they benefit a large number of constituents (voters) and are generally mandated by law. One cannot fail to pay the interest on the national debt because of the need to borrow in the future, and much of the "fat" has been removed from the other 15 percent of the budget. That leaves the defense budget, which is particularly vulnerable because approximately two-thirds of it is appropriated annually and is somewhat easier to cut than expenditures that are made automatically (entitlements and debt service). The only alternative is to open the "lockbox" of social entitlement programs for the future.

All of the factors listed thus far influence the strategies we contemplate, adopt, or reject. Mostly, they do not have a direct impact on the operational levels of strategy, but instead help form the outer parameters of what is acceptable and possible. The factors leading to the conservative bias, for instance, dictate that national security concerns will always operate within a bounded set of intellectual ideas. Technological levels and economic constraints will influence what we can or are willing to do. In addition to these influences, however, there is the more general attitude of the country toward defense and strategic matters, something known as strategic culture.

Strategic Culture

The strategic culture of a country is the combination of historical experience, geography, and political tradition and how these help to shape the country's attitudes toward the military instrument of power. For example, previous results from using the military instrument greatly affect current perceptions of the places and ways the instrument can be appropriately and effectively employed. Thus, experience has much to do with how different countries assign roles to military power in achieving their goals. Each of the factors in strategic culture has acted quite differently in shaping the strategy process in the United States and other countries. The cumulative experience of countries is likely to produce a distinctive, collective view of military power and appropriate strategies for its use—a unique strategic culture. The contrast between the United States and Russia—two of the world's largest and most powerful states but with very different experiences—illustrates the impact of these factors.

Historical experience may be the most basic factor. In the broadest sense, how we view our history at war and at peace predisposes how we look at present and future uses of military force. As a point of contrast, history has taught Americans and Russians very different lessons.

At least prior to our involvement in the Cold War, the American experience with military affairs had been episodic but positive. For most of the American experience, military force has not been as central a part of our national consciousness as it has been for other countries living in close proximity to enemies or potential foes. Because of this, war has been viewed as the interruption of prolonged and more normal interludes of peace in which there has been little need for sustained concern with national defense. Because no foreign invaders have seriously menaced American soil since the War of 1812, when the United States has had to go to war, we have historically had no need for constant vigilance or the elevated gratitude for the protection provided by the military. Instead, the United States usually fought in an expeditionary manner, sending troops far from home in defense of extended interests rather than the more-immediate and personal defense of hearth and home.

At the same time, the experience before Korea and Vietnam was one of success. American political purposes were served by the experience at arms (the War of 1812 being a single exception not often acknowledged). From this experience has grown the traditional American self-image of an essentially pacific people, slow to anger but effective once mobilized. We believe in the description attributed to Adm Isoroku Yamamoto when he learned that Pearl Harbor had been attacked before the Japanese ultimatum was delivered in Washington. He was quoted as saying that Japan had "awakened a sleeping giant and filled him with a terrible resolve."[3]

The Russian experience, as well as that of many European countries, has been quite different. For Russians of whatever political persuasion, national survival has always been a major concern, and failures to prepare for military action have exacted a high price. Russian history is replete with invasion and expansion. The list of foreign invaders goes back at least as far as the Golden Hordes of the Mongols and forward through the Polish princes and Napoléon to Hitler. In the twentieth century alone, there were four major invasions of Russian soil: the Russo-Japanese War, World War I, the Russian Civil War of 1919–22 (when one of the invaders was the United States), and World War II. The last of these experiences, known in the then–Soviet Union as the Great Patriotic War, is the most instructive. In that war upward of 20 million Soviet citizens lost their lives, and the Soviet Union was nearly defeated before the German armies were stopped in the environs of Moscow by the Russian winter. The result has been a "Barbarossa complex" (from the code name of the German invasion) that teaches that the Russians must never again be unprepared for war. The slow acceptance of NATO's eastward expansion since the end of the Cold War reflects this Russian suspicion of hostile outsiders approaching, surrounding, and even attacking their soil.

Geography also influences strategic culture. In the American case, once again, that influence has been largely positive in at least two related senses—protection from assault and the absence of dependency on the outside world.

First, the geographic position of the United States has protected us from foreign invasion. In geopolitical effect, the United States is essentially an island protected by broad oceans. Moreover, the United States borders on only two other countries, neither of which poses any military threat to the integrity of American soil. As a result, we have been afforded the luxury of being militarily unmobilized for much of our history.

The geographic inheritance of the United States has also been benevolent in the sense that the North American continent is exceptionally well endowed with natural resources (fertile soil, mineral and energy resources, etc.). Thus, for much of our history, we have been essentially self-sufficient in natural resources. Only recently, as some resources have been depleted and as needs have arisen for exotic materials (e.g., titanium), has the United States become dependent on foreign sources. The idea of defending access to something like the petroleum reserves of the Persian Gulf is thus a far more recent and alien concept to Americans than it is to the energy-deficient countries of Europe and Japan. In short, geography has had the effect of shielding Americans from the geopolitics of natural resources, a major concern for countries like resource-poor Japan, whose economy and prosperity are highly dependent on foreign sources.

Geography has not been so kind to the Russians. Although Russia occupies more territory than any other state in the world, with a rich endowment of mineral and energy resources, it is also physically vulnerable. European Russia is part of the northern European plain that has been a historic east-west invasion route in both directions over the centuries. Moreover, a look at the map shows that the old Soviet Union was ringed by real enemies and reluctant allies from Norway in the northwest to the Korean peninsula in the east. Many of these enemies were richly earned through a series of Russian military adventures from the czars to the commissars, but nonetheless they are sources of the need for military preparedness. If American history suggests that geography is a buffer against military threat, Russian history equally suggests that geography means a need for vigilance.

Political tradition manifests itself in several ways. One manifestation is national political ideology concerning the relationship between man and the state and the proper function of government. The Russian and American experiences stand in contrast. The Russian tradition, under the czars of the Russian Empire and their latter-day counterparts in the Soviet Union, offered a state-centered, messianic, expansionist, and authoritarian worldview in contrast to the liberal democratic, capitalistic American view. Both ideologies view themselves as universally applicable (representing an order that all countries should adopt), and both countries have supported like-minded groups around the globe. The current emphasis of the neoconservatives in the United States on spreading political democracy around the world reflects this tradition, and it may be less than coincidental that a number of the neoconservatives were originally Marxists.

The impact of political tradition is also evident in historical and current ideas about the proper levels of political participation. The Communist regime in the Soviet Union inherited and perpetuated an extremely closed, authoritarian political system that contained no tradition of broad-based, mass political participation. In some ways, the attempt to transform that country into a political democracy is made more difficult by the absolute absence of any kind of liberal, participatory tradition. This tradition contrasts sharply, of course, with the open, highly participatory American democratic tradition.

The effects of political tradition on strategic culture are ambiguous and, to some extent, contradictory. At one level, closed societies tend to be more militaristic than open societies. The relationship between the regime and the military is often synergistic. Since these societies are not based on popular consensus, helping to keep the regime in power is an important military function. To gain and sustain military support for the regime, military preparedness is a higher priority for political authorities than would otherwise be the case. At the same time, the absence of open political debate means that the government of a closed society has less difficulty in allocating scarce resources to military purposes rather than to more-popular priorities, such as agricultural productivity or consumer goods. Finally, a closed society has historically been able to control access to information to a much-greater degree than is possible in an open society, and this has facilitated manipulation of knowledge about military actions. The Orwellian prediction about control of information and regime control has, of course, been reversed since the telecommunications revolution. States that have attempted to manipulate and control information have been more prone to opposition and overthrow than more-open societies. Technology has become the ally of openness and the opponent of suppression, not the other way around, as Orwell feared.

Many observers contend that the need to develop political consensus for military employment makes pursuit of limited political objectives in war extremely difficult for open societies. Explanations for this phenomenon vary and generally have complex psychological roots. The basic line of thought is that unlimited objectives (e.g., unconditional surrender) are more concrete and understandable than are more-limited objectives. Since they portray the enemy as an absolute evil who must be defeated absolutely, they justify the sacrifices entailed by warfare to a greater degree than limited objectives. Put more simply, absolute objectives are easier to "sell" to the public than limited political objectives.

The tendency of open societies to prefer "all-or-nothing" military solutions alarms many observers in a nuclear-armed world, but it is instructive to officials responsible for framing American policy. Of the four major conflicts fought by the United States in the twentieth century, the two (World Wars I and II) that enjoyed more popular support had unlimited political objectives; whereas the two largely unpopular conflicts (Korea and Vietnam) had limited political objectives. In the latter cases, opinion surveys clearly indicated that the public never understood the objectives, hence, never embraced the goals. Moreover, the limited nature of the objectives in the Korean and Vietnamese wars lacked the moral force of total objectives. Most future American military actions are likely to be for limited purposes (the overthrow of Saddam Hussein was an exception), so these dynamics are likely to continue in the future.

Summary and Conclusions

This chapter has discussed the web of idiosyncratic factors that, in effect, places boundaries on American use of military force. These factors are, of course, politically derived and politically expressed limitations that strategists must anticipate and accommodate, because a military strategy that is unacceptable politically is a strategy that is likely to be rejected by the public and thus be incapable of implementation.

On occasion some good military advice may be lost in the process of being weighed against political criteria, and that can be frustrating. The frustration can, however, be lessened by knowing what the criteria are. Other elements that must be understood include actors in the national security policy process and their institutional positions, to which the discussion now moves.

Notes

1. Carl von Clausewitz, *On War*, ed. and trans. Michael Howard and Peter Paret (Princeton, NJ: Princeton University Press, 1976), 88.

2. B. H. Liddell Hart, *Strategy* (New York: Meridian Printing, 1991), 338.

3. The quote, long attributed to Adm Isoroku Yamamoto, is believed to have originated in the film *Tora! Tora! Tora!* (1970) and was never actually spoken by the Japanese fleet commander.

Chapter 5

Grand Strategy Actors and Institutions

Decisions about the content of grand strategy and the resources available to implement that strategy are products of political processes within the federal government. Therefore, a basic understanding of how the federal government makes national security policy decisions and who in the various institutions of government makes those decisions is a critical element in the making of strategy. While the political system may not have a controlling role in the details of strategic decisions at all levels, it does provide direction about the interests the country will pursue and the resources that will be available for strategists to use in the name of national opportunities and risk reduction.

By way of introduction, two aspects of decision making in the national security area should be mentioned: the unique role of the National Security Council system in making and implementing policy, and the more-general political principle of checks and balances as it applies to the national security area.

The system by which national security policy is made within the executive branch of government is known as the NSC system. The basic structure of this system was created by the National Security Act of 1947, which, among other things, established those statutory institutions most responsible for coordinating the various actions of government that affect national security. The individuals who comprise the NSC are the key players in making grand strategy. It is basic to understanding national security policy to recognize that policy is the result both of the interactions of formal institutions and the personalities of the individuals who operate them. Membership in and evolution of the NSC system are discussed below.

The basic principle by which the system works is that of checks and balances. At the formal, constitutional level, this principle regulates the interaction between the executive and legislative branches of government and, when the system works the way it is intended, guarantees that neither branch acts arbitrarily without the consultation or approval of the other. Within this relationship, the executive—the president—often appears to have the primary responsibility and power, but that power is counterbalanced by the Congress, principally through the power of the purse, oversight of presidential actions by congressional committees, and constitutional responsibilities that correspond to and limit specific constitutional mandates given to the president.

The checks and balances system also acts in a more informal manner, especially within the executive branch, to ensure that the widest possible range of policy perspectives is aired before policy is made. This means that the NSC system—augmented in individual policy cases by other agencies where their interests are also affected (e.g., the Department of Agriculture for embargoes on foreign grain sales)—ensures that all institutional perspectives on given problems have a chance to be heard before key decisions are made. When the system works as intended, the result is an effective system in terms of creating the greatest practical level of review and the most likely chance that wise policy will result. At the same time, the very thoroughness of the system often makes it time-consuming and frequently inefficient. As a practical matter, there is always some tension between effective and efficient operation, and this tension and dynamic are even more obvious in the relations between the executive and the legislative branches.

With this very basic introduction in mind, one can look at the various influences on the system. This chapter begins by examining the role of the executive branch, since it is most visible within the national security policy system from which most strategic mandates arise, and notes the checks and balances built into executive power. It then looks at the bases of congressional authority and finally at the influence of other actors, principally interest groups and public opinion, on the process.

Executive Branch

The executive branch of government has the major responsibility for the formulation of foreign and national security policy. At the pinnacle of this system, of course, is the president, whose powers are both constitutional and political in nature. The president is assisted by relevant executive branch agencies, organized around but not limited to those advisers and agencies named by the National Security Act, as it has expanded across time.

The constitutional responsibilities of the president in the national security area are stated succinctly in Article II, section 2, of that document. By constitutional provision, the president is designated as commander in chief of the armed forces, has the sole authority to negotiate treaties with foreign governments, and has the power to appoint and remove ambassadors and other officials. In addition, he is both the chief executive (head of government) and the head of state and is the only official who can recognize (and remove recognition) of foreign governments. This short listing reflects both the compactness of the Constitution as a whole and the relative simplicity of the time in which it was written. In 1787, after all, governmental activity was considerably more restricted than it is today, and the international role of a young and physically isolated United States was marginal and circumscribed, which is both an accurate depiction of the nation's role in the world and the preference of most Americans at the time. Each of these basic roles has changed and generally expanded as the United States' role in the world has increased.

As the size of the US armed forces has increased and US commitments with security implications have become global, the president's role as commander in chief has become much greater. The power of the president to act in this capacity, particularly in the actual employment of armed forces, is shared with the Congress and is highly controversial. Important checks and balances are built into this role. For one thing, the president commands only those armed forces explicitly raised and maintained by the Congress, and only the Congress has the authority to declare war. War declaration was originally a significant limitation of presidential power, but since countries now seldom formally declare war, it has become less important and has effectively reduced this constitutional limitation on presidential authority.

To attempt to retrieve some of their authority over how armed forces are used, the Congress has passed—over presidential objection—such mechanisms as the War Powers Act (which places reporting and approval requirements on the employment of US forces in combat) and the Arms Export Control Act (which limits the size of arms exchanges that can be undertaken without specific congressional approval).[1] In recent years, presidents have tried to smooth congressional concerns about proposed military actions, either by consultation with key congressional members before employing armed forces or by seeking and obtaining joint resolution of the Congress in support of proposed military action in advance; both the Gulf War of 1990–91 and the invasion of Iraq in 2003 were "authorized" in this manner.

The treaty-making power has also expanded. According to the Constitution, only the president or his representatives invested with full power (plenipotentiaries) can negotiate treaties with foreign governments. The framers of the Constitution assumed that agreements between the United States and other countries would be in the form of treaties and, as a result, gave the Congress a check by requiring the president to secure the advice and consent of two-thirds of the Senate on any treaty before it becomes binding on the United States.

The sheer volume of foreign affairs does not allow all international interactions of the US government to be handled through the treaty process. Instead, the overwhelming majority of all formal relations now takes the form of executive agreements— formal obligations between the United States and other governments that have the force of law but do not require senatorial approval. In these cases the congressional check is informal. If the agreement requires spending American monies (they usually do), the Congress can exercise the powers of the purse and effectively veto the agreement by not providing the funds necessary to implement it. If there is no funding involved in what the Congress thinks is an obnoxious agreement, it can retaliate against the president in some other area of public policy.

The third presidential power is the authority to appoint and remove officials. The advantage this confers to presidents is in helping to ensure the loyalty of key decision makers and implementers of policy. The power to appoint allows presidents to name to important positions people who share their views, and the power to remove assures continuing loyalty. Originally, the Constitution envisaged that this authority would apply mainly to ambassadors, but as the power and size of the federal government have expanded, so have the numbers of important officials who work for the president. Now literally thousands of so-called political appointees (presidential appointees who do not have civil service protection and thus serve at the pleasure of the president) are named at the senior- and middle-management levels of various cabinet and other agencies.

Once again there is a congressional check in that almost all important presidential appointments require confirmation by the Senate. The confirmation process does not encompass the personal staff of presidents, including the professional staff of the NSC and other parts of the White House Office. The Congress, which does not have the time or resources to examine all appointees exhaustively, uses the check selectively and thus reserves its detailed consideration for controversial positions and individuals.

The president is designated as both the chief executive (or head of government) and head of state. As head of government, the president is effectively the chief executive officer (CEO) of the executive branch of the government and is responsible for formulating the policies of that government. Because of his position as CEO, essentially the entire federal bureaucracy "works for" the president. At the same time, his role as formulator of policy makes him the leading partisan politician in the country. This designation often clashes with his largely ceremonial position as head of state. In that role, he is the leading political symbol of the United States, a position not unlike the role of the Queen (or King) of England.

These two designations often create some difficulty in how we deal with presidents. In systems like that of Great Britain, the two roles are separated, and their positions thus differently defined. The British prime minister is head of the governing party, is viewed (quite correctly) as the leading partisan politician in the country, and has his or her policies and person criticized as such with no notion that doing so somehow injures Great Britain. That is because the Queen, who does not engage in any partisan activity, serves as the rallying point for the country, the symbol of the British Empire. Thus, British citizens can hate and berate the prime minister but still not deride the crown.

It is more confusing in our system, where we fuse the two roles into one position and person. When someone criticizes the president as a partisan politician with whom they disagree, are they also besmirching the presidency as the symbol of the country? This was an issue during the impeachment of former president Richard M. Nixon. Many Americans, regardless of whether they thought Nixon was guilty of the charges against him, opposed impeachment on the grounds that impeaching the man would also degrade the office.

Sixth, and finally, the president is the recognizer of foreign governments. This power technically derives from Article II, section 3 of the Constitution, which deals directly with receiving "Ambassadors and other Public Ministers." Since these officials are representatives of their governments, either accepting or rejecting them has the effect of extending or denying recognition and approval to the governments they represent. Although this power is seldom used (the refusal to recognize the government of the People's Republic of China between 1949 and 1972 was a major exception), it is a potentially significant power, since it can be wielded without congressional action.

If the constitutional prerogatives of presidents convey power, their political powers can be even more impressive. Presidential political powers are in areas that are not subject to congressional checks and balances and thus can yield advantages over the Congress. At least six such powers stand out.

The first is presidential singularity. The president is the only nationally elected official. Thus, a president is the only politician with a national constituency and the only person who can legitimately claim to be the representative of and speaker for "all the people." By contrast senators and representatives can only speak for their states or districts. As a consequence, their individual views are generally not accorded the same weight as that of the president. It is no coincidence that presidents get their busts chiseled into Mount Rushmore; members of the Congress do not.

The second advantage presidents have is that, at least nominally, the entire federal bureaucracy works for them. Although presidents rapidly learn the limits of their control over elements of the bureaucratic structures (especially those structures run by people with civil service protection), the advantage in terms of access to information and expertise on the range of public matters is great, since the resources available to the Congress are considerably smaller.

The third advantage is the mantle of office. Simply occupying the presidency bestows prestige, credibility, and deference to the holder of the office. As the political leader of the world's most powerful country, the president is automatically a world leader whose opinions and actions have global consequences. Aside from the simple prestige this provides, the position means presidents routinely have access to other world leaders and as a result can claim more personal, even intimate, knowledge of such contemporaries than any other American official. At the same time, what presidents do and say is important simply because they are presidents.

The importance of the presidency and its occupants leads to a fourth advantage—unparalleled access to the electronic and print media. Whatever any president does is news. There is an entire White House press corps whose livelihood and success are based on its surmises about presidents. If a president wants publicity for a position that he does not wish to officially endorse, all he has to do is wander down to the pressroom, declare his remarks off the record (at which point the president becomes a "well-placed spokesman" or the like), and the total resources of the electronic and print media are at his beck and call.

Fifth, presidential power in the national security area has been enhanced by de facto delegation of authority from the Congress. With certain high-profile exceptions, the Congress does not enmesh itself in the day-to-day workings of national security policy, and with good reason. For one thing, national security affairs are almost invariably complex and multifaceted, and most members of the Congress have neither the expertise nor the interest to follow them in-depth. For another, the sheer volume of national security affairs is beyond the capabilities of congressional scrutiny, especially since the Congress must consider public affairs across the range of public policy areas. Many security problems are time-sensitive as well. The structure and nature of the Congress are best suited to situations that allow thorough deliberation and debate, both of which are time-consuming. National security situations often move faster than the pace of congressional debate so that a president must act after only informal consultation with the leaders of the houses of the Congress and the chairpersons of relevant committees. Since national security matters often involve physical danger to the country or to American citizens, the public is likely to turn, in times of crisis, to the national leader—the president.

A sixth advantage of the president is his ability to issue presidential doctrines. While these statements of policy have no real binding authority attached to them, they are nonetheless important statements of the policy preferences of the presidents who declare them, and they have proven difficult positions for subsequent presidents to renounce or downgrade, even if they may personally disagree with them.

Not all presidents issue doctrinal statements, but those who have are remembered for them. The most famous is the Monroe Doctrine (1823), of course, which has guided US policy toward Latin America (no colonization or interference in the Western Hemisphere) for nearly two centuries.[2] More recently, the Carter Doctrine of 1980, by declaring US access to Persian Gulf oil to be a vital interest, has been a standard that subsequent presidents have all given homage to as the basis of policy in that region.[3] Most recently, the Bush Doctrine—American military superiority, preference for multilateral action but the willingness to act unilaterally, and the assertion of a right to take preemptive action—has set the grounding for American security policy. Its endurance may be as great as the Monroe Doctrine or as fleeting as the Nixon Doctrine of 1969 (which specified in what limited cases the United States would come to the physical aid of beleaguered Third World states during the Cold War).[4]

The cumulative effect of the president's constitutional and political position is effective political dominance of the national security system. Generally speaking, presidential advantage has been expanding throughout the period since World War II. Before that war, foreign and security policies were relatively uncomplicated. The chief, and virtually sole, institution responsible for carrying out US foreign policy was the State Department. Concerns that we now routinely label as national security considerations were of comparatively minor importance.

The emergence of the United States as a major world power in competition with the Soviet Union after the war changed that. Clearly, a major motif of that postwar competition was military.

As a result the national security implications of foreign policy became more important, and the terms *foreign policy* and *national security policy* came to be used more or less interchangeably.

This change in orientation was recognized statutorily and organizationally in the National Security Act of 1947. In addition to creating an independent Air Force, the Central Intelligence Agency (CIA), and the Department of Defense (DOD), the act provided a structure within which to fashion national security policy: the National Security Council. The statutory members of the council are the president (who convenes it and serves as chair), the vice president, the secretary of state, and the secretary of defense. The president may appoint additional members, and the act specifies that the director of Central Intelligence (DCI) and the chairman of the Joint Chiefs of Staff (CJCS) serve as advisers to the NSC. Finally, the act contains the provision for a professional staff to coordinate the council's activities. The position of national security adviser (NSA) evolved from this provision.

The institutional complexity and inclusiveness of the NSC system began to expand during the Eisenhower administration, assuming a form resembling its present parameters during the 1980s and 1990s, and is now often referred to as the interagency process. In addition to the NSC itself, the system has three additional formal sets of institutions of descending authority. Directly below the NSC is the Principals Committee (PC). It is composed of the same members as the NSC itself, except that the president is not physically present at these meetings. The reasons for convening the NSC as the PC include providing a forum for matters not important enough to require presidential presence or to provide a forum for frank exchange of views that might be less candid if the principals were concerned about pleasing the president (this use was invoked by John F. Kennedy during the Cuban missile crisis; the PC was then called the Executive Committee or ExComm).

Directly below the PC is the Deputies Committee (DC). As the name implies, the members are the principal deputies of the major members of the NSC/PC. Their job is to handle details of policy recommendations going up to the NSC/PC or to begin implementation of decisions reached from above. At the bottom of the expanding pyramid is a series of Policy Coordination

Committees (PCC). These are organized geographically (chaired by the relevant assistant secretary of state) and functionally, with the chair appointed from the most relevant agency (e.g., the PCC for economics is chaired by a representative of the Treasury Department). The PCCs perform functions such as monitoring ongoing situations, implementing policy orders, and providing staff work on proposals in the system.

The NSC system has proven a very durable tool that has remained intact despite changes of party in the White House for more than 50 years. In addition it has been the model for other security-related initiatives. In 1993, for instance, President Clinton used the concept as the basis for forming the National Economic Council (NEC) as a parallel advisory organ in the field of international economics (the principal difference between the two is that the NSC was created by statute and the NEC was created by executive order of the president). After the 9/11 tragedy, President Bush created the Homeland Security Council (HSC), with a structure that includes a PC, a DC, and PCCs, to coordinate the response to international terrorism.

The institutions represented on the National Security Council and prominent at other levels of the interagency process are the core actors who examine national security policy within the executive branch. They bring to bear different institutional perspectives on foreign and defense concerns and thus, when the system operates properly, guarantee that the range of institutional concerns is addressed before policy is made. This is especially true at the lower levels of the process where more than the statutory agencies are routinely represented.

Despite its historically preeminent role as the foreign policy agency, the State Department's influence has been in gradual decline. The department is still responsible for US embassies and consulates and their personnel up to and including the ambassadors. Most American business with foreign governments is still conducted through the embassy system, but, particularly in high-profile situations with national security overtones, other actors have infringed on traditional State Department "territory."

There are several reasons for this. The business of the State Department is diplomacy, and its preferred instrument of power is the diplomatic instrument. As the economic and especially the military instruments have become more prominent, their "advo-cates" have assumed more importance in the decision system. Moreover, the State Department's preference for diplomacy has earned it, rightly or wrongly, a reputation within other segments of the national security community for being "soft" on policy is-sues. The very public struggle for primary influence over na-tional security policy between Secretary of State Colin Powell and Secretary of Defense Donald Rumsfeld during crises con-fronting the Bush administration brought these differing and contrasting perspectives into particularly vivid relief.

A second source of decline has been the tendency of a number of post-1945 presidents to actively conduct their own foreign policies, and in the process, to draw into the White House a number of policy functions historically associated with the State Department. This was especially true during the Nixon adminis-tration, when a good deal of the real responsibility for making security policy was given to the NSC staff and particularly the national security adviser, Dr. Henry Kissinger. During the 1990s, President Clinton showed a tendency to insert himself person-ally into the process, notably in the Israeli-Palestinian dispute and in Northern Ireland. After two years of relative aloofness, Pres. George W. Bush placed his personal prestige on the table in attempting to sell the "road map" for a Middle Eastern peace.

A third source of decline is the revolution in communications. In earlier times, embassies in foreign countries were distant in time as well as space from Washington, DC. As a result, ambassadors had to have real decision-making authority because of the impos-sibility of timely communication with Washington. Today, that au-thority has diminished; generally, ambassadors serve as little more than communications links between the governments of their host countries and decision makers in Washington. This dilution of im-portance also applies to the information-gathering function that used to be central to the embassy system. Formerly, the embassy was the chief government source for information on activities in foreign countries. Today, the government in Washington routinely receives its initial information on world events from global televi-sion. The embassies are relegated to verifying television reports and interpreting news provided over global airwaves.

The other statutory member of the NSC (other than the vice president) is the secretary of defense. The Department of Defense is, of course, the largest actor in the system in terms of manpower and budget, and it also serves as the implementing arm for the military instrument of power.

The role of the DOD has increased as foreign policy problems have been redefined as national security problems. Its role has been more or less enhanced, depending on the predisposition of administrations to look to the military instrument as the proper tool for dealing with foreign problems. Thus, the Reagan administration elevated that role to a much higher level than did the Carter administration, and the Bush administration relies more on the military instrument than did the Clinton administration.

It is the genius of the NSC system to set these competitive agencies as coequals in forming policy and to force their cooperation in making that policy most of the time. In important national security decisions, both the secretaries of state and defense have a prominent voice at the NSC and PC levels, and this interaction occurs at the assistant secretary level or below at the DCs and PCCs as well. The secretaries bring to bear the unique institutional perspective and the accumulated expertise and judgment of their agencies. In this process of review and consultation, the relevant arguments and counterarguments are likely to be aired and presented to the president for his or her final determination. It should be noted that no votes are ever taken at the NSC because to do so might influence or confine the president's option, which is not the purpose of the NSC; it is merely to advise. Although wise policy is not always the result, policy is at least well informed.

Three statutory advisory assistants to the NSC aid the statutory members in reaching decisions. The CJCS has the responsibility of offering military advice on various policy options as the chief statutory military adviser to the president (a designation created by the Goldwater-Nichols Defense Reorganization Act of 1986). The DCI, as head of the CIA and chair of the intelligence community (a collection of all the agencies within the government with some intelligence function), has the primary responsibility of gathering and providing intelligence information on the activities of foreign governments. This information is provided through a daily summary of intelligence collected worldwide by various agencies and collated by the CIA and by the National Intelligence Estimates (NIE), summaries, and recommendations based on intelligence gathered over longer periods of time. Finally, the NSC staff, headed by the national security adviser (whose original role was NSC office manager), has as its primary responsibility coordinating the activities of the action agencies and providing whatever level of policy advice the president wants. Because the NSA, as head of the staff, has his or her (Condoleezza Rice was the first female to hold the post) physical headquarters in the White House, the incumbent often has superior access to the president.

Controversy has surrounded, to varying degrees, both the DCI/CIA and the NSC staff. The major source of controversy regarding the CIA has centered on those activities within its Directorate of Operations that fall under the title "covert actions." The directorate's ability to engage in secret actions against foreign governments had been severely curtailed under the Carter administration and DCI Stansfield Turner. President Reagan appointed William Casey, an old friend and former spymaster under the legendary William "Wild Bill" Donovan of World War II fame, to the DCI position. One of Casey's chief goals was to revitalize the agency's covert-action capabilities.

In the wake of the Iran-Contra affair of the mid-1980s, the NSC staff came under careful scrutiny. When it was first formed, the staff's role was viewed largely as clerical, collating and transcribing the actions of the NSC. Gradually that role expanded, especially under Presidents Kennedy and Johnson, both of whom elevated the national security adviser to a policy adviser. Nixon further expanded the NSA role to policy formulation. In the Iran-Contra affair, the NSC staff adopted the role of policy implementer, albeit clandestinely, conducting secret negotiations with the Iranian government of Ayatollah Ruhollah Khomeini and providing congressionally forbidden assistance to the Nicaraguan Contras (the two major aspects of the Iran-Contra scandal).

Two concerns have arisen as the NSC role has expanded. First, there is concern about the propriety of the NSC staff acting as a policy implementer. Many would like to see staff functions reduced to the original intent as essentially staffers with little policy responsibility. Others argue that, since the NSC staff is a personal staff of the president, the president should be able to organize it in the way that best fits his or her own style. Second, the NSA and other NSC staff are not confirmed by the Senate nor are their activities subject to direct congressional oversight, as are the activities of most government agencies, thus raising the question of accountability.

The activities of the CIA and other intelligence agencies have similarly been controversial and subject to public scrutiny. So-called covert operations emanating from the CIA's Directorate of Operations have long been questioned because they sometimes involve the clandestine commission of acts that violate US (and foreign) law. These activities—curtailed by Carter and reinstituted by Reagan—were further reduced by Clinton in the 1990s to the chagrin of some analysts following the 9/11 tragedy. At the same time, scandals such as the Aldridge Ames affair (a CIA officer exposed after years of selling US secrets to the Soviets and later the Russians) and intelligence failures, such as the questionable performance of the intelligence community in anticipating and thwarting the 9/11 attacks, have further tarnished the intelligence community's—and especially the CIA's—reputation.

Legislative Branch

The Congress is the other major institutional actor in the national security policy process. Within the checks and balances system that underpins the US Constitution, there is planned tension between the executive and legislative branches, sometimes referred to as "an invitation to struggle." In attempting to ensure that a too powerful executive did not emerge to threaten the republic, the Constitution assigns a major role to the Congress to oversee and restrain the actions of the executive; this is accomplished constitutionally and politically.

The constitutional restraints given to the Congress, as pointed out earlier, are largely reactive and seek to review presidential actions to ensure they are in the national interest. These restraints operate in shared areas of responsibilities, or what are otherwise known as concurrent powers exercised by both branches. As noted in the last section, these include raising and maintaining armed forces, declaring war, advising and consenting on treaties, and confirming officials.

The political powers of the Congress in the national security area consist of two related powers. The first is the power of the purse. All appropriations bills, by constitutional provision, must originate in the House of Representatives, and the executive branch of government cannot spend any money in the national defense (or for any other purpose) that has not been specifically appropriated by the Congress for the purpose mandated. Since virtually everything the executive branch does costs money, this is not an insignificant power.

The power of the purse can be exercised both directly and indirectly. In a direct sense, the Congress can refuse to fund all or part of the monies requested by the president for national security projects. Prime examples of this direct application in the 1980s included the MX (Peacekeeper) missile system and the Strategic Defense Initiative (SDI), both of which were funded at levels considerably lower than those sought by the administration.

There are some things that, as a practical matter, the Congress cannot directly control, such as providing support for military personnel in a combat zone. In these instances, the Congress can voice its displeasure indirectly by such means as threatening to deny funding for other presidentially backed programs. The Congress used the power of the purse to force extrication of American combat forces from Vietnam by announcing a cutoff date for the appropriation of funds in support of combat operations there.

The other political tool of the Congress is known as "watchdogging." A primary purpose of the Congress is to monitor executive policies and programs, both in terms of their wisdom and the degree to which they are exercised. The primary tool for this is the web of standing committees in the two houses of the Congress. The committee-system structure, in fact, is designed to reflect the organization of the executive branch, with a pair of committees—one in each house—designated to oversee each major executive agency and function. Most of the interaction between the Congress and the executive branch in matters of national security occurs in these committees, and the most powerful (and usually the most knowledgeable) members of the Congress in the area of national security policy are the chairs and ranking minority members of the relevant oversight committees. In the area of national security, the most relevant Senate committees (with their House equivalents in parentheses where the title is different) are Foreign Relations (International

Relations), Armed Services, Finance (Ways and Means), Select Committee on Intelligence, and Appropriations. When important national security concerns arise, statements by the chairs (almost always members of the majority party in the relevant house of the Congress) and the ranking member (the leader of the minority party who would normally become chair should control be reversed) are bellwethers of congressional opinion.

Other Actors

In addition to the governmental actors with formal responsibility in the policy process, other actors directly affect the substance of strategy. Three major sources of influence outside formal governmental channels are readily identifiable—interest groups, public opinion, and the media—and will be discussed below.

At the most general level, an interest group is a collection of individuals who share common interests different from other groups' interests and who act in concert to promote their common interests. In the political sphere, many such groups represent the gamut of interests on general issues of grand strategy and more-specific policy issues. Each group attempts to influence public policy in directions compatible with its beliefs.

Interest groups operate in several ways. Two of the most prominent tools interest groups employ are lobbying and education to transmit policy options and positions from the private sector to governmental actors who make policy decisions. Lobbying refers to direct attempts to persuade public officials to support their positions. Education (which is also used in lobbying) refers more generally to efforts to convince people to support interests based on enlarging citizen awareness of the interest group's position and its desirability as a part of public policy.

A more controversial form of interest-group activity is "pressure," a form of influence-peddling that attempts to coerce political figures into compliance with interest-group positions, not so much on the virtue of the position as the negative consequences of opposing that interest. The most obvious mechanism for bringing pressure is the political action committee (PAC), and the most extreme of pressure activities is using the resources of the PAC either to promote or oppose the election or reelection of targeted officials or candidates. Among domestic interest groups, the National Rifle Association is among the most famous (or infamous, depending on one's position on these matters) practitioners of pressure; among more internationally oriented groups, the American-Israeli Political Action Committee (AIPAC) stands out.

Classifying the different kinds of interest groups in any neat, precise way is difficult, but there are at least four criteria that can be used for distinguishing different kinds of groups. Certain groups can be distinguished by the breadth of the issues in which they take an interest. At one extreme are the general interest groups, such as the League of Women Voters or the AFL-CIO, who take positions on virtually all issues. These generalist groups differ from more-specific groups who may take positions only on foreign and national security policy problems (e.g., the Council on Foreign Relations) or some subset of foreign policy (e.g., the Association of the United States Army on Army matters). Generalist groups are larger and have higher public visibility, but quite often the more specialized groups possess greater expertise in their particular areas of interest and, hence, are more effective in influencing decisions.

A second perspective on interest groups relates to their organizational permanence. Most organized groups persist over time and attempt to promote enduring interests, but the last several decades have seen the rise of so-called single-interest groups. These groups usually begin as loose, ad hoc coalitions responding to a discrete interest and have mixed records in terms of permanence. The various anti-Vietnam war groups represented a single-interest group that dissolved after their issues disappeared. The antidraft registration movement of the early 1980s is another example. The groups organized by Ralph Nader are examples of single-interest groups that have shown more permanence by widening their purviews.

A third way to view interest-group activity is the degree to which they focus on strategic issues. Such organizations as the Foreign Policy Association or the Veterans of Foreign Wars have foreign policy/strategic interests as primary concerns, and they generally develop elaborate positions encompassing the broad range of strategic policies. Others become directly interested in specific issues when their other interest areas become relevant to foreign policy (e.g., the American Farm Bureau Federation and the National Association of Manufacturers regarding import of foreign goods).

Fourth, interest groups may be distinguished in terms of whether they represent "public" or "private" interests. An important phenomenon paralleling the rise of single-issue groups has been the emergence of groups purporting to protect broad public interests (e.g., the public at large) rather than more parochial interests. Such groups as Common Cause or Moral Majority are controversial because their views of what constitutes the public "good" are often based on ideological precepts (liberal or conservative) and because many suspect that their apparent piety in professing the interests of all masks more parochial concerns. It is virtually a contradiction in terms for a group to claim to represent the interests of all citizens on any policy area. There are essentially no areas in which everyone agrees, and if everyone did, there would be no reason to form an interest group.

The most controversial interest groups represent private interests that may profit directly from policy outcomes. These "vested" interests exist across the whole range of policy areas (e.g., pharmaceutical firms in relation to food and drug laws), but they have gained particular prominence in the security area due to the large amounts of money traditionally allocated to defense spending. Private interests are often quite active in pressure tactics, such as raising campaign funds for and against particular candidates.

In any open society, public opinion provides the final and ultimate restraint on governmental decision making. Principles of responsibility and accountability embedded in our constitutional system mean that decisions must be justified as being in the public interest, and the public must be willing to bear the burdens that policy decisions create. The perception of public willingness to support policy is a particularly important consideration in the defense and security area because of the potentially extraordinary burdens that decisions may impose on members of the public and the society as a whole (e.g., policies may result in war). In less extreme cases, however, public opinion as a determinant of what policies can and cannot be sustained is more constrained.

The point to be made in the national security area (as in other policy areas) is that there is no single public opinion. Instead, the public can be divided into several categories, based on their knowledge of and interest in public affairs. The distinction is important, because most Americans fall into the lowest category, and this limits the effectiveness of the public as a whole in overseeing and judging policy.

For better or worse, the vast majority of the US citizenry has no developed or sustained interest in foreign policy issues. This uninformed public does not regularly seek information about foreign or national security affairs, and it does not consistently form opinions unless its own interests are directly affected by events (e.g., the Iraq war), an event receives wide publicity (e.g., Saddam Hussein's alleged weapons of mass destruction), or efforts are made to mobilize it (e.g., support for the "war" on terrorism). Participation by the uninformed public tends to be sporadic, and its members' opinions are highly malleable; rather than shaping foreign policy, its opinions are shaped by it.

The second largest public sector is the informed public. This segment of the public is defined as citizens who regularly keep up with, and form opinions about, foreign affairs. Its opinions tend to be generalized rather than specific (e.g., "pro-defense" or "anti-defense" spending as opposed to being for or against specific weapons deployment). Access to information for this group is generally limited to the electronic and popular print media, and most of its members are professionals whose work does not directly involve them in foreign affairs. This group generally contains local opinion leaders (e.g., clergy and journalists) who perform the important task of transmitting information to the uninformed public. With its limited information and greater focus on other areas, however, the informed public's role in the policy process is more reactive than formative.

The most important influence on decision makers comes from the effective (or elite) public. This segment is made up of that part of the public that actively puts forward and advocates various policy alternatives. It includes interest-group representatives, national opinion leaders (e.g., the national media), and individuals whose lives and livelihoods are directly affected by foreign affairs (e.g., executives of corporations doing business overseas). In the areas of grand strategy and military strategy, the expert community of defense intellectuals—scholars and analysts at "think tanks" and retired military officers, for instance—are particularly influential. These individuals seek to influence policy by advocating positions in scholarly and professional journals, testifying before committees of the Congress, and the like. Members of this group are often seen on television locally or nationally as "talking heads," analyzing and explaining events and crises and thus, presumably, expanding the expert base of the media outlets.

The other, and in some ways most controversial, outside influence on the process is the news media. There are two distinct forms the media take—print and electronic journalism. In recent years the electronic media have become the more prominent and, to the extent that media coverage is controversial, most of the controversy resides with television journalism. This has become especially important in an age of 24-hour-a-day news coverage through outlets such as Cable News Network (CNN) and its numerous clones worldwide.

The media play several increasingly controversial roles in the governmental process. The first and most traditional function is collecting and reporting news. Observing and reporting what goes on in the world is the most basic thing that journalists do. When questions arise about this function, as they often do in areas such as national security, they tend to come from one of two sources. One is the question of qualification: are journalists well trained or educated enough to observe and understand complex reality in events such as war? This is particularly a problem in the current generation, since hardly any journalists have served in the military (previous generations were subject to the draft, and as a result, some journalists had served). The other question is objectivity. For years there was a common accusation of a "liberal bias" among journalists that caused them to see events in a distorted manner. More recently, an opposite accusation has emerged that there is a "conservative bias" that has intruded into the process (primarily, according to the charges, the product of large advertisers and media moguls threatening to punish journalists who veer from the conservative interpretation of events).

A second form of media activity is investigation and watchdogging. At the simple level of reporting, journalists do little more than reiterate what public officials tell them. Traditionally, journalists have felt the need to go beyond acceptance of official positions to try to determine the veracity of those statements and to be sure that officials are indeed carrying out the public trust. When the media in effect suggest officials may be lying or doing things they should not do, the results are tension and an adversarial relationship between the media and the government. Such an adversarial relationship is, however, exactly why the First Amendment called for a free and unregulated press to place a check on the malfeasance of government officials. This tension became a major national security problem during the Vietnam War—especially after the Tet offensive of 1968—when reporters concluded they had been lied to in reports of progress in the war and that, by dutifully reporting those lies, they had been deceiving their readers and viewers. The tension has remained in the media-government relationship ever since.

The media also interpret news for a public that often does not have the expertise to determine the deeper meaning of events and actions in the public realm, and this is particularly true in a highly technical and political area such as national security. This is certainly an important and legitimate service for the media to perform for the public, but it is subject to the same criticisms as those that attach to reporting in general. Are reporters systematically biased in how they interpret events on ideological bases? Is the result a distortion of what they report? Do reporters really have the expertise to make interpretations that are any more valid than the average citizen (who probably is unqualified to question the reporter's qualifications)? Who should you trust?

More recently, there has been the question of whether interpretation that is dissenting of governmental positions is suppressed because of fear of the consequences. One of the more notorious, recent examples of government punishing a dissenting media member was the 2003 case of Associated Press correspondent Helen Thomas. The dean of the White House press corps, it had been tradition to recognize her to ask a question, often the first one, at presidential press conferences since the early 1960s. Because Thomas had angered the White House by printing a critique of the then-mounting campaign to invade Iraq, she was not recognized, sending a chilling message to other journalists. The official White House explanation, that she was not recognized because she was no longer a reporter (she was retired) but only a columnist, did little to assuage concerns.

A final role—or at least accusation—is that the media act as an agenda setter for government. The idea is that media publicity of some events and ignoring of others has the effect of forcing government to respond to some situations not on the basis of their assessment of what is important but because of what the media forces them to consider. One of the most poignant examples of this force was a response by Tony Lake, Clinton's first national security adviser, to a question from a reporter as he was entering the White House. When the reporter asked what was on the agenda for today, Lake replied, "I don't know. CNN hasn't told me yet." Journalists deny that they set agendas, but simply report the agendas established by others.

Conclusions

The process of formulating grand strategy is not a sterile, analytical procedure in which changes on one side of a magic formula automatically suggest or produce reactions on the other side. Nor is it an exercise in deductive logic, where first principles produce axioms and corollaries that cascade downward to culminate in a comprehensive plan to confront hostile forces. Rather, the grand strategy process is inherently a political process with all the untidy characteristics of any political process.

The product of such a thorough process is usually compromise. In a closed society, a small elite can largely impose its will on the majority, but the interplay of interests and ideas within and outside various levels and branches of government in a democratic society requires some kind of consensus. Reaching consensus usually involves all sides giving something to get something else. For those in search of constancy and clarity of guidance in translating abstract ideas into concrete operational strategies, the result can be confusion and even frustration. Much of the strategists' purpose is to try to bring some order to the chaos of conflicting events, the most extreme of which is the employment of military force. Those strategies, in turn, have as their primary purposes protecting the chaotic, even messy, political process that frustrates creating the order fundamental to protecting it.

Notes

1. The *War Powers Resolution of 1973* was initially vetoed by Pres. Richard Nixon but later enacted by the 93rd Congress (H. J. Res. 542, 7 November 1973) as Public Law 93-148. (See *US Code*, vol. 50, secs. 1541–48). Section 2778 of the *Arms Export Control Act* provides the authority to control the export of defense articles and services and charges the president to exercise this authority. Public Law 90-629 (*US Code*, vol. 22, secs. 2751–2799).

2. For additional information, see http://www.ushistory.org/documents/ monroe.htm.

3. Pres. Jimmy Carter, State of the Union Address, 23 January 1980, as cited by Secretary of State Cyrus Vance, "US Foreign Policy: Our Broader Strategy," 27 March 1980, Department of State, Current Policy no. 153, as reprinted in *Case Study: National Security Policy under Carter*, Department of National Security Affairs, Air War College, AY 1980–1981, 98.

4. The Nixon Doctrine—"United States Foreign Policy for the 1970s: A New Strategy for Peace" (submitted to the Congress on 18 February 1970)—can be found at http://www.presidency.ucsb.edu/ws/print.php?pid=2835. It outlined a policy of reducing US overseas military commitments in favor of economic and military aid. The Vietnamization process is a classic example of this policy.

SECTION III
THE MILITARY DIMENSION

Chapter 6

Military Strategy

The discussion of the overall strategy process in chapter 2 indicated that military strategy consists of four distinct elements: force development, force deployment, force employment, and coordination of these actions in pursuit of national objectives as directed by grand strategy. This chapter discusses these four elements in broad, fundamental terms. Development, deployment, employment, and coordination appear, at first glance, to provide a logical sequence for the discussion that follows. Any discussion of military strategy, however, should begin with anticipated force employment. How, where, and against whom one plans to employ military forces are factors that should determine to a major degree what forces should be developed, where those forces will be deployed, and the coordination required.

Force Employment Strategy

At the military strategy level, force employment refers to the use of forces in a broad, national sense. Employment decisions revolve around the perceived threat and can be discussed in terms of two basic questions. First, where would forces be employed? Second, against whom would they be employed? The answers to these questions were relatively obvious until the end of the Cold War but since have fallen into a state of considerable confusion. We consider each question separately while bearing in mind that they are interrelated.

Where Would Forces Be Employed?

The fundamental "where" issue concerns whether military forces are required for direct defense of the homeland or whether they will be required to project power abroad to protect national interests around the world. Prior to the dawn of the nuclear age, the United States had not faced a serious externally based threat to its borders since the War of 1812. Blessed with broad oceans to its east and west and nonhostile, lesser powers to the north and south, the United States did not require a significant military establishment to counter external enemies until it entered the international arena in a serious way. As late as the beginning of World War II, the United States relied on a small, professional military force that could be augmented in times of crises by citizen-soldiers. In the years between the two world wars, for example, the US Army was only the 18th largest in the world. But even in wartime, a large standing military force was not required for homeland defense because an invasion of the continental United States was a very remote possibility. Clearly, US military forces, if employed, would only go into combat overseas. This circumstance also helps explain why the United States has maintained a world-class navy since before the turn of the twentieth century, even in periods when its other military services languished. Naval forces could protect American shores and, before the age of long-range airpower, were the only means of projecting American power overseas to protect US interests abroad.

Not all countries have had such good fortune. Some perceive themselves to be physically threatened from every quarter and thus plan to employ their forces on the defensive "at home." The best-known modern example of this situation (perhaps an extreme case) is Switzerland. A small state surrounded on all sides by powerful, oft-warring neighbors, the Swiss devote their entire military establishment to homeland defense. Thus, where forces might be employed can be the result of happy—or unhappy—geographic accidents.

Although a happy geographic circumstance simplified the American defense equation for over 200 years, the terrorist attacks on 11 September 2001 added a significant new twist to the problem. The attacks revealed that so-called unconventional attacks by shadowy nonstate organizations could cause serious damage and therefore posed a significant threat to the American homeland. The bulk of the defense against such attacks requires significant actions by many nonmilitary institutions in such areas as immigration control, customs, the Border Patrol, and the like. However, there is also a significant military component in the renewed focus on homeland defense including the designation of a new joint theater command, Northern Command, which is responsible for military homeland defense. It is important to note that although defensive efforts, both military and nonmilitary, to counter the terrorist threat were significant, the major US reaction to the threat was offensive, not defensive, and overseas, not in the homeland. Attacks on the Taliban government of Afghanistan that had supported the terrorist organization responsible for 9/11 and on the terrorist headquarters and training camps in Afghanistan took the struggle to the enemy, thus projecting homeland defense abroad.

Technology can also play an important role in the military employment equation. The development of long-range aircraft and missiles with intercontinental range has put all countries at near-immediate risk regardless of their geographic circumstances. The advent of nuclear weapons coupled to intercontinental delivery systems raised the stakes to the level of national survival. As a result, the United States diverted a significant portion of its military establishment during the Cold War to homeland defense. Air defense forces were obviously intended for this purpose. Nuclear retaliatory forces fulfilled, in a somewhat perverse way, the same purpose.

The newest problem, as of this writing, posed by technological development is the "cyber" threat. Ubiquitous personal, commercial, government, and military computers linked together on the World Wide Web (WWW) have revolutionized communications, the international financial system, commercial transactions, and international trade, to name but a few areas. Interlinked computer systems have also had a major impact on every facet of the military and have revolutionized the command and control of modern military forces. At the same time, these electronic advances have created significant new risk factors. The prospect of an adversary wreaking havoc on the economy or on the military establishment through a few keystrokes on a computer half a world away is frightening. What overall impact these new vulnerabilities (and opportunities) will have on the employment of military forces is not yet clear but is almost certain to be significant. In terms of the "where" question in military employment, the question becomes nearly irrelevant. The WWW brings the electronic world together at the speed of light, making the physical location of a cyber attack moot.

Where one intends to employ forces is obviously important to force deployment decisions. It is also important to force development decisions because the characteristics of forces

105

needed for homeland defense are usually far different from the characteristics of a force intended for expeditionary use. For example, the development of expeditionary forces would probably emphasize airlift and sealift assets, highly transportable ground forces (i.e., light, no oversized cargo, etc.), and forces to control air and sea lines of communication. However, if one knows with certainty where forces will be deployed, they can be prepositioned—thus allowing for the development of much heavier forces. Such was the case during the Cold War when the United States prepositioned military units and heavy equipment in NATO Europe and the Korean peninsula. More recently, heavy equipment has been prepositioned on the island of Diego Garcia in the Indian Ocean for quick transport to the Middle East or Southwest Asia, as required. The development of forces for homeland defense, on the other hand, might emphasize "heavier" forces, fortification of key positions, and defensively oriented weapons (e.g., mines).

After this brief look at how geography and technology—two influences on the strategy process—can influence where forces will be employed and how the place of employment can influence force development, the discussion now moves to the second basic question about force employment.

Against Whom Would Forces Be Employed?

This issue is of crucial importance to both force development and deployment. To know the enemy is to know the nature of the threat. If strategists know the enemy, they will understand how the enemy is armed and with how much, in what manner the enemy might use his forces, and ultimately, what is required to counter the threat.

For more than four decades, the United States identified the Soviet Union as the primary threat to its security interests. Clearly, this Cold War perception was correct in terms of a direct threat against the United States or its European allies in NATO. Only the Soviet Union had the ability and possible motive to be a credible direct threat. The result of this perception was the development and deployment of a force structure calculated to deter or, if required, fight the Soviets and their Warsaw Pact allies. Ironically, and thankfully, although the United

States fought two major wars during the Cold War period in the three decades following the end of World War II (Korea and Vietnam), neither was against the Soviets. The United States was also involved to varying degrees in a number of other conflicts during the Cold War (Quemoy and Matsu Islands, Bay of Pigs, Lebanon twice, three Arab-Israeli wars, Angola, Nicaragua, Grenada, and Panama), none of which directly involved the Soviets. American actions in some of these conflicts were justified by the perceived need to limit Soviet influence in the zero-sum game of superpower politics. However, the nature of the military threat to American interests in these Third World conflicts was far different from the threat of direct confrontation with the Soviets. As the United States bitterly learned in Vietnam, the force structure, weapons, tactics, and training needed to confront the Soviets in a high-speed, mechanized war in Europe were not necessarily appropriate for combating insurgents in the jungles of Southeast Asia.

During the Cold War, the Soviets were the enemy, and the United States prepared forces accordingly. In the post–Cold War world, there is no clearly defined adversary and yet, during the first 13 years of the period, US forces engaged in combat operations six times—in Iraq, Somalia, Bosnia, Kosovo, Afghanistan (against both the Taliban government and the al-Qaeda terrorist group), and Iraq, again. Situations that would appear to threaten US interests continue to brew around the world. As a result, the post–Cold War "who" question becomes muddled at best.

This situation led to a still-ongoing military policy debate that began during the Clinton administration. The debate began over the "how much is enough" question, morphed into questions concerning what kind of capabilities were required, and in its latest incarnation is sporadically addressing what sorts of functions are appropriate for the military. The last issue currently centers on peacekeeping and nation-building activities following the second war in Iraq.

The "who" question has a direct impact on the entire military strategy decision-making process. The diverse nature of the threat (or threats), however, presents strategists with several dilemmas and forces them to undertake a policy of risk management. This problem is addressed later in this chapter when discussing the *coordination* portion of military strategy.

Force Development Strategy

Force employment strategy decisions ideally determine, in a broad sense, what needs to be done, where it needs to be done, and how it should be done. These decisions are also the primary driving force behind force development strategy decisions. Force development concerns resources for getting the job done—how much, what kind, and how these resources are molded and shaped into a force structure. It is important to remember that although force employment drives force development, these two facets are interactive. For example, many force employment decisions depend on the raw resources available for development. A small, poor, isolated, and backward state would find it difficult to wage modern, high-intensity, mechanized warfare in far-flung overseas locations. The requirements would overwhelm its available resources. In another sense, a country confronted by a contingency requiring immediate action is forced to rely on forces already developed regardless of raw resources available for future development. Consequently, force employment and force development are dependent variables.

Resources are the key to force development. The key resources are well known. Among them are raw materials (or access to them), an industrial base (or access to one), population, technological sophistication, and economic wherewithal. These are the primary factors in determining the force structure that can be developed in response to force employment decisions. Strategists' function is to manipulate these primary factors to develop a force structure in concert with force employment strategy.

Strategists' manipulation of resources is controlled by the obvious need to take advantage of a country's strengths and to offset its weaknesses. Some states with large populations, but relatively backward industrial and technological bases, have emphasized massive force structures whose effectiveness relied on the sacrifice of ordinary soldiers employed in overwhelming numbers. Some Asian societies have followed this path, as did czarist Russia. Life was not "cheap" in those societies, as some have claimed. Rather, lives were the most plentiful and available resource to use against enemies who were often industrially and technologically superior.

Western countries that prospered by industrial development and technological sophistication have tended to rely on the mechanized forces and firepower generated by industry and technology. This trend became most pronounced after World War I. The predisposition to substitute fire and steel for flesh and blood has been most obvious in the American experience. Incredible industrial output and the mastery of technology have allowed the United States to substitute things for people, a trend which fits well with its dominant Judeo-Christian ethic emphasizing the worth of the individual and the sanctity of life (at least the sanctity of American lives).

Toward the end of the Cold War, some critics claimed that the American penchant for technology had gone too far. The quest for more sophisticated weapons had dramatically increased unit costs, therefore limiting the number of weapons that could be purchased and, in turn, limiting the size of the force structure. Further, some of the technology being fielded appeared at that time to be unreliable. The so-called military reform group called for less-sophisticated weapon systems that could be bought in larger quantities. This was the path that had been followed by the Soviets, who fielded weapon systems that were often somewhat less sophisticated, considerably cheaper, and far more plentiful. The critics' fears turned out to be without substance. The high-tech weaponry developed by the United States performed well on the battlefield in the Gulf War and in later conflicts. The quest for high-tech solutions to battlefield problems has continued at an ever-increasing pace. The US military is committed to making the most of its technological edge.

It is worth noting, however, that a significant reliance on high technology does have its own set of risks. Achieving a favorable balance is a particularly vexing problem for several reasons. First, technology advances rapidly, and the military advantages offered by any given technological development are almost always temporary. Even if the adversary cannot respond in-kind, it may be able to find low-tech counters. Second, new technology is not battle-tested before one is forced to rely on it. Third, possession of superior technology is no guarantee that the technology will be employed effectively or, in fact, that it will be employed at all (note, for example, that the United States did not employ nuclear weapons in either Korea or Vietnam). Finally, an adversary's clever operational strategy can often off-set a technological advantage. In Vietnam, America's enemies were inferior in virtually every measure of military power. Un-fortunately for the United States, a clever strategy, often based on guerrilla tactics combined with a campaign to sap US home-front support for the struggle, eventually frustrated the Ameri-can effort. This problem is discussed in much greater detail in chapters 8 and 13.

In sum, force development decisions revolve around the most effective use of resources to meet the requirements of force employ-ment decisions. The decisions involved are difficult, and the situa-tion is always fluid. But the decisions must be made so that the force structure can be properly constructed and finally deployed.

Force Deployment Strategy

Understanding who the enemy is and where forces would likely be employed will obviously be driving factors in the de-ployment of forces. The design of the force structure will like-wise be an important consideration, especially force size, equipment characteristics, and lift capacities. Geography also plays an important role, particularly in wartime. The United States, for example, has broad and immediate access to mari-time transportation routes across both the Atlantic and Pacific Oceans, making large deployments by sea and the sustain-ment of deployed forces overseas a relatively easy task. Other countries, such as Germany, could only deploy forces by sea through narrow choke points that can be easily closed. None of these factors prevents deployment by air, of course; but the fact is, large-scale deployment and long-term sustainment by air are difficult, expensive, and can be risky propositions. For "heavy" forces, large-scale deployments by air are impractical.

Strategists must perform a delicate balancing act when mak-ing decisions about deployments forward during peacetime. This is particularly true for any state that has many security interests in different parts of the world. Strategists must bal-ance three factors: time, vulnerability, and flexibility.

Time, of course, is the centerpiece of peacetime deployment. The primary military reason for deploying forces forward (i.e., overseas) is to reduce the time required to respond to enemy actions. Certainly, there may be other reasons for forward deployment, such as providing a deterrent, demonstrating resolve, or strengthening alliance relationships, but the hard, practical military reason involves time. Having forces in place should increase their readiness for employment and facilitate their training in a realistic environment. Further, the availability of in-place maintenance facilities and logistics depots can be of inestimable value, particularly in remote areas.

Forward basing, no matter how valuable in terms of response time, is a risk-laden undertaking because it increases vulnerability. Although more quickly available for combat, forward-based forces are more vulnerable to enemy fires, air raids, and possibly to quick encirclement and destruction by a rapid enemy thrust. The German blitzkrieg into the Soviet Union in 1941 offers a good example. Large segments of the Soviet military were deployed far forward. They were caught by surprise when the Germans struck swiftly into rear areas, surrounding huge pockets of Soviet formations. Many of the trapped units were destroyed or forced to surrender. Consequently, strategists are faced with a dilemma. On one hand, forward deployment decreases response time and increases readiness. On the other hand, forward-deployed forces may be so vulnerable that readiness becomes irrelevant.

The third factor strategists must consider in deployment decisions is flexibility. If forces are deployed forward, one assumes they are deployed advantageously. However, if conflict erupts in another corner of the world, redeployment of forward-deployed forces could be time-consuming and, perhaps, politically difficult.

During the Cold War, US strategists were confident that they knew where our forces should be forward deployed. They knew the Soviet Union was the threat they had to meet, and they knew the most likely place for trouble to erupt was along the inter-German border. Further, they understood the political and practical necessity of defending Western Europe. The result, of course, was a major forward deployment of US forces into Western Europe. Today, strategists do not have the luxury of such clear-cut adversaries or political imperatives carved in stone.

111

If strategists had perfect knowledge of the places where forces would actually be needed, deployment would pose few problems. If a country had few vital interests overseas, the deployment problem would be mitigated. The fact is, of course, that perfect knowledge is rarely available. As the world becomes more interdependent, worldwide security interests multiply, particularly for a superpower such as the United States. As a result, deployment dilemmas increase, and the need for a coordinated military strategy becomes paramount.

Coordination of Military Strategy

Coordination of the three parts of military strategy—employment, development, and deployment—is essentially an exercise in risk management. In the American experience, neither the will nor resources to create adequate forces to meet every contingency have ever existed. Strategists must, therefore, make hard choices and understand the risks involved with each choice.

The fundamental problem is that enemies seek to exploit weaknesses. An enemy will attack where the adversary is weak or will seek to wage the kind of war the adversary is least capable of waging.[1] Every military strategy decision is made in response to a threat but at the same time forecloses other options because of limited resources. Thus, countering one kind of threat in a particular place creates opportunities for the adversary elsewhere.

How can these risks be managed? The American answer to that question in the Cold War was based on worst-case analysis. In essence, the United States concentrated its efforts on preparing for the war it could least afford to lose—a nuclear war. Thus, for four decades the United States concentrated much of its effort on developing and deploying a nuclear retaliatory force designed to convince the Soviets that a nuclear attack on the United States or its allies would certainly result in disaster and devastation for the Soviet Union. That is, the United States viewed nuclear deterrence as its first priority and nuclear war as *the* worst case to be avoided.

At a lesser worst-case level, the United States concentrated on conventional forces designed, equipped, and deployed to counter possible Soviet conventional aggression in Western Europe. It is true that the United States also developed and

112

deployed conventional capabilities elsewhere—most notably Northeast Asia—but the primary focus remained on Europe throughout the Cold War.

In the post–Cold War world, a firm American military strategy has yet to emerge. The forces developed during the Cold War were reduced significantly in anticipation of much less need. Unfortunately, a succession of military operations in East Africa, the Balkans, Southwest Asia, and the Middle East tasked those forces heavily with operations tempos higher than had been seen for decades. The situation became so serious by the end of the second war in Iraq that serious talk about reinstituting compulsory military service (the draft) spread through the news media. There is little indication that such heavy demands on the US military will soon abate. To the contrary, the specter of North Korean nuclearization, continued animosity between India and Pakistan, unending problems in the Middle East, and chaos in much of sub-Saharan Africa would seem to indicate continued demands on US forces throughout the world. Such is the price paid to be the world's only superpower.

Conclusions

As discussed in this chapter, the issues involved in coordinating the development, deployment, and employment of military forces—military strategy—are very complex and remain so in the "new world order." Strategists face new and, in many ways, more challenging dilemmas in the post–Cold War world. How should these new risks be managed? Should strategists prepare for the worst case or the most likely case? Is there a worst case? Is there a most likely case? Can one prepare for both possibilities, or would that raise the specter of not being prepared adequately for either case? Resolving such risk-management dilemmas is the essence of military strategy. The chapters in the next section explore these contingencies and the strategy problems they pose.

Note

1. Saddam Hussein provides excellent evidence to support the notion that one should not wage war on the opponent's terms if the opponent is stronger.

In both 1991 and 2003, Saddam essentially waged a conventional defense against US-led coalitions that possessed overwhelming conventional power and expertise. The disastrous results for the Iraqi ruler and his armed forces bear witness to his folly.

Chapter 7

Operational Strategy

Chapter 1 traced the evolution of warfare since the eighteenth century when wars often consisted of only one or two decisive battles. In the intervening years, truly decisive battles became things of the past, victims of the democratization of warfare that created mass armies and the Industrial Revolution that created the technology that allowed the rapid replacement and reinforcement of defeated forces. Most modern major wars have become long, drawn-out affairs, often spread over large theaters of operation. They consist not just of battles, or even combinations of related battles (operations), but combinations of operations (campaigns) aimed at particular objectives. Because of that reality, chapter 2 defined operational strategy as the art and science of planning, orchestrating, and directing military campaigns within a theater of operations to achieve national security objectives.

The contrast between the eighteenth-century tradition and the realities of modern warfare came to a head in American military history during the Civil War. Early in the war, Union leadership sought to bring the war to a quick conclusion through decisive battles in front of the Confederate capital, Richmond, Virginia. On the Confederate side, Robert E. Lee was obsessed with the vision of achieving a decisive Napoleonic-style victory. But the war dragged on without decisive victories by either side. Union generals Ulysses S. Grant and William T. Sherman finally realized that the quest for a decisive victory was illusory and, instead, concentrated on a series of campaigns (e.g., Vicksburg, Atlanta, and Northern Virginia) that destroyed, in a methodical fashion, the Confederates' ability to resist and eventually forced their surrender.

The Civil War also emphasized the importance of coordinating different campaigns, perhaps best illustrated by the synergistic use of naval and land forces in such campaigns as the Union drive to capture Vicksburg. With the advent of air forces in the twentieth century, the situation has become so complex and important that to speak of "coordinating" campaigns is no longer descriptively adequate. *Orchestrating*—molding the disparate parts into a symphonic whole—is a much more descriptive term.

Orchestrating Campaigns

Operational strategy links the national-level concerns of military strategy with the battlefield concerns of tactics, a very wide-ranging area for decision making. As one would expect in such a large decision-making area, campaign concerns range from broad questions bordering on very general military strategy issues on the high side, down to narrow issues closely related to tactics on the low side. To organize this examination, one must view the orchestration of campaigns at three interconnected levels, beginning with the broadest campaigns and working toward the narrowest. Finally, these interconnected levels are combined into the complex whole that is theater-level warfare.

Combined Campaigns

For the foreseeable future, any US engagement in theater-level warfare will almost undoubtedly take place overseas, thanks to nonhostile neighbors and neutral oceans on its borders. Further, any engagement by American expeditionary forces will almost certainly involve allies and thus will create the requirement to orchestrate the campaigns of American and allied forces. The amount of orchestration required between allies will vary by the level of participation in the struggle by each ally.

Combined-campaign orchestration involves difficulties that can arise from various sources. First, the United States and its allies may have different political objectives or hidden political agendas that result in divergent military objectives. In World War II, for example, the United States, Great Britain, the Free French, and the Soviet Union (among others) were united in their basic objective of inflicting total defeat on the Axis powers. Great Britain and France, however, also sought to regain control over those portions of their colonial empires occupied by Axis forces. The United States was lukewarm and at times hostile to those objectives. The result was friction between the Allies, particularly in Southeast Asia, as the war drew to a close.

The Soviets' desire to establish control over the East European countries they liberated from the Nazis led to a number of problems between the Allies, most notably in Poland, over support for the Warsaw uprising and over the composition of the provisional Polish government.

Cultural heritage can also cause problems in orchestrating efforts between allies. Again using an example from World War II, the British were haunted by the memories of World War I trench warfare and the slaughter of British manpower on the fields of Flanders. They vowed never again to suffer such losses as they did in the first battle on the Somme in 1916 when more than 57,000 British soldiers were casualties in the first day of fighting (nearly 20,000 were killed).[1] As a result, the British sought to attack the Axis only on its most exposed and difficult-to-defend perimeter areas (North Africa, Sicily, and Italy) and through strategic bombardment and naval blockade. The British resisted as long as they could a cross-channel invasion into France and into the teeth of German resistance. American military leaders, on the other hand, continually pressed for an early invasion of France because they sought the shortest and fastest road to Berlin and victory.

In more recent combined campaigns in which US forces and leadership dominated the proceedings, orchestrating the campaign in the face of differing national objectives and cultures still proved to be a difficult and at times a very frustrating task. The NATO campaign in Kosovo is a case in point. It was primarily an aerial bombing campaign. The air forces used and most of the senior leaders were American. However, every target proposed for bombing had to be approved by every NATO member—a process that was often lengthy and at times very contentious. Further problems arose because of differing levels of technological sophistication and resulting differences in capabilities among the allies. In the Kosovo case, this was particularly true concerning precision weapons delivery capabilities. Some allies flying with the US forces lacked certain equipment required for precision delivery and as a result could only bomb those targets for which a high level of precision was not a critical requirement.

Apart from differences caused by objectives and culture, military professionals from allied states can differ in their professional judgment on appropriate methods, timing, and enemy vulnerabilities. The timing of the cross-channel invasion involved not only cultural heritage (the ghosts of the Somme) but also professional military judgment. Another example centers on the conduct of the strategic bombing campaign against Germany. The British favored night area bombing while the Americans favored day precision attacks. At the Casablanca Conference in early 1943, the two allies agreed to capitalize on the different approaches and bomb around-the-clock. Unfortunately, the separate campaigns were not well orchestrated. Germany was bombed continuously but rarely was a specific target given continuous treatment, much to the disappointment and anger of American airmen. The bombing raids on the ball-bearing works at Schweinfurt are a case in point. American aviators believed that destroying German ball-bearing production would be a key—perhaps *the* key—to bringing down the German war machine. However, the costly American daylight attacks on the German factories were not followed up by British night raids on the town of Schweinfurt and its skilled workforce. The Royal Air Force (RAF) had bigger fish to fry. Believing that attacks on the ball-bearing industry were a false panacea and that the town of Schweinfurt was insignificant and too difficult to hit at night, the RAF concentrated on raids on major German cities.

Joint Campaigns

For modern military establishments, warfare in the twenty-first century has become four-dimensional. Although land, sea, air, and space forces have unique characteristics and capabilities; and although at times each seems to be independent of the others; in truth, most battles, operations, and campaigns are joint in nature. Thus, a primary job of operational strategy is to capitalize on the unique capabilities of land, sea, air, and space forces. More importantly, operational strategy should meld together ground, sea, air, and space operations into a synergistic whole.

Orchestration of joint campaigns is often hindered by several factors with which the operational strategist must cope. The most fundamental factor is the differing worldviews held by soldiers, sailors, and airmen—a subject that will be discussed in considerable detail in chapter 11. Ground forces face immediate physical obstacles and thus tend to concentrate on near-term problems. Hence, the immediate land battle must be the first priority for ground forces and must have first call on all available forces. Naval forces, faced with fewer immediate physical obstacles, tend to focus on a bigger picture. Those with a traditional naval perspective understand the importance of the land battle but maintain that control of the high seas and narrow choke points can control events on shore. They believe the battle to gain sea control must have the first priority. Air and space forces face no real physical barriers except the limitations of their aircraft and spacecraft. Their viewpoint is theater-wide or global in perspective. To airmen, the overwhelming first priority is to gain control of the air so that they can effectively attack the sources of the enemy's power, which are often in its industrial base. Space operations are, of course, the newest dimension in military capability, but a widely accepted "space power" perspective on war fighting has yet to emerge.

The traditional worldviews of air, ground, and naval power briefly outlined above have been stated as rather stark absolutes. In truth, few hold such austere views. A renewed emphasis on "jointness" that began in the 1980s has taken the edge off traditional views and led to much higher levels of interservice cooperation. However, differing priorities can still lead to major problems in a joint campaign, particularly since resources are limited. For example, while ground forces may be in desperate need of air support, airmen may be in the midst of waging their own desperate struggle for control of the air, an enterprise that might well absorb most of the resources that could otherwise be used to support ground forces. Naval air support might also be needed by ground forces, but it, too, could be tied down defending the fleet, the loss of which would mean loss of sea control.

Examples of such problems abound. In World War II, American airmen attempted to concentrate on the strategic bombing campaign against Germany, believing that the attacks would eventually bring the Germans to their knees. However, much to the frustration of the airmen, resources intended for the bombing campaign were often diverted to other theaters—for example, to the campaign to liberate North Africa—or to other kinds of targets within the European theater, such as the German submarine pens on the coast of occupied France.

Conflicting priorities exacerbate problems of command and control. Ground, naval, and air forces fear control by commanders who do not understand and appreciate their priorities. There is great reluctance to give total control to theater commanders from other services who might squander the scarce resources they do not fully understand.

The debates over command and control are particularly important to sailors and airmen. Naval assets are extremely difficult to replace because of their cost and the time required to construct a modern warship. In a sense, a naval war could be lost in one afternoon if the fleet were destroyed. To a somewhat lesser extent, the same problems apply to aerial forces. Air assets are not easily or quickly replaced and are relatively scarce because of their cost. Figuratively speaking, an air war could also be lost in one calamitous afternoon. Such high stakes contribute to the great reluctance to cede command and control of forces to those who may not be well versed in the use of naval and air forces.

The same attitudes will, no doubt, someday affect space forces because the fundamental problems are so similar. Many of the most valuable space assets are literally one-of-a-kind, and as a result are incredibly expensive and would be very time-consuming to reproduce. To "true believers," space is the place where future wars will be won or lost. The nature of the space capabilities that should be developed is a matter of considerable controversy. Whatever the outcome of the controversy, the advent of space-based weaponry will be a major complication for operational strategy.

The other side of the command and control problem is the broader issue of orchestrating various kinds of forces into synergistic, four-dimensional campaigns. Without a firm command and control arrangement, synergies may not be possible. The operational level of war and operational strategy require difficult decisions that leave many less than satisfied, depending on their worldview and priorities. But the fact remains that someone must be in firm command and complete control. The American approach to this problem—in addition to appropriately balanced joint staffs for combatant commanders—has been to increase the jointness of individual military leaders through education, exchange duties, and joint assignments, much of this mandated by the Congress in the mid-1980s through the Goldwater-Nichols Act. The objective of these efforts has been and remains to broaden the perspectives and knowledge of the officer corps beyond parochial service-based interests.

Component Campaigns

In the previous section, the discussion centered on orchestrating the efforts of ground, naval, and air components so that they work well together in joint campaigns. The discussion now turns to the inner workings of the components and the orchestration of campaigns *within* components.

Ground forces have long recognized the synergy that can be achieved by careful orchestration of various efforts in ground campaigns. Infantry, artillery, cavalry, and other ground components have demonstrated time and again that the whole of their orchestrated efforts is far greater than the sum of their individual efforts. Achieving such synergistic effects often has not been easy. Technology often changes the optimum relationships between the various component elements. A case in point is the relationship between infantry and armor in ground warfare. In World War I primitive tanks were used as infantry support weapons. By World War II armor had developed to the point that the relationship reversed itself, at least in the German army—much to the chagrin of those in other armies who had not realized that technological development permitted and encouraged a different and more highly mobile role for armor.

Naval forces have also recognized that synergies can be achieved by careful orchestration. The use of marines to seize and hold forward naval bases has long been recognized as important to fleet operations. The advent of subsurface forces and their operations in concert with surface fleets changed the nature of naval warfare even before World War II. During World War II, of course, naval aviation again changed the nature of war at sea, working hand in hand with surface and subsurface forces.

Although ground and naval operations have extensive histories, aerial operations are, relative to their surface cousins, newcomers to warfare. As a result, synergies within air operations are not as well recognized. But they do exist and have been well exploited. One of the most significant synergies is between fighter and bomber aircraft. In World War II, American bombers acted as bait when they attacked German aircraft-production facilities in 1944 as part of the campaign to achieve control of the air. The presence of the bombers and the importance of their targets drew the enemy fighters into the air where the US fighters escorting the bombers could engage them. The effects of the combined fighter-bomber partnership were much greater than using either force separately.

Orchestrating component campaigns is not a simple task, nor do definitive guidelines exist. Much depends on technological developments and strategists' insights in seeing how such developments can affect the optimal relationships between operating elements. A great deal depends on the nature of the enemy, its strengths, weaknesses, and vulnerabilities. Orchestration is further complicated by the requirements of joint campaigns (e.g., it is difficult for bombers to attack aircraft plants in a campaign for control of the air if they are required to attack submarine pens as part of a joint campaign for control of the sea).

Operational Strategy: Design Choices

All of the foregoing is important for strategists to understand when designing and implementing an operational strategy. But what strategy? What are the fundamental approaches for designing an operational strategy? What follows is a discussion illustrating some of the most basic approaches to operational-level strategy. Admittedly, the list of approaches is not exhaustive nor are the approaches necessarily mutually exclusive. Although many of the approaches are discussed in pairs of what appear to be extreme opposites, in some cases these seemingly opposite approaches have been used simultaneously in the same theater of operations.

Sequential and Cumulative Strategies

First proposed by RADM J. C. Wylie in his marvelous little book, *Military Strategy*, sequential and cumulative may be the most elemental of all strategy distinctions.[2] A sequential strategy is a series of actions, each one dependent on the action that preceded it, and generally dependent on the success of that previous action. Examples are most obvious in the World War II island-hopping campaign in the Pacific. Each island captured became a naval, air, and logistics base to capture the next island as American forces "leapfrogged" across the Pacific toward Japan.

Conversely, a cumulative approach is one in which no action is dependent on the action that preceded it. What counts is the overall cumulative effect of all actions. We can again find examples in the Pacific during World War II. The American submarine campaign against the Japanese merchant marine consisted of independent actions sinking Japanese shipping—no individual attack depended on the attacks that preceded it. However, the accumulated tonnage of Japanese ships sent to the bottom of the Pacific could not be replaced, and Japanese war industries began to starve for want of raw materials, particularly materials from Southeast Asia.

The air campaign against Japan was also cumulative. B-29 fire-bombing raids were methodically planned to burn down Japanese industrial cities and thus destroy their industrial capacity. No raid depended on any previous raid. Ultimately what mattered was the accumulated damage, death, destruction, and misery.

Graduated and Parallel Strategies

Graduated and parallel strategies are subsets of sequential and cumulative strategies. In sequential strategies, each action generally depends on the success of the previous action. In a graduated strategy, each action is the result of the failure of the previous action. The bombing campaign in Kosovo provides a clear case in point of a graduated strategy. The bombing started with very few sorties per day in the hope that the Serbian leadership would call a halt to the ethnic cleansing taking place in Kosovo. The failure of the early raids to force capitulation resulted in steadily increasing numbers of daily sorties, bombs dropped, and targets destroyed as the Serbian leadership continued to resist. The same sort of approach was used during the Rolling Thunder bombing campaign in Vietnam.

Parallel strategies are closely related to cumulative approaches but are really the product of advancing technology. First seen in the 1991 war with Iraq, rather than bombing raids against a particular target set one night and another target set on another night, parallel approaches use advanced technology (particularly stealth and precision munitions) to destroy several target sets at once—in parallel. But, as with the cumulative approach, it is the cumulative effect on the adversary that is important.

Direct and Indirect Strategies

Direct approaches to strategy tend to match strength against strength. This was a common strategy in the ancient world and down through the nineteenth century. Much of it also appeared during the trench warfare on the Western Front in World War I. While such direct strategies have had both success and failure, they have nearly always been terribly bloody and costly affairs for victor and vanquished alike. Indirect approaches, a term popularized by Sir Basil Liddell Hart, seek to pit one's strength against an enemy's weakness and thus put the adversary in an untenable situation, forcing either capitulation or retreat. This concept is at the heart of maneuver warfare. A near-classic but recent example of the indirect approach was the "Great Left Hook" by coalition forces against Iraqi forces in the Gulf War. While Iraqi troops dug in behind formidable defenses on the Kuwaiti–Saudi Arabian border, the main coalition blow fell far to the west with an armored thrust around the Iraqi right flank that quickly threatened to either trap or destroy the entire Iraqi army. In 100 hours, the Iraqis had signed a humiliating cease-fire agreement.

Outside-In and Inside-Out Approaches

Outside-in approaches to strategy are very traditional ways of waging state-versus-state warfare. Outside-in postulates subduing a hostile state by invading across its border, defeating the hostile army, marching on the hostile capital, and capturing the seat of government including, perhaps, the government itself if it has not already sued for peace. This is a close relative of the direct approach.

Its opposite number, the inside-out approach, is a close relative of the indirect approach. It has roots in naval blockades but is really the child of the airpower age. The idea is to destroy the adversary's economy and military infrastructure through strategic bombing, naval blockade, and so forth; turning his fielded forces defending the country into a fragile shell that will crumble at the first sign of an invading force.

There are many other approaches to strategy, but most are subsets of those discussed above. For example, in the wake of the terror attacks on New York City and Washington, DC, in 2001, there was considerable discussion concerning symmetric and asymmetric strategies. Unfortunately, these remain ill defined. The most common definition refers to one side fighting in an entirely different manner than the other in the sense of guerrilla or terror tactics opposed by modern high-tech, high-intensity, mechanized operations. While the terms wait for agreed-upon meanings and nuances, it would appear the concepts are subsets of the direct and indirect approaches. These distinctions are discussed more fully in chapter 8.

The Essence of Operational Strategy: Orchestrating Theater Campaigns

To this point, the discussion concerning the orchestration of campaigns has moved from the macrolevel (combined campaigns) to the microlevel (component campaigns) in an attempt to illustrate the functions of operational strategy, considerations for strategists, and major problem areas. All of this has been only a preliminary to the main event. It is now time to discuss putting all of these things together in theaterwide, mutually supporting, and synergistic campaigns. This is the essence of operational strategy.

The goal of operational strategy is to win the theater war; that is, achieve the military objective and ensure that achieving the military objective contributes in a positive sense to the achievement of the political (national) objective. The task of operational strategists is to orchestrate military campaigns to take maximum advantage of the strengths of friendly forces and to attack crucial enemy targets. At the same time, operational strategists must protect crucial friendly targets and offset enemy strengths. Strategists must remember that the enemy strategists are attempting to do exactly the same thing. The winner in this battle of wits is determined, to a large extent, by who best uses strengths (orchestrates campaigns) and who most accurately identifies crucial enemy targets.

Orchestrating campaigns has already been addressed in some detail. But what are "crucial targets"? They are best described by the Clausewitzian term *center of gravity* (COG), the hub of the enemy's power. The center of gravity is that on which everything else depends and thus is a vulnerability against which all efforts and energies should be directed. Although this concept is simple enough in theory, identifying the enemy's COG can be very difficult in practice.

Worldviews and their resultant priorities, as discussed earlier in this chapter, influence strategists' opinions of the enemy's center of gravity. Ground force strategists are likely to believe that the COG is within the enemy's deployed forces or is some particularly important geographic location. Airmen tend to look deeper to the industrial base and to certain targets within that base that seem particularly crucial. Naval personnel lean toward raw material supply lines. Indeed, there may be more than one COG. Ideas about the COG abound—accurate perceptions, in practice, can be more difficult to find.

Clearly, much depends on who the enemy is. The nature of the war and the objectives of both antagonists may also play roles. Several examples may help clarify the issue. In World War II, the Japanese COGs were relatively clear. Japan was waging a modern mechanized war. Industrial production was crucial to its success. Further, being a resource-poor country, its ability to import raw materials was also crucially important. Thus, two COGs became quickly evident—raw materials and the industry they fed. If raw materials were cut off, war industries would be useless. If the industries were destroyed, the raw materials would be useless. If either or both were destroyed or reduced, deployed forces could no longer be sustained, replaced, or reinforced; and the Japanese war effort would collapse.

By way of contrast, in the American Civil War, the Confederacy was not fighting a high-tech, mechanized war. Its lack of industry was, in fact, a major shortcoming. The Confederate COG clearly resided in the Confederate army itself. The army could not be replaced or adequately reinforced because of severely limited manpower; and without the army, the Confederacy could not continue to resist. This was not immediately obvious to many

Union generals at the beginning of the war. They were more enamored with the capture of Richmond, the Confederate capital. They assumed the Confederacy would collapse in political disarray if the capital city were eliminated.

Perhaps the strangest example comes from the American experience in Vietnam. In that war the United States had overwhelming resources of troops, materiel, firepower, and technology. Still, in the end, the United States withdrew in disarray in 1973 and refused to become involved again when the final crisis approached in 1975. The American COG in that war was the will of the American people to continue the struggle. Although the war effort had considerable support when large-scale American combat involvement began in 1965, that support gradually declined. On the battlefield, American victories mounted, but progress in actually winning the war was difficult to judge. The turning point for American morale, particularly on the home front, came in early 1968 when, in spite of three years of continuous American victories, the enemy mounted a major offensive across South Vietnam. The offensive was a failure and, in fact, ended in crushing military defeat for the enemy, but the point was that the enemy was still able to mount such an offensive in spite of American efforts. American willingness to continue, our COG, was overcome.

These three examples are relatively clear-cut and illustrate the variety of centers of gravity. Correctly identifying the enemy's COG is often not an easy task and generally requires great insight and considerable analysis. There are many less clear-cut examples throughout history.

The reason the authors focus on this notion is that attacks against the enemy's COG are generally the most effective, efficient, fastest, and least expensive (in terms of both blood and money) method of achieving victory, but wars can be successfully prosecuted without its identification or without effective attacks directly against it. An analogy illustrates this notion. In American football, a team can score by long, tedious, offensive drives (campaigns)—"three yards and a cloud of dust" football. This sort of campaign may be the only choice if one cannot detect a significant vulnerability in the opponent's defense. If a critical vulnerability (COG) in the opponent's defense is spotted, the offense can take advantage of that weakness and perhaps score in a short campaign consisting of only one play that covers the length of the field. Both kinds of campaigns can have the same result—points on the scoreboard. The longer campaign consumes much time and resources, while presenting numerous opportunities for mistakes. The shorter campaign is clearly more efficient. However, one must have the ability to attack the enemy's COG, which raises the subject of how such attacks can be undertaken; that is, how theater campaigns can be orchestrated.

To illustrate the variety of operational strategies and the kinds of campaigns used to attack an enemy's COG, consider the three examples discussed earlier to see how the identified COGs were attacked in each instance. In the Japanese example, the United States took a two-sided approach. To attack the Japanese natural resource vulnerability, the US Navy expended great efforts to destroy the Japanese merchant marine, particularly through submarine warfare. In addition, the drive across the Central Pacific was aimed at cutting off merchant marine traffic from the South and Southwest Pacific, areas that contained a wealth of vital natural resources. In the second stage, when island bases had finally been seized within range, Army Air Forces B-29s bombed Japanese industrial cities, eventually gutting many in fierce firebombing raids. Although this all sounds very straightforward, it was no easy task. It required much hard fighting, major fleet actions, and large-scale ground fighting before the Japanese COGs could be attacked directly.

In the American Civil War, Union forces did not get into high gear until General Grant took command. Grant understood that the Confederate army itself was the enemy's COG. In 1864 he also undertook a two-phased plan. The first phase was to send General Sherman south from Chattanooga to capture Atlanta and then on through the heart of the South (across Georgia and then north into the Carolinas) on a rampage of pillage and destruction. In addition to the direct damage to the Confederate heartland, there was the panic among the population of the affected areas. The impact on the front lines in Virginia was a serious morale problem resulting in a rapid increase in desertions from those units that came from the areas ravaged by Sherman. In short, many of the troops simply quit and went home. In conjunction with Sherman's march, Grant began a grinding campaign in northern Virginia (phase two) aimed at the direct destruction of General Lee's Confederate army. Rather than taking time to recuperate after each battle or to withdraw and refit after a setback, Grant plunged after Lee without letup, hurling superior Union manpower against the outnumbered Confederates. Grant often suffered the greater casualties, but he could replace his losses; Lee could not. The struggle was not marked by great finesse, but eventually Lee was forced to surrender.

In our third example, the North Vietnamese and Vietcong waged a war calculated only to frustrate the United States. During the critical period from 1965 to 1968, their tactics were designed to prolong the war, to avoid decisive defeat, to hit and run, to inflict casualties, and thus to send body bags home to an increasingly impatient and skeptical American population. They also made clever use of propaganda, manipulating journalists from the West and those who sympathized with their cause. The South Vietnamese aided them in no small measure. The South Vietnamese government was admittedly and obviously corrupt, largely incompetent, and led by men who were less-than-sympathetic characters in the eyes of many Americans.

All of the foregoing illustrates that there are no standard ways of attacking the enemy's COG. It also illustrates that finding the COG is not a magic solution to end a war quickly. Much hard campaigning may be required even to get into a position to attack the COG (e.g., the Japanese case). Once in position, considerable bloody fighting may still be required (e.g., the Civil War case).

But consider the alternatives. Had the Americans not gone for the Japanese jugular, they would have faced an even longer, slower, and bloodier road to Tokyo, a discouraging prospect and one in which the American people might have grown weary. If Grant and Sherman had not achieved obviously significant results in 1864, Lincoln might not have been reelected. Significant peace candidates opposed his reelection, and there was widespread war weariness and dissatisfaction in the North. As to Vietnam, the enemy had little choice. There was never much of a possibility that the Vietcong or North Vietnamese could defeat the Americans on the battlefield.

It is also significant in these examples that where Americans met with success, it came not with one sweeping campaign or battle but through well-coordinated and mutually supporting campaigns. Few modern wars have been quickly settled by a decisive battle or even one decisive campaign, the two campaigns against Iraq being notable exceptions if one considers them to be "wars." Most often, campaigns must be orchestrated to achieve the required results, and that is the essence of operational strategy.

Conclusions

All of the foregoing discussion applies to "conventional" warfare; that is, warfare fought without nuclear weapons and fought on what can be called the "European" or symmetrical warfare model. Much of the discussion may apply across the entire spectrum of conflict; however, there are two special cases, two kinds of warfare, in which some of the conventional rules and wisdom do not apply. Both asymmetrical warfare and nuclear warfare fundamentally differ from conventional war on the European model. How, for instance, do you develop operational strategies for the four media of modern warfare against an opponent that only uses one of those media (land), and then does so in ways that negate the lessons of campaigning and the like that form the basis for conventional, symmetrical planning? Conversely, how do you plan for operations where the use of the weapons around which the combat would center (nuclear weapons) would likely overwhelm any purposes for which they might be employed and make a mockery of any reasonable notion of success?

Notes

1. Data found at http://www.firstworldwar.com/battles/somme.htm.
2. See J. C. Wylie, *Military Strategy: A General Theory of Power Control* (Annapolis: Naval Institute Press, 1989).

Chapter 8

Asymmetrical Warfare Strategies

As noted in the introduction, warfare using unconventional means or ends (or both) has had many names. The currently vogue term is *asymmetrical warfare*, which has been adapted as the title for a chapter dealing primarily with these kinds of wars, which are often internal in nature. The term *asymmetrical warfare*, however, refers more to an approach to fighting when one is at a disadvantage than to a strategy as such. Asymmetrical warriors have determined that they cannot succeed by fighting in the accepted way of waging war and must change the rules to give themselves a chance. Once the determination to break the rules and fight another way has been reached, then it is the role of strategists to adopt the proper means to the end.

As also noted in the introduction, insurgent warfare strategy was a problem for the United States during the Cold War, normally in the form of revolutionary insurgent warfare by groups opposing US-backed Third World governments. The prime example was Vietnam, and although the United States has not directly confronted such a foe since, variations of insurgent warfare are still being conducted in parts of Asia and Africa, making an understanding of that strategy and how to counter it of continuing relevance.

Today there is a new set of strategies for conducting asymmetrical warfare. These new variations differ from "traditional" insurgent warfare chiefly in that they are not always fought by an insurgent group against a government and by the use of even less-conventional forms of warfare—including terrorism. One way to describe these variations is *fourth generation warfare*; another is *new internal war*. In a world where American military superiority is as great as it is, some variation of asymmetrical warfare may be the prime—and possibly sole—form of opposition the United States faces, making a knowledge of its variants a necessary prerequisite to countering them. This process, in turn, touches on the subject of homeland security and thus less-than-totally military responses to these problems.

This chapter attempts to survey the strategic problems associated with the current variations of asymmetrical warfare. It begins with the most prevalent form of such warfare in the twentieth century—insurgent warfare—because of its historic significance, the number of underlying principles it raises that affect other forms of asymmetrical warfare, and its current relevance in places like Iraq. It then moves to more contemporary variants already suggested—new internal warfare, fourth generation warfare, and terrorism—and concludes with some commonalities among the examples.

Insurgent Warfare

Insurgents wage revolutionary warfare and, for the most part, insurgencies have been revolutions—attempts to overthrow and replace governments. Revolutionary insurgent warfare has played an important role in the military history of the twentieth century, particularly in the so-called Third World, and it continues to be important in this century. In the earlier part of the twentieth century, insurgencies often resulted from emerging nationalism and anticolonialism within the empires of the European powers. Political and economic inequities played a major role in motivating these anticolonial movements, and the spark for revolution was often provided by perceptions of minimal chances for political and economic betterment. The postcolonial era did not produce much improvement to the situation. Many colonial administrations in the Third World were replaced by indigenous regimes that were more repressive, corrupt, and inept than their colonial predecessors. Thus, the stage was set for further revolutionary wars.

Although there are many examples of both colonial and postcolonial insurgencies, the protracted conflict in Vietnam exemplifies both types of struggles. While some tend to think of Vietnam as a single conflict, it had four phases that are distinctive enough to be thought of as separate wars. In what can be called the First Vietnam War (1946–54), Vietnamese insurgents (the Vietminh) defeated their French colonial masters in a prolonged anticolonialist struggle but were forced (some would say tricked) to settle for a partial victory. After the French defeat in 1954, the Geneva Accords divided Vietnam at the seventeenth parallel between Ho Chi Minh's victorious Vietminh in the North and a non-Communist regime supported by the United States in the South. In 1956 or 1957 (opinions differ on when it actually began), fighting broke out between the Republic of Vietnam (South Vietnam) and the National Liberation Front (more commonly known as the Vietcong), aided by North Vietnam. This second Vietnam war—internal to Vietnam, but an international war if the divided Vietnam is considered two countries—ended in 1965 when the United States intervened to stop the collapse of the South. In the third Vietnam war (known to most Americans as *the* Vietnam War), the United States and South Vietnam opposed the Vietcong and North Vietnam. This phase lasted from 1965 (when the first American combat forces arrived) until 1973 (when the last US combat troops were withdrawn). In the fourth war (1973–75), North and South Vietnam fought for control of the country.

The purpose of this convoluted chronology is to introduce the complexity of this kind of warfare and how different styles and strategies coexist in what appears to be a single war. In Vietnam, not only did dominant parties change (the French in the first war, the Americans in the third), but so did the style. The Communists, for instance, fought guerrilla style (asymmetrically) against the firepower-superior French and Americans, while the North Vietnamese fought conventionally against the South Vietnamese but mostly unconventionally against the Americans. Such variation in strategies is not uncommon in insurgent warfare.

In the Cold War, many insurgencies involved the superpowers to one degree or another. The United States and the Soviets, time after time, backed opposing sides in attempts to gain influence in the Third World and wrest advantage in international power politics. As a result it was all too easy to forget that insurgencies are, first and foremost, internal struggles for political power and only secondarily East versus West confrontations, as they were during the Cold War. They are, after all, civil wars de facto if not de jure. For example, because of the circumstances and politics of the struggle, Americans often forget that even the third Vietnam war could be seen as a civil war. From the viewpoint of the United States, North Vietnam was committing aggression against South Vietnam, a viewpoint that provided justification for American intervention. However, from the perspective of the North Vietnamese and the southern insurgents they supported, the struggle was a civil war for political control of greater Vietnam. Particularly when contemplating involvement in one of these kinds of affairs, it is useful to realize that the internal issues are most important to the local population and that outside involvement will be judged by its effects on that population, a dynamic the United States is learning painfully in postwar Iraq.

Nature of Insurgent Warfare

Revolutionary insurgent warfare has had many theorists. They differ from one another in some respects, but they agree far more than they disagree. The fountainhead for most Third World revolutionaries in the twentieth century was Mao Tse-tung, who put his ideas to the test in the long civil war in China as he overthrew the government of Chiang Kai-shek. The fact that he was ultimately successful has given Mao's theories great credibility as a model for others seeking to overthrow what they view as tyrannical governments.

Mao visualized peasant-based "peoples' revolutionary wars" that were protracted struggles waged to wear down and discredit the government while at the same time gaining support from a larger and larger proportion of the peasantry. By basing the insurgency in the countryside (where it was beyond the physical reach of the government) and by expanding its support, Mao ensured that the government would become evermore isolated, impotent, and surrounded in the cities. Mao viewed the struggle as a flexible, three-phased conflict.

In the first stage, the insurgents establish secure operating bases in remote areas (or in sanctuaries across an international border if necessary) virtually inaccessible to government troops. Stage two involves ever-increasing guerrilla warfare—attacking and overrunning government outposts, seizing arms, demoralizing government forces and their supporters, and demonstrating the government's inability to control and protect the populace. Following the principles set forth by Chinese strategist Sun Tzu

3,000 years ago, guerrillas only attack when they are certain to be successful, abandoning their positions when they are vulnerable. In the third and final stage, the balance of power shifts decisively to the insurgents, who can then openly take to the field in large units using conventional tactics to destroy demoralized government forces and overthrow the government. Although Mao envisioned these as progressive stages, his concept is flexible. If the situation dictates, the revolutionaries can fall back to a previous stage and work to create a more favorable opportunity for progress. This was, of course, exactly what the North Vietnamese did during the fourth segment of their civil war. When their opponent was the relatively weak South Vietnamese, they fought symmetrically, eventually crushing the resistance in 1975. Against the Americans, they reverted to guerrilla-style (asymmetrical) warfare to avoid annihilation.

However, according to Mao, military action is only a small part of a complex program designed to disaffect the population from the government. Revolutionary warfare relies on a sophisticated package of political, psychological, and economic programs, all designed to take advantage of grievances against the existing power structure and to win support (or at least neutrality) from the population. Winning that support—Lyndon Johnson's battle for "the hearts and the minds of the people"—is the key to changing the correlation of forces away from the government to favor the insurgents.[1]

Mao's basic theory of insurgent warfare has been adapted and modified by other insurgent theorists (e.g., Che Guevara in Latin America and Ho Chi Minh in Vietnam) to fit local conditions and cultural differences. As a result, every insurgency has its unique characteristics; however, successful insurgencies also have had certain characteristics in common that constitute the basis of insurgent warfare doctrine. Four characteristics are particularly significant to the American military: the protracted nature of such struggles, the central role of the insurgent political infrastructure, the subsidiary role of insurgent military forces, and the use of guerrilla tactics in military operations.

The first characteristic of successful insurgencies is that they are almost always protracted struggles. Rebels attempting to overthrow an entrenched government usually cannot achieve a quick victory because they generally enter the contest considerably weaker than their opponent. However, in the hands of an insurgent, time becomes a weapon that cuts into support for the government and its allies. On one hand, the rebels require time to build their support and strength relative to the government they seek to overthrow. On the other hand, insurgents use time as a weapon in itself to weaken that same government. Every day that an insurgent movement continues to exist (not to mention continues to operate and grow) discredits the government and its ability to govern and control its own destiny. Every day that an insurgent movement continues to exist adds a degree of legitimacy to its cause and can eventually create an air of inevitability surrounding an eventual victory for the rebels. In Vietnam both France and later the United States found that their enemies used time as a potent weapon. The Vietminh and later the Vietcong/North Vietnamese protracted their struggles, waiting for the French and Americans to tire of the endless bloodletting and to abandon their efforts.

The second characteristic of insurgencies is the central role played by their infrastructures. The primary source of an insurgency's strength is its underground organization—the hostile political infrastructure within the target population. This infrastructure is the single, most important ingredient in the insurgent recipe for success and performs several functions vital to the survival, growth, and eventual success of the insurgency: intelligence gathering and transmission; provision of supplies and financial resources; recruitment; political expansion and penetration; sabotage, terrorism, and intimidation; and establishment of a shadow government.

Accurate and timely intelligence is vital to insurgent success in both political and military actions. Well-placed agents within the government and its military can provide information that simultaneously can make government counterinsurgency actions ineffectual and increase the effectiveness of insurgent actions. Even those agents or sympathizers who are not well placed can provide significant information to the insurgent command structure simply by observing government troop movements or reporting the unguarded conversations of minor government officials. Such agents can also deny information (or plant false information) with the government or its supporters.

Insurgent sympathizers provide their military forces with important supplies that are readily available within the society under attack. They can obtain simple medical supplies and clothing in small amounts without suspicion. For those supplies not readily available, "taxes" voluntarily paid by sympathizers and coerced from others provide the means to obtain such needs from foreign sources or corrupt government officials.

If the proselytizing efforts of the insurgent underground succeed and the infrastructure spreads through the population, the government is obviously weakened. In addition, as it spreads through the society, the infrastructure taps into a larger and larger manpower pool from which to draw recruits (volunteers and conscripts) for the rebel armed forces. This phenomenon explains why it is possible for the size of the rebel military force to increase despite heavy casualties inflicted by government forces. Indeed, if the government concentrates its attention on the insurgent military threat, and thus provides the infrastructure the opportunity to grow unimpeded, the government's military problem is exacerbated.

Members of the underground are often in positions from which they can effectively conduct sabotage operations against government resources and installations. Moreover, because they are embedded deeply within the general population, clandestine insurgent cells can effectively engage in or abet acts of terrorism designed to intimidate portions of the population. These activities further weaken support for the government (particularly if the perpetrators are not apprehended) and weaken the will of the population to resist insurgent efforts.

Finally, the insurgent infrastructure can establish its own government as a rival to the authority of the government under siege. This is a particularly effective ploy if certain geographic areas are effectively under the control of the insurgents. A shadow government challenges the legitimacy of the established government by virtue of its announced political program (calling for solutions to the grievances that produced the insurgency), its control in certain areas, and the inability of the government in power to destroy the insurgency. Further, a shadow government can provide a "legitimate" conduit for support from friendly foreign powers.

The rebel political infrastructure feeds on the perceived grievances that led to the birth of the insurgent movement. The infrastructure is difficult for the government to attack because it is essentially "bulletproof." (One could not attack a three-person insurgent cell in a Saigon high school with heavy bombers or artillery.) Moreover, if the infrastructure is well constructed (e.g., small cells with little knowledge of other cells), government forces will have great difficulty in rooting out and destroying the infrastructure with nonmilitary means, such as counterintelligence activities and police actions.

The importance of the insurgent infrastructure is mirrored in the third characteristic of successful insurgencies: the subsidiary importance of insurgent military actions. Without question, rebel military actions play an important role in the insurgency, but success on the battlefield is not crucial to the success of the insurgent movement. This explains why insurgent forces can lose virtually every battle and still win the war. It is also why it is important for governments, and those who support them, not to be too hasty in claiming victory against an insurgent movement.

The fourth and final characteristic successful insurgencies have in common is the use of guerrilla tactics. Guerrilla tactics are the classic ploy used by the weak against the strong, and as such, are at the conceptual heart of all asymmetrical approaches to war by one name or another. Rather than military operations designed to win a quick victory (as in the conventional or symmetrical model of fighting), guerrilla tactics are designed to avoid a decisive defeat at the hands of a stronger enemy. Understanding the dynamics, purposes, and methods of success of insurgents is a necessary step to designing effective strategies for countering them, a problem that has yet to be decisively mastered.

The first contrast is organizational and philosophical. While conventional forces are constructed around the mobility of large units, guerrilla forces base their operations on the mobility of the individual soldier. Operating in small units, guerrillas avoid presenting themselves as tempting targets for government forces that usually have vastly superior firepower at their disposal. As a result, guerrillas seek to negate the major advantage of government forces. Guerrillas fight only when it is to their advantage to fight, often quickly concentrating a superior force against an isolated government unit, attacking, and then disappearing as quickly and mysteriously as they appeared. Rarely do these forces using guerrilla tactics attempt to hold terrain, for to do so invites destruction by superior enemy forces.

The purposes of employing guerrilla war tactics are numerous. Even if apparently unsuccessful militarily, insurgent military actions shift government attention away from the activities of the insurgent political infrastructure so that the underground can continue to grow and spread with minimal opposition from government forces or officials. Guerrilla attacks harass, demoralize, and embarrass the government, its forces, and its allies by their continued existence and the government's inability to destroy them. With any luck, guerrilla actions can elicit draconian reprisals from a frustrated government. Although these reprisals can take a heavy toll on insurgents, they almost inevitably exact a fearful price from bystanders, the very people on whose continued loyalty the government depends. As a result, such reprisals are often counterproductive because they further alienate the population from the government, which is much of the purpose of the guerrillas.

If successful, rebel operations using guerrilla tactics can achieve several favorable results. Support for the insurgents increases, or the people take a neutral stance, because the government is unable to protect itself or the people from guerrilla actions. Fatigue and war-weariness set in as the struggle becomes more protracted, particularly if the government seems to be making little if any headway against the guerrilla forces. Morale among government forces begins to deteriorate, and desertions from the government ranks increase as the insurgent underground infrastructure continues to expand, thus compounding the government's problem almost geometrically. Eventually, according to classic insurgency doctrine, the correlation of forces changes in favor of the insurgents. Insurgent forces mass into large units, using conventional tactics and administer the coup de grace in rapid order.

Fundamental Differences

When taken together, the unique aspects of the insurgent warfare variant of asymmetrical warfare indicate that such

139

struggles are fundamentally different from conventional warfare. For the United States during much of the twentieth century, the tendency was to downplay those differences because doing so made them more familiar in terms of how to deal with them. This approach was largely unsuccessful because it made strategists conceptualize the problem incorrectly and hence the nature of its solution. Rather than a large war made small, insurgent warfare is at least as different from conventional war as conventional war is considered different from nuclear war. Two fundamental differences, which apply in varying detail to other forms of asymmetrical warfare, are of interest here.

Perhaps the most important difference is that in an insurgency, both antagonists have virtually the same ultimate objective, which is the loyalty and support of the population of the country. This support is known as the center of gravity, what Pres. Lyndon Johnson labeled "the battle for the hearts and the minds of the people," as mentioned above. In most insurgencies, the winner of this battle also wins the war.

The center of an insurgency's strength and the key to its survival and growth is the covert political infrastructure deeply embedded in and permeating the general population. Without some support from the people—or at least their neutrality in the struggle (neutrality is a net benefit to the insurgent and is, in effect, passive support)—the underground infrastructure would be quickly exposed and eliminated. Without an infrastructure, the insurgency has no political arm, is devoid of its intelligence apparatus, and is bereft of its principal source of military manpower and logistical support (e.g., food). No insurgency can persist without some support from the population, and it is imperative for anyone contemplating countering an insurgency to recognize that if the insurgency has lasted over a period of time, it almost certainly has some popular support.

The besieged government's power also ultimately depends on the support and loyalty of the general population. In the long run (and insurgencies certainly qualify as long-run situations), no government can survive without the acquiescence of the people—least of all, a government actively opposed by an attractive and aggressive insurgency. Put another way, an enduring insurgency also suggests that the government has been less-than-totally successful in winning the contest for public loyalty.

Thus the COGs of each side in an insurgency are located within the general population. For the insurgency, the center is its infrastructure with its active and tacit supporters. For the government, it is its supporters. The groups commingle and are virtually indistinguishable. Whichever group becomes dominant in the population—government or insurgent supporters—will likely prevail in the long run.

In conventional warfare, military professionals have long accepted the concept of centers of gravity, but with a different connotation. The basic military objective in such warfare is to conduct operations that lead to the destruction of the enemy's COG while at the same time protecting one's own vital centers. There are, in other words, two separate centers: theirs and ours. However, in insurgent warfare, the existence of commingled COGs calls this basic military doctrine into serious question. Using traditional military means—fire and steel on a target—to destroy the insurgent's COG may well also destroy one's own vital center by attacking and alienating the population mass that each side must court and ultimately win over to succeed.

A second unique feature of insurgent warfare is the different criteria for success for the government and the insurgents. Although it may initially sound paradoxical, insurgent military forces win whenever they do not lose. Although forces using guerrilla tactics often "lose" small tactical engagements, their dispersed nature and their focus on small-unit actions are designed to avoid anything approaching a decisive defeat. Their survival in the face of often vastly superior government strength adds to their credibility and the aura of success they must nurture to change the odds in their favor. Conversely, conventional military forces lose whenever they do not win. The failure to decisively defeat a military force over which they have great advantages in firepower discredits the government's military and the government as a whole. The longer the insurgency avoids defeat, the more likely it is to prevail in the long run. The longer the government fails to destroy the insurgents, the more likely it is to lose.

The kind of military warfare conducted by insurgents is therefore the antithesis of conventional warfare. Conventional military forces have continually sought, particularly over the past two centuries, ways to concentrate forces in time and space to achieve quick and decisive victories, a quest that has been most successfully mastered and applied against similar forces in symmetrical warfare. Insurgent military forces take the opposite approach by dispersing in space and protracting in time to avoid decisive defeat. While conventional forces attempt to achieve victory by acting faster than the enemy can or is willing to react, insurgent guerrilla forces seek victory by acting longer than the enemy can react. While conventional forces attempt to provide their enemy with insufficient time, guerrilla forces try their enemy's patience—time becomes a weapon.

Counterinsurgency Concepts

From the foregoing analysis, it should be clear that countering an insurgency is no easy task. This observation should come as no surprise, since the most basic underlying purpose of any asymmetrical approach to warfare is frustrating the calculation of conventional strategists by presenting them with problems about which they have not adequately thought and thus for which they have not properly prepared. This is, in some measure, the situation in which strategists find themselves today. They can, however, derive some concepts for a counterinsurgency strategy with considerable confidence.

The most clearly evident concept is that any successful counterinsurgency strategy must incorporate a three-pronged approach. Sources of popular unrest must be excised, the covert infrastructure must be identified and destroyed, and insurgent military forces must be defeated. Each of these tasks is critically important. The longer the insurgency operates and imbeds itself into the population, the more difficult it is to accomplish each of these goals, and especially all of them.

The second concept is that population control and intelligence gathering are key factors in the implementation of a successful counterinsurgency strategy. Superior intelligence operations are always an important factor in military operations and are even more important when attempting to defeat forces employing guerrilla tactics because guerrillas are exceedingly difficult to find and bring to battle. Additionally, identification and destruction of the covert insurgent infrastructure require criminal intelligence operations (identification, correlation, tracking, and apprehension). These are requirements not unlike those involved in the suppression of terrorists (see below). The intelligence task is much more difficult if population movement is not tightly controlled. A key ingredient of intelligence, when working against the infrastructure, is knowing who is not supposed to be where and identifying aberrations to the pattern. This knowledge can be gained much more easily in a controlled environment, or at least one in which you have adequate sources of reliable information of your own to monitor the situation. Further, population control presupposes a high degree of security within the controlled area. If effective control and security exist, those who might otherwise be intimidated by the insurgency infrastructure may feel confident enough to aid in the identification of insurgent agents.

The third concept is that the single, most important factor in countering an insurgency is time—just as time is the most important tool in an insurgent's kit. Counterinsurgent actions are far more likely to succeed if they begin early, long before the situation becomes a crisis. In the same light, counterinsurgent actions should be sudden and decisive rather than gradual and graduated actions that provide time for insurgent reaction. Once again, insurgencies are most vulnerable in their infancies, before they can imbed themselves in the population and begin to develop the popular support that makes them difficult, and may ultimately make them impossible, to defeat.

From all of the foregoing, it is clear that the complex world of insurgent and counterinsurgent warfare strategy is a "special case" for strategists. Insurgent warfare is the conceptual "base case" for looking at other forms of asymmetrical warfare, since most of the concepts and problems associated with new internal war, fourth generation warfare, and terrorism are outgrowths of dynamics and problems that are present in traditional insurgency. With a basic understanding of asymmetry in warfare flowing from the insurgency example, the discussion turns to its more-contemporary variations.

New Internal War

During the 1990s a distinctive subset of insurgencies emerged. The traditional kinds of insurgencies already discussed, while asymmetrical in the means used to prosecute them, were traditional in the sense of the reasons for which they were fought: an insurgent group sought to overthrow and replace a government which responded by seeking to avoid that fate through the defeat and destruction of the insurgency. Using force to maintain or overthrow governments is, of course, the heart of the Clausewitzian dictum that war is the continuation of politics by other means.

The new internal wars (or NIWs, a term one of the authors coined in *UnCivil Wars*) are different.[2] While they are asymmetrical, in that they reject or ignore conventional rules of war, they have been more overtly unconventional than traditional insurgencies, both in their methods and their underlying political purposes.

What sets these conflicts apart has been the extreme disorder-liness, violence, and apparent senselessness of the suffering they have exacted, mainly against civilian populations of their fellow citizens. These conflicts have been extremely bitter, bloody, and hideous in their conduct, often involving the brazen commission of crimes against humanity, and usually for ends that are more often venal than lofty. The purpose is often not to replace one political order with another one; rather, as often as not, it is to destroy any form of order as the means to create political chaos in which the "rebels" can flourish in nefarious endeavors. It can vary as widely as protecting or nurturing the narcotics trade (a subset of NIWs sometimes referred to as narco-insurgency) or providing an environment in which the diamond trade can be illegally controlled (also known as criminal insurgency).

The fact that these kinds of wars emerged in the 1990s sug-gests a Cold War connection that is at least partly justified. During the Cold War, most insurgencies had an East-West as-pect, with the United States supporting one side (usually the government) and the Soviet Union or China the other (usually the insurgents). For fear either of escalation to direct super-power confrontation or of being embarrassed by allies' actions, the result was to place some constraint on the quality of vio-lence employed, especially against the mutual center of gravity. A consequence of the Cold War's end was the withdrawal of both the United States and Russia from Third World conflicts, and whatever constraint they had imposed on internal conflicts left with them. At the same time, that withdrawal also meant less attention was paid to the more geopolitically obscure parts of the world in which NIWs tend to occur. Having said that, what is arguably the prototype of the NIW was the Cambodian civil war of the middle 1970s; however, it was distinctive in that the sponsoring parties were not the superpowers but the two communist giants, the Soviets and the Chinese.

The list of prominent instances of NIWs from the 1990s is familiar. The post–Cold War prototype was Somalia, where the combination of a long drought and the use of international relief supplies to influence a clan-based war threatened to produce massive starvation until an international peacekeeping operation involving the United States prominently interfered with the suffering in 1992. That conflict continues at a more subdued level, in that no recognized national government has yet emerged. "Ethnic cleansing" was added to the language of international politics when Serbs, Croats, and Bosnian Muslims struggled to partition the Bosnian successor state to Yugoslavia, a process dramatically reprised in Kosovo at the end of the decade. Between the Bosnian and Kosovar outbreaks, the United States intervened in Haiti, and the tragic Rwanda genocide occurred. The problem of narco-insurgency in places like Colombia and Peru spanned the Cold War's end; criminal insurgencies blossomed in African locations like Liberia (where it periodically recurs, as in 2003, causing the United States to join an international peacekeeping effort there) and Sierra Leone. The bloodletting in East Timor provides an Asian variant as well.

These conflicts sent contradictory signals to the international system—including the United States—during the 1990s. Almost all of these conflicts, although geographically distributed across the globe, tended to occur in the geopolitical peripheries where vital national interests were not involved, and the consequences of ignoring them were minimal. At the same time, their emergence coincided with the maturing of global television and especially 24-hour news outlets like CNN. The result was an unprecedented level of coverage of the atrocities that are a signature part of the NIWs: the distended bellies and rail-like arms and legs of Somalian children; Bosnian refugees peering through barbed-wire fences eerily reminiscent of Nazi concentration camps; the bloated bodies of Rwandan victims of the rampage there; the amputees of Sierra Leone; and the panicked victims of East Timor fleeing as their homes burned behind them, to cite some examples. The effect was to make these tragedies much more unavoidable than they would have been otherwise. The added fact that these conflicts were occurring in an international environment where they were essentially the only interruptions to the peace further highlighted them.

The events of 11 September 2001 and the ensuing dynamics of the "war" on terrorism diverted our attention from these kinds of wars, and the campaign promise by candidate Bush to refrain from committing American forces to peacekeeping seemed to signal a further diminishing of US attention to the NIWs. But they do not seem to go away, and when Liberia boiled over once again during the summer of 2003, President Bush discovered that avoiding involvement in these humanitarian disasters was easier said than done, and US attention to these wars was rekindled.

Nature of the Problem

Like more traditional insurgencies, NIWs are both a political and a military problem. At the political level, however, these kinds of conflicts tend to distort traditional political goals in such a way as to contribute to the extreme brutality and atrocity that often mark the military signature of this form of warfare.

Unlike traditional civil wars, the control of government is often not the clear objective of both (or all) sides. In a number of instances, the insurgent force articulates no political objectives or statements about the principles by which it would govern if it prevails. The Revolutionary United Front (RUF) of Sierra Leone, for example, has never issued a political manifesto of any kind, and this is not unusual, especially in African NIWs. Generally, the reason is that the movement's purpose has little to do with positive governance and more with creating a condition of anarchy where it destroys government authority with no intention to replace it. In the case of the RUF, its principal motivation was to remove government control of the diamond fields of Sierra Leone to facilitate its criminal control of the diamond trade. In the case of the various "revolutionary" groups in Colombia, their function is to protect the drug trade from a government that might seek to interrupt it. Often, this absence of a positive political purpose is masked behind high-sounding

146

rhetoric (e.g., the so-called Lord's Army of Uganda) to obscure its basic criminality.

Because NIWs are often not fought for positive control of the political system, there is much less emphasis on the battle for the hearts and minds of men than is the case in traditional insurgencies. There is no common COG in the target population to which both sides must appeal to succeed. Rather, one segment of the population seeks to impose its will on the other for one purpose or another: control of territory through ethnic cleansing (the Balkans), to avoid secession of an area of a country (East Timor), or for a variety of criminal purposes. In these circumstances, one segment of the population seeks to intimidate or eliminate others to gain its ends. In this sense, the dynamics of NIWs more resemble the dynamics of symmetrical interstate wars (wars between countries) than traditional insurgencies (countries at war with one another normally do not have conversion of the enemy population as a major objective until the fighting is concluded). The principal difference, of course, is that there are accepted—and usually honored—conventions of interstate war that do not exist in NIWs.

The major consequence of this political dynamic is the absence of moderation or limits in the ferocity with which NIWs are fought. The contest for a common COG may be (and usually is) partly conducted through violence and intimidation, but it must also have a positive element that places some boundaries on behavior toward the target population for fear of alienating it. In NIWs, by contrast, that regulator of violence is totally missing. The Hutu of Rwanda did not want to convert the Tutsi in anticipation of a postwar reconciliation; they wanted to kill as many of them as possible, hopefully eliminating them from the population.

The military characteristics of NIWs follow from these nontraditional political characteristics and provide a parallel and preview for the military characteristics of fourth generation warfare. Since there are no clear political goals (other than destabilization), they do not provide any Clausewitzian guidance for the development of military objectives and operations, as discussed in earlier chapters. The military units that conduct these kinds of wars are typically highly irregular, not wearing uniforms or organized into coherent orderings of officers and soldiers, poorly trained and disciplined, and utterly unaware or contemptuous of normal conventions of warfare (these are also characteristics of fourth generation war). It is not unusual for these troops to be referred to as "fighters" rather than "soldiers"—an apt distinction. Moreover, the global concern with the number of children engaged in war in fact largely describes the forces in NIWs, where it is not unusual for 10- to 12-year-olds to be used to do the fighting. The Lord's Army, for instance, often raids orphanages, kidnaps children, and forces them into service, threatening to kill them if they refuse or attempt to escape.

The kinds of reasons for conducting NIWs and the kinds and qualities of forces that are involved have resulted in the unique savagery that NIWs have added to the landscape of international violence. One trend of the twentieth century has been that the victims of war are increasingly civilians. In World War I, for instance, an estimated 15 percent of the casualties were civilian. That proportion has steadily risen to the point that, in modern internal wars, upwards of 90 percent of the victims are noncombatants. A prominent reason for that change is that civilians are the conscious targets in the NIWs.

Fundamental Differences

While the new internal wars present some unique operational problems largely shared with fourth generation warfare and to a lesser extent terrorism (discussed in the conclusions), the real differences they present to American strategy are political. These consist of two sequential questions, neither of which was entirely satisfactorily answered during the 1990s, and which were further blurred in the early 2000s.

The first question was whether the United States should respond to outbreaks of NIWs, especially with armed force. Viewed in traditional realist terms of vital interest as the trigger for military involvement, almost none of the NIWs of the 1990s justified US intervention, but the United States in fact involved itself in four of these situations (Somalia, Haiti, Bosnia, and Kosovo). In each case, the American intervention was as a peacekeeper, although the situations into which the United States thrust itself varied from latent hostilities (Somalia) to negotiated (Bosnia) or imposed (Kosovo) cease-fires to the Haitian "interaction" (part intervention, part invasion) to restore the Aristide government to power. At the same time, the United States declined to become involved at all in other events (Rwanda is the notable example) or only indirectly (East Timor).

The experience of the 1990s thus leaves no clear guidance about when and where the United States needs to be prepared to insert itself into NIWs, and early pronouncements and actions of the Bush administration have not clarified this situation. During the 2000 election campaign, Bush and his spokespersons argued for a reduction of US overseas deployments, with specific reference to peacekeeping duties in the NIWs. By contrast, the Bush administration actually increased the "ops tempo" in places with situations not entirely different from the sites of the 1990s' NIWs, such as Afghanistan. The Bush administration abruptly (if implicitly) reversed course with the short-term dispatch of US peacekeepers to Liberia in 2003 in apparent contradiction to its 2000 campaign assertions, further muddying any precedents for action or inaction based in prior experience.

If there is not clear policy about which NIWs to be involved in, neither is there much clarification about what the United States should do and how it should go about doing it. Generally speaking, the purpose of outside intervention is to stabilize war zones and improve conditions so as to leave the target country better off than it was when the peacekeepers arrive (and hopefully better off than before fighting began). These efforts fall broadly under the rubric of nation building and consist of both political actions (stabilizing, and hopefully democratizing, the political system in heretofore unstable political climates) and economic actions (improving the lot of the population to the point they will not be predisposed to a return to violence). These kinds of activities extend to non-NIW situations (such as Afghanistan and Iraq) as well and share some common problems with fourth generation warfare and terrorism. There is less than unanimity about the military role in these kinds of operations; therefore, discussion of the principles for countering these situations will be deferred to the conclusions of this chapter.

Fourth Generation Warfare

The idea of what is now called fourth generation warfare is not a particularly new concept, as is generally true with various types of asymmetrical warfare. Rather it is the accumulation of a body of thought among some military historians and analysts that have argued for sometime that conventional, Western-style warfare conducted using Clausewitzian principles represents an aberration in the history of warfare, and that what is generally called asymmetrical warfare represents the much more universal case. The term *fourth generation* derives from what these analysts see as the evolution of modern warfare through a series of generations: a first generation dominated by linear formations of armies clashing in open fields with smoothbore muskets (classic eighteenth-century warfare); a second generation that was introduced when more-accurate rifles and muskets made linear formations suicidal and created defense dominance epitomized in World War I; and a third generation where mechanization of warfare made rapid mobility possible and returned the dominance of offensive warfare (blitzkrieg techniques). The fourth generation is the logical successor to these forms of symmetrical warfare that leaves traditional warfare techniques and principles obsolete.

The analysts who argue fourth generation warfare represents the future maintain that the world is entering a period of radical change in who makes war, how they make war, and why. One of the major apostles of this change is Martin van Creveld who argues that the old Clausewitzian conceptualization on which so much of current strategy and philosophy of war is based no longer holds and "should these trends continue, the kind of war that is based on the division between government, army, and people seems to be on its way out." Instead, he (and others like him) argues, "In the future, wars will not be waged by armies but by groups whom we today call terrorists, guerillas, bandits, and robbers. Their organizations are likely to be constructed along charismatic lines rather than institutional ones, and to be motivated less by 'professionalism' than by fanatical, ideologically based loyalties."[3] This prophecy eerily suggests the actions of al-Qaeda on 11 September 2001 but was published a full decade earlier.

What is notable for strategy and strategists about fourth generation warfare is the degree to which it turns conventional ways of thinking about war on their heads. Most of our strategic thought is based upon the military interaction of sovereign states fighting against one another for traditional political objectives such as control of the state or the righting of some difference between the combatants. Those who project the fourth generation obviously gaze into the future and see a very different reality and one that challenges most of our ways of thinking about planning the use of force.

Nature of the Problem

In 1989 William Lind and a group of colleagues laid out six characteristics of fourth generation warfare.[4] At least two of these are historical and could be derived from the American experience in Vietnam, whereas the others are extrapolations from the past into the future. Cumulatively, however, they help define the problem of fourth generation warfare.

The first characteristic identified refers to the physical conduct of hostilities. In this view there will be no distinctions in future warfare between military forces and civilians in terms of targeting—society is the target set in the new warfare. There will also be no definable battlefield, and the places where fighting occurs will be dispersed and undefined—everywhere and nowhere is the front line. The result is a much more fluid military situation where traditional concerns, such as land gained or lost, will lose much of their meaning as measures of military success.

The purposes of fighting will also change for those who adopt fourth generation warfare. The goal, Lind argues, will not be military defeat of the opposition but instead the internal political collapse of the enemy and its willingness to continue the struggle. Manipulation of the media will be a major tool of fourth generation practitioners, and the purpose of much of the campaign will be popular support among the opponent's population, what the authors have referred to as "cost-tolerance" in *From Lexington to Desert Storm.*[5]

To this point the characteristics of fourth generation warfare may challenge symmetrical, Western conceptualizations, but they hardly break ground from other asymmetrical experiences. A fluid battlefield where civilians were targets was a feature of the Vietnam War, and it has been argued that much of the war, and notably the Tet offensive of 1968, was aimed principally at destroying support for the war effort within the American public. The fourth generation, however, extends beyond these historical bases.

A third characteristic of the fourth generation is its explicit roots in the Asian style of warfare, which emphasizes maneuver and surprise more than it does the direct clash of armies on the battlefield. Sir John Keegan, defense editor of the *London Daily Telegraph*, describes and applies this characteristic: "The Oriental tradition, however, has not been eliminated. It reappeared . . . particularly in the tactics of evasion and retreat practiced by the Vietcong against the United States in the Vietnam War. On September 11, 2001, it returned in an absolutely traditional form. Arabs, appearing suddenly out of empty space like their desert raider ancestors, assaulted the heartlands of western power, in a terrifying surprise raid and did appalling damage."[6]

Lind and his colleagues further maintain that the terrorism described in the previous quotation by Keegan is a standard part of the arsenal of those practicing this form of asymmetrical warfare. The reason is straightforward, given the other characteristics of the genre. Since fourth generation warfare represents the actions not only of the weak (the basis for asymmetrical warfare), but often the very weak, terrorism—which is a tactic of the weak (see discussion in the next section)—is a logical tactic to adopt. Terrorism is also attractive because the countries against which fourth generation warriors will fight will often be Western democracies whose openness makes them more vulnerable to terrorist attacks. The use of terrorism is further reinforced by a fifth characteristic of the fourth generation, which is to attack opposition states by attempting to disrupt their normal, orderly societal bases—what Lind terms the "culture of order."

Finally, the practitioners of fourth generation warfare often will not be nationally or territorially based states but will instead be so-called nonstate actors (terrorist groups are an obvious example of this kind of entity). These kinds of opponents—who may have sanctuary or sanction (and occasionally even sponsorship) by state governments—have an ambiguous standing in international law. The notion of declaration of war, for instance, is traditionally intended to be by one state against another. Hence, it will not always be entirely clear who or what to attack in attempting to defeat nonstate actors. When a non-state actor confronts a state actor, and especially a powerful state, then the dynamics that lead to the choice of asymmetrical warfare methods are virtually dictated.

Fundamental Differences

The kinds of asymmetrical problems addressed in this chapter clearly represent ascending orders of challenge to traditional conceptualizations about strategizing for war. The fourth generation is no exception to this, and it adds at least two fundamental challenges to the mix. It provides something of a definition of the "rule changes" that the asymmetrical warrior may present in the future, and it further complicates the problem of responding to these kinds of problems with extraordinarily sophisticated and powerful, yet thoroughly conventional, forces of our own.

The characteristics of the fourth generation rather clearly define some of the ways that future asymmetrical warriors may change the rules of engagement to reduce their disadvantages against superior opponents. As noted, not all of these rule changes are unique. The blurring, if not extinction, of the boundary between civilian and military targets and the attempt to render conventional measures of success, such as territory lost or gained, are problems the United States confronted in Vietnam, but it is not clear they have been surmounted. In Iraq, for instance, there were pockets of ongoing resistance that popped up in one locale or another, faded away, and sometimes returned. Which parts of the map were blue (American) and which parts green (whatever form Iraqi resistance took)? It was not always clear. At the same time, part of the purpose of the Vietcong campaign against the United States was rather clearly aimed at undercutting the morale of the American public by causing unacceptable levels of American casualties, a tactic apparently revisited in Iraq in 2003.

Adding an Asian overtone to warfare illuminates the challenge. The Asian tradition, dating back to Sun Tzu, does not glorify the Western code of warfare but does indeed encompass tactics and methods generally considered illegal or immoral under Western standards of war. Indiscriminate terrorist attacks against civilian targets are a prime example and illustrate how the asymmetrical warrior changes the rules. Purposely attacking noncombatants is outlawed under the Geneva conventions of war, but asymmetrical warriors may decide that they have no chance of success unless they can adopt this tactic, which allows them to attack Lind's culture of order as one of the few ways they may impose their will on an otherwise entirely superior opponent. Conventional strategists find these actions reprehensible, but do they also find them incomprehensible? More to the point, how can they compel the enemy to abandon this tactic? Can strategists defeat its application? Can they compel the enemies' return to the rules? If so, how? Conventional thinking does not necessarily provide good answers.

The other new ingredient the fourth generation adds to the mix is the problem of countering this breed of asymmetrical warrior. In some important ways, Western—especially American—military strength has become so enormous as to be unchallengeable, at least in terms of symmetrical responses. But is that enough to assure that the United States will prevail? American firepower is overwhelming, but is it responsive to an opponent which imbeds itself into the civilian population and justifies doing so by erasing the distinction between military and nonmilitary targets and argues all society is fair game under the new rules of war? Precise airborne weapons can reduce the collateral damage of trying to excise the opposition from the civilian web, but does it convince the opponent to reverse its rejection of the conventional rules? The development of counterinsurgency strategy has always been a difficult business, and the adoption of the tenets of fourth generation warfare only adds to this difficulty.

Terrorism

Terrorism is the final form of asymmetrical warfare to be discussed. In some ways it is the ultimate method of the asymmetrical warrior. The use of terror more fundamentally assaults conventional mores and conventions about the legitimate uses of force more than any other form of "warfare," thus representing the greatest challenge to the rules of warfare of any method. It is typically (although by no means exclusively) the form of action of nonstate actors, at least in the contemporary system where it is more difficult for governments to terrorize their own populations than it was in the past. Moreover, it is a method that allows a far inferior force to attack directly the target society and its cost tolerance in a way that other applications of violence cannot so easily do.

Among the sources of controversy surrounding terrorism is where it fits into the hierarchy of military problems. Is terrorism a strategy in the classic sense, or is it merely a tactic that is a part of implementing broader strategies? Without going into details, the answer is probably that terrorism can be both a strategy and a tactic, depending on the situation and the nature of the terrorists. Entities like states with a number of capabilities available to them may occasionally employ terrorist techniques for tactical advantage; whereas, small, isolated groups with no other means at their avail may think of terrorism more strategically. Regardless, terrorism is a distinctive *problem* for the United States (and others) that is important enough to rate inclusion in a discussion of strategic challenges.

The term *terrorism* derives from the Latin word *terrere*, which means to frighten, and that is exactly what terrorists seek to do. The heart of terrorism is to create fear in the target population, whether it be a state or a group of people inside a state, to the point that the population decides that acceding to whatever demands the terrorists have is preferable to living in a continued condition of fear of being victim to the terrorists' violent acts. Terrorism does not, like fourth generation warfare, generally seek to physically defeat an obviously militarily superior enemy; rather it seeks to cause the target's morale to collapse by disrupting the culture of order. In terms used before, the terrorists attempt to exceed the target's cost tolerance. When they do and the target complies, the terrorists win. If they cannot overcome cost tolerance or are defeated and suppressed, the terrorists lose.

A key element in terrorism's success is surprise. Terrorists create fear by making their actions as unpredictable as possible. From their viewpoint, the ideal psychological condition of the target population is a constant fear of random, unpredictable acts that psychologically disables the target and creates so much stress and anxiety that the population comes to value a reduction in that anxiety more than holding out against the terrorists' demands. Therefore, the successful terrorists will choose and attack those targets the population least expects to be attacked in the least-predictable manner and will develop no pattern that could lead to a sense of predictability.

Terrorism and how to deal with it also has a unique position in a book like this, the primary purpose of which is to deal with military strategy. If the various forms of asymmetrical warfare discussed in this chapter are distinguished by being progressively less conventional in their approach to the use of violence, terrorism adds another strategic consideration. Terrorism is not a military problem per se, and thus its solution is not the exclusive province of military strategy. Rather terrorism is a problem for which the solution is partially military but also (and in some ways more fundamentally) nonmilitary. Dealing with terrorism contains some military elements (e.g., reprisals against terrorist camps or selective raids by highly specialized military units), but much of the problem requires intelligence gathering/interpreting and law enforcement skills and activities, both of which are only marginally military. As mentioned in the introduction, suppressing terrorism is thus a semimilitary problem, and it is also a semistrategic problem in the terms previously used.

Since 9/11, terrorism is also a high-priority national problem in the United States that occupies a good deal of the attention of the American government. While the first vestiges of the contemporary problem have their roots in the 1990s' attacks in the United States (the World Trade Center in 1993) and overseas (the Khobar apartment complex in Saudi Arabia and the American embassies in Dar es Salaam, Tanzania, and Nairobi, Kenya), the 9/11 attacks were the riveting event that created the national priority. The inclusion of terrorism in this volume is partly justified because it is such a high-priority concern for national security policy, but also because its primary dynamics, if not its total content, is certainly part of the problem of asymmetrical warfare.

Nature of the Problem

Because terrorism is only partially a military problem, it cannot be discussed exclusively in military terms or even in the standard geopolitical terms associated with traditional insurgency warfare. Instead it is approached in terms of a series of characteristics of the phenomenon. These include terrorist objectives, justifications, sponsorship, and forms.

For what objectives do individuals and groups engage in terrorism? If, as Clausewitz proposes, "war is the continuation of politics by other means," terrorism is one of those means to achieve political objectives.[7] Because the means are normally vile and in violation of criminal laws and laws of warfare, this fact tends to be overlooked when terrorism occurs. Osama bin Laden, for instance, had been stating his objectives against the United States for years before September 2001 (the removal of the American presence from Saudi Arabia and abandonment of Israel are the primary demands), but hardly any Americans knew this even after the attacks.

There are at least two reasons why the target population may not recognize the objectives of terrorists. One is that the objectives may not be fully or well articulated. Beyond a general contempt for the American government and its actions against the Branch Davidians at Waco, Texas, it is not clear why Timothy McVeigh bombed the Murrah Federal Building in Oklahoma City, Oklahoma, or why Libya apparently authorized the destruction of Pan American Flight 103 over Lockerbie, Scotland.

The other problem is that the political objectives may be so far outside the political mainstream as to seem too incredible to be believed. It is the nature of terrorist organizations, after all, that their appeals are very limited within the target population. In that case they have no realistic prospect of attaining their goals through normal political processes, leaving them with terrorism as one of the few remaining chances to succeed. If the objective is sufficiently obscure and unorthodox, the target may simply not believe it.

Understanding terrorist objectives is not the same thing as accepting them, however. The goal of the Provisional Wing of the Irish Republican Army (IRA)—the forceful removal of Great Britain from Northern Ireland—has been quite well known by citizens of the United Kingdom for some time. Understanding that goal, and enduring the terrorist campaign against them, has not produced a greater sympathy toward the idea of detaching the seven counties of Ulster.

How can terrorism be justified? Or can it be justified? Put another way, is terrorism a *legitimate* means to achieve political goals? The answer is that it is a matter of perspective.

One thing is absolutely clear about terrorism: it is illegal. Terrorism invariably involves acts of violence against people or property that constitute criminal activity under any national or international standard. Those who oppose terrorism tend to emphasize the criminal nature of terrorism and hence to favor bringing terrorists "to justice."

Proponents and practitioners of terrorism counter that they are engaged in acts of war. People get killed and property gets destroyed in war, and it is legal within certain limits. The terrorists maintain that what they are doing is an act of war and should be treated accordingly. As the saying goes, "one man's terrorist is another man's freedom fighter." Whether committing the illegal acts is justified thus depends both on the typification of terrorism as crime or act of war and, in the mind of the justifier, the legitimacy of the cause for which the acts are committed.

Is terrorism crime or war? The answer is that it is partially both and can, to some extent, be justified either way. There is a nuance involved here, however, that is important to understand in assessing the phenomenon. One way to think about acts of terrorism is they are both crimes and criminal acts of war, in which case they are crimes regardless of how they are justified. Thus, terrorists are both common criminals and war criminals. Killing civilians by blowing up buses in Jerusalem is clearly an act of murder under Israeli law, but it also violates codes of permissible conduct under the Geneva accords. Either way, it is viewed as reprehensible.

But it is also a form of asymmetrical warfare. The fourth generation warrior, as noted, makes no distinction between civilians and military personnel or property; society is the opponent. In that case, rejecting the illegitimacy of suicide bombing is just another way that terrorists seek to change the rules to give themselves a chance of succeeding. The Palestinians engaging in suicide bombing apparently have reached the entirely reasonable conclusion that they stand no reasonable chance of attaining statehood by confronting the Israeli Defense Force (IDF) frontally in symmetrical warfare under the existing rules of war (for one thing, they lack an army). If they are to force Israel to comply with their demands for statehood, they must exceed Israeli cost tolerance in the only way that they can, and the rules cannot get in the way. To say this is not to make the tactic of suicide bombing more acceptable; it is to make it more understandable.

Who sanctions or sponsors terrorism? There are four general categories of sponsorship, each of which suggests a different means of dealing with the terror produced. The first category is *state terrorism*, the situation where the state authorizes and carries out acts of terror. The object of this terrorism can be domestic (seeking to suppress or eliminate elements of one's own population) or international (acts against foreign nationals or countries). Historically, state terrorism was the largest category of terrorism, as ruthless authoritarian governments from Stalin's Soviet Union to "Papa Doc" Duvalier's *Tonton Macoutes* in Haiti regularly terrorized their populations. A reduction in the number of authoritarian regimes and greater transparency in what occurs in countries has reduced this phenomenon. General international condemnation and effective counteraction have also reduced international terrorism conducted by governments. Libya, for instance, was a long-time practitioner of state terror but abandoned the practice after the American 1986 retaliatory raid against Mu'ammar Gadhafi.

The second form is *state-sponsored terrorism*, where states authorize and support terrorist organizations financially and otherwise but do not directly engage in the specific direction or commission of the acts carried out by the terrorist groups they sponsor. Normally these sponsoring states deny their involvement and try to obscure the relationship to be able to engage in "plausible deniability"—the criterion for success of covert operations. Iran has often been identified in this role, notably as the major sponsor of Hezbollah.

A third form is *state-sanctioned terrorism*. In this form, a state may approve of a terrorist group and give it some support but have an otherwise limited relationship to the terrorists. This form of involvement is related to state sponsorship but comes up short of that level in terms of the amount of involvement. The provision of sanctuary by the Taliban government of Afghanistan for al-Qaeda is a classic case of state-sanctioned terrorism.

Finally there is the condition of *private or no sponsorship*. Some terrorist groups, whether because of their small size, the unappealing nature of their objectives, or their level of notoriety, cannot or do not seek state sponsors of any kind. Instead, the scope of their activities is so limited that they do not require, for instance, outside financial assistance, or they can raise the funding they need from private sources. Since its expulsion from Afghanistan, al-Qaeda, which apparently receives generous funding from private sources in the region, falls into this category.

What means do terrorists employ to try to achieve their goals? A representative list would include: hijacking; arson; kidnapping of public officials, corporate executives, or common citizens; hostage taking; assassination; raids against installations; property seizure or destruction; and sabotage. And there are probably more acts that do not fall under one of these categories.

Two things stand out about this list. The first is its sheer size and diversity. The potential "target set" for terrorists seeking to carry out any of these acts is impressive, especially in a country the size of the United States. It is, as a practical matter, essentially impossible to protect all of the possible victims of all of these forms of attack all the time, and trying to reduce risk in this area is one of the true horrors for those involved in homeland security. The second observation relates to diversity. As one tries to nullify the ability to carry out each of these forms of attack, one quickly realizes how little transferability there is from one form of attack to another. Learning how to protect airliners from being hijacked does not help a great deal in protecting the Golden Gate Bridge from attack or provide much guidance for designing means to prevent corporate executives from being kidnapped or assassinated.

There is the added problem of terrorists coming into possession of or using weapons of mass destruction in attacks. The ultimate fear of those engaged in homeland security is the scenario where terrorists employ a chemical, biological, or worse yet, a nuclear device against some civilian target. Although it is arguable that the threat is not as great as is sometimes argued (clandestinely building and transporting a nuclear device to an American target is not an easy task), it remains the ultimate danger.

Fundamental Differences

Terrorism is both a distinctive problem and part of the continuum of forms of asymmetrical warfare. Its distinction is that it is not entirely a military problem, and thus strategies and solutions cannot be entirely military. Certainly, dealing with other forms of asymmetrical warfare presents political elements as well as military ones, but the configuration when dealing with terrorism is different. At the same time, terrorism is the result of the same kinds of conditions that breed other forms of asymmetrical warfare. All forms of this kind of war have their bases in conditions of deprivation and despair that nurture and protect groups that engage in one form or another of asymmetrical warfare. Thus, the tasks facing those charged with suppressing terrorism have common ground with those seeking to defeat other kinds of asymmetrical warriors.

There are two basic methods for dealing with terrorism, each of which has a military element but is by no means strictly military. The first method is *antiterrorism*—defensive measures used to reduce the vulnerability of potential targets to attack and to lessen the effects of terrorist attacks that do occur. Antiterrorist activities are at least implicitly based on the presumption that preventive measures will not always succeed in avoiding the mounting of such an attack, and that as a result, efforts must be made to lessen the effects.

Antiterrorism entails two kinds of activities: those that make terrorism more difficult and those that make it less effective. Examples of making acts more difficult include enhancing airline security to make it more difficult for terrorists to board airliners or get to cockpits and posting increased numbers of Marine guards at overseas embassies. Efforts to make such attacks less effective include surrounding public facilities with cement fencing that can absorb bomb blasts or limiting close access to public buildings, such as closing Pennsylvania Avenue in front of the White House to vehicular traffic.

The other method is *counterterrorism*—offensive and military measures taken by the military and other agencies against terrorists or their sponsoring agencies to prevent, deter, or respond to terrorist acts. The major emphasis of counterterrorism is to disable or dissuade terrorists from carrying out their actions before they occur by means such as penetrating their organizations and taking disabling actions against them. When this fails then the emphasis shifts to retribution, both directly to punish the transgressors and to issue warnings to others who might contemplate similar actions. The raids against Gadhafi in 1986 and against bin Laden's training camps in 1998 in Afghanistan are examples of the latter.

The problem with either of these approaches is that competent terrorists can be quite adept at negating antiterrorist efforts or at countering counterterrorism. Achieving the randomness and un- predictability that makes terrorism effective is facilitated by an enormously large and diverse set of potential targets that can be attacked in a variety of ways. It is literally impossible to "terrorist proof" a place as large as the United States against a terrorist threat that one cannot anticipate (counterterrorism) and thwart when at- tacks are attempted (antiterrorism). An emphasis on knowing and thwarting is an emphasis on intelligence and law enforcement, which are the ultimate tools for suppressing terrorism.

Interestingly, the tasks that flow from this description are akin to those already described for counterinsurgency, where three tasks were identified. The first is to undercut support and to de- stroy the infrastructure and forces of the insurgent. Penetration of terrorist organizations (an act of counterterrorism) is a parallel activity. The second requisite of counterinsurgency is intelligence superiority, knowing who the enemy is and what the enemy is doing, which clearly also applies in suppressing terrorism. The third requisite of counterinsurgency is timing, trying to identify and destroy insurgent movements in their vulnerable, formative stages. Domestic attempts at penetration to deal with terrorists are generally assigned to law enforcement (the Federal Bureau of Investigation), while overseas efforts are normally assigned to intelligence agencies.

Conclusions

Asymmetrical warfare has moved to the center stage of stra- tegic concern for the United States in the early twenty-first cen- tury. Although there is clearly nothing novel about unconven- tional applications of force by inferior powers facing superior opponents, the degree to which asymmetrical warfare has come to represent the major strategic challenge facing the United States is virtually unprecedented in the American experience. The United States last faced a symmetrical foe in the Kuwaiti desert in 1991; that same Iraqi foe largely chose not to make a contest of the second opportunity in 2003. In between there has been a string of applications of force in one or another of the categories of asymmetrical warfare described above. Is there any reason to believe this problem will change?

The overwhelming answer is that not only will devising strategy to deal with asymmetrical challenges likely not fade, it will probably intensify. The major reason for this likelihood, hinted at in the introduction, is an ironic, unintended consequence of the US military superiority that is a centerpiece of the Bush Doctrine: the United States has become so overwhelmingly superior in fighting conventional, symmetrical warfare against any potential foe that no one will present that threat to us in the likely future. Fighting the United States asymmetrically may or may not be successful, but fighting the United States on its own terms is openly suicidal. Thus, the design and application of asymmetrical strategies that dilute or negate American conventional power is the only logical way for potential opponents to go (with the possible exception of becoming a nuclear power, a problem discussed in the next chapter). The counterstrategy for American symmetrical dominance is asymmetrical approaches to war. The strategic problem for the United States is how to find ways to counter those counterstrategies: counter-asymmetrical-warfare strategy.

As the discussion in this chapter has suggested, asymmetrical strategies are becoming progressively more unconventional and thus presenting multiplying military and political problems for the United States. The problem, in other words, is getting harder, not easier; and there is no particular reason to believe it will not get more difficult in the future as potential opponents search for effective ways to nullify American power.

Insurgency warfare, most prominently associated in the American mind with Vietnam, was not so radically asymmetrical in retrospect as it seemed at the time. At the political level, for instance, it was highly traditional and Clausewitzian, a traditional contest for control of government by two contending sides. In its guerrilla phase, that war was asymmetrical at the tactical level but not so much so at the strategic level. Mao, after all, was a reader and follower of Clausewitz, and ultimately it showed in his and others' applications of insurgency, notably in Vietnam.

When looking at other asymmetrical approaches, the problems have become more complicated. The new internal wars add a chaos of purpose and military action that the application of organized force can contain as long as that force is in place. The experience in places like Bosnia and Kosovo, extended to Afghanistan and Iraq, suggests that the creation of postwar stability that can endure after outside force is removed may be another problem. Liberia, which has been in a state of chaos since 1989, is just the most recent test case. Fourth generation warfare extends warfare to the comprehensive definition of society as target and nonstate opponents to confront. International terrorism adds significant nonmilitary elements to the asymmetrical problem. Each permutation further complicates the problem of counter-asymmetrical-warfare strategy. What is next?

Iraq is an important test of the evolution of asymmetrical warfare in at least two ways that bear close observation. The US military might have successfully overthrown the Saddam Hussein regime, but will it succeed in transforming Iraq? If Iraq does not evolve into the region's exemplary democracy that was always the underlying neoconservative dream for the operation, what will the world conclude about overwhelming American superiority? Does that force translate into positive change, or is it primarily good for negative tasks? Is it possible that the United States has power to conquer but not to transform? Only time will tell, but the answer could have considerable strategic significance in the evolution of asymmetrical warfare strategy and counterstrategy.

Notes

1. Pres. Lyndon B. Johnson (remarks, dinner meeting of the Texas Electric Cooperatives, Inc., Austin, TX, 4 May 1965), http://www.presidency.ucsb.edu/ws/index.php?pid=26942&st=&st1=.

2. Donald M. Snow, *UnCivil Wars: International Security and the New Internal Conflicts* (New York: St. Martin's, 1996).

3. Martin van Creveld, *The Transformation of War* (New York: Free Press, 1991), 192, 197.

4. William S. Lind et al., "The Changing Face of War: Into the Fourth Generation," *Marine Corps Gazette*, October 1989, 22–26.

5. Donald M. Snow and Dennis M. Drew, *From Lexington to Desert Storm: War and Politics in the American Experience*, rev. ed. (Armonk, NY: M. E. Sharpe, 2000).

6. Sir John Keegan, editorial, *London Daily Telegraph*, 8 October 2001.

7. Carl von Clausewitz, *On War* (Middlesex, England: Penguin Books, Ltd., 1968), http://www.clausewitz.com/CWHOME/CWZSUMM/CWORKHOL.htm.

Chapter 9

Nuclear Strategy

The advent of nuclear weapons, the threat of nuclear war, and the devising of nuclear strategies to regulate these awesome weapons formed the centerpiece of military thinking during the Cold War. The reason was simple; the Cold War was ultimately a military competition. War between the superpowers and their blocs was its ultimate expression, and a war entailing a general exchange of nuclear weapons could—and probably would—destroy both sides. In an atmosphere where most people believed the only outcomes of the Cold War were either its indefinite continuation or "hot" war, avoiding the heat of nuclear confrontation was clearly the highest priority.

Given the way the Cold War actually ended and our growing distance from those events, the subject of nuclear strategy has clearly lost its urgency; some would argue even its salience. To paraphrase George H. W. Bush during the 1992 presidential campaign, we no longer go to bed worrying about nuclear war.

So why continue to discuss nuclear war in a volume such as this? There are three reasons. First, nuclear strategy was a dominant form of thinking that produced some unique constructs that may be useful for current strategists dealing with contemporary problems. Second, the continued possession of sizable nuclear arsenals by countries like Russia reminds us that nuclear war may be a diminished problem, but it has not disappeared altogether. Third, older nuclear constructs may provide some guidance for dealing with current problems such as WMD proliferation.

The original American research into the weapon potential of the atom was commissioned in 1939 by Pres. Franklin D. Roosevelt in response to reports of German nuclear investigations and continued even after reliable intelligence concluded the Nazi effort had been abandoned. The result was a successful fission reaction under the grandstands of the University of Chicago football stadium in 1942. The first successful nuclear weapon demonstration occurred in the White Sands, New Mexico, desert on 16

July 1945; and on 6 and 9 August 1945, the only employment of nuclear weapons in war was consummated with the bombings of Hiroshima and Nagasaki.

The enormous impact of nuclear weaponry required considerable adjustment by those who plan military strategy. Part of the problem was that even the scientists who designed the original devices had only a vague idea of what they had created. After viewing the White Sands test of July 1945, Robert Oppenheimer, the physicist generally considered the "father of the A-bomb," said, "There floated through my mind a line from the Hindu scripture, the *Bhagavad-Gita*: 'I am become Death, the destroyer of worlds.' I think we all had this feeling, more or less."[1]

Analyses of the effects of nuclear bombing were profoundly sobering. In deciding to attack Japanese cities with these weapons, Pres. Harry S. Truman and his advisers underestimated their destructive effect and viewed nuclear munitions as no more than a dramatic extension of developments in strategic bombing that had evolved during the war. In one sense, nuclear bombs simply armed advocates of the strategic-bombing theory with an explosive device that would adequately and efficiently carry out the promises of aerial bombardment proclaimed by prewar enthusiasts. Others argued that nuclear weapons were unique and that deterrence of nuclear attack was now the major military task. In the ensuing debate, a whole new branch of and outlook on military strategy was born.

Three initial points must be made about the evolution of thought on nuclear weapons. First, most sources agree that nuclear weapons create such a qualitative departure from conventional weaponry that their military usefulness is highly questionable. Indeed, the entire body of nuclear thought is often described as the study of nuclear deterrence, hence questioning or denying a war-fighting purpose for these weapons. Second, these judgments about the consequences of employing nuclear weapons lead to a general agreement that this area of strategy is unique. The applicability of strategies and doctrine governing other military instruments has been deemed conceptually inadequate or irrelevant for understanding nuclear dynamics because of the physical effects of employing these weapons in war. The result is development of nuclear strategies of deterrence divorced from, or only tangentially related to, prior strategic and doctrinal formulations. Third, the area of deterrence theorizing has been largely left to civilians. Whereas professional military theoreticians had developed strategies and doctrines of aerial bombardment before World War II, strategies regarding nuclear weapons have evolved almost entirely outside the professional military community.

These factors tended to make nuclear strategy a distinct and independent area in the study of strategy. The area abounds with complex concepts and ideas that are, at first encounter, forbidding and alien, even for people with a detailed knowledge of nonnuclear (conventional) strategy. To understand the role of nuclear strategy in overall strategy and the dynamics of nuclear thought requires examining briefly two separate but interrelated topics: the evolution of the nuclear age and how evolving reality has affected thinking, and concepts of nuclear strategy and their relationship to a condition of nuclear deterrence. These concerns can then be applied to contemporary nuclear issues such as proliferation of WMD and missile defenses.

Dynamics of Nuclear Evolution

Nuclear weapons development was, in many ways, the model for the extreme dynamism that marks modern weapons development. Nuclear weapons indeed qualitatively transformed the prospects of future warfare. Unlike modern weapons that have made warfare more efficient and raised the possibility of war fought with decreased military and civilian deaths, nuclear weapons raised the opposite prospect of warfare so destructive and gruesome as to be virtually unthinkable, with results increasingly hideous. This development was progressive.

Although development and change were continuous and dynamic throughout the thermonuclear age, four events stand out as most important in defining the "ground rules" for nuclear strategy: development of nuclear (atomic or fission) weapons themselves, advent of the hydrogen (fission-fusion) bomb, perfection and deployment of the ICBM, and development of the multiple independently targetable reentry vehicle (MIRV). The prospect of missile defenses is conceptually equivalent, although effective versions were unavailable during the Cold

War. Collectively, these events have provided the context for nuclear deterrence, but each has had a different impact.

The Atomic Bomb

Although early atomic weapons greatly increased the destructive power of airborne munitions, the changes they introduced in military employment strategies were matters of degree, although admittedly a high degree. The primary difference was a quantum increase in the destructive capacity of an airborne "launcher"—a single airplane armed with a single atomic bomb could now accomplish area destruction formerly attainable only by repeated mass aerial bombardment. As strategist Bernard Brodie and others quickly realized, this capability alone substantially changed the calculation of warfare.[2] First, it made massive destruction of industry and civilian populations incredibly more rapid and "efficient." Second, these weapons accelerated "demilitarization" of traditional warfare. The swift cataclysm produced by a single atomic bomb meant that devastation, formerly possible only after a victor had vanquished an opponent's armed forces, could now be accomplished independently of the military situation on the ground and at sea.

These effects were, in large measure, what airpower enthusiasts before World War II had maintained would be the impact of strategic bombardment on warfare. As a qualitative change in the military calculus, however, these effects were mitigated by two factors. First, the original atomic devices were crude and difficult to build. The bombs that leveled Hiroshima and Nagasaki weighed approximately five tons apiece, greatly strained the capacities of the B-29 bombers that carried them to the targets, and developed only 15 to 20 kilotons (thousand tons of TNT equivalent) of destructive force. Detonation of the second bomb temporarily exhausted the world's arsenal of nuclear weapons. Second, conventional bombers were the only means of delivering the original atomic bombs, and defenses could succeed in interdicting bombers. Thus, the result was more quantitative than qualitative. Atomic bombs were certainly a great deal more powerful than conventional bombs, but questions about defense strategy, detection, interception, and losses were fundamentally the same.

The Hydrogen Bomb

The hydrogen bomb, known also as the thermonuclear or "super" bomb at the time, again produced a quantum increase in the amount of destructive power that could be produced by a single bomb. Fission bombs had been measured in kilotons, but the new hydrogen bombs could produce explosions measured in megatons (*millions* of tons of TNT). The destructive potential of even a few thermonuclear weapons penetrating defenses became much more frightening to contemplate, and people began to wonder whether any conflict fought with this weaponry was winnable in any meaningful manner.

The "bigger bang for the buck" and weight produced by hydrogen weapons, combined with improved warhead designs, raised the possibility of using a different means of delivery. The primary candidate was strategic rockets, which had first been used by Germany during World War II.

The Intercontinental Ballistic Missile

Rocket research begun before World War II continued after the war, but weapon applications were limited by the weight and size of early nuclear bombs. Using the new developments, rocket programs accelerated; and in 1957 the Soviets successfully tested a ballistic missile and launched Sputnik into space. The quantitative change in warfare had become qualitative.

Introduction of ballistic missile delivery systems fundamentally altered traditional notions about defense. Although the prospects of nuclear warfare had raised terrible specters of death and destruction, the fact remained that, before the advent of ballistic missiles, it was possible to design a defensive strategy to intercept enough of an incoming enemy force to minimize the resulting destruction. A society absorbing a nuclear attack might be greatly damaged, but it could still reasonably expect to survive.

Ballistic missiles changed that expectation and, in the process, Americans recognized a fundamental qualitative difference between bombardment by manned aircraft and by ballistic missiles. The basis of the change was the realization that, at the time, defense against ballistic missiles was impossible. John F. Kennedy described the problem during the 1960 election campaign as trying "to shoot a bullet with another bullet." Facing nuclear-tipped rockets, it was no longer reasonable to expect to be able to defend the homeland in any conventional way. Realization that the Soviets could reach the United States with rockets we could not defend against was shocking. If the United States could no longer avoid devastation in a nuclear war, then the only way to avoid the consequences of nuclear war was to ensure that war did not occur at all. Deterrence became the prime (many would argue sole) purpose of nuclear weapons.

Ballistic missiles also raised questions about how to implement a deterrence strategy. In traditional military thinking, the deterrent purpose of military force had been based on making one or both of two threats. On one hand, a potential adversary could be deterred from attacking by the credible threat that one's forces would thwart its aggressive design and hence render the effort futile (a denial threat). On the other hand, an aggressor could be dissuaded by the believable threat that one would punish him in excess of any potential gain (a punishment threat).

The denial threat has effective defense as its basic ingredient. Thus it was an unrealistic threat when applied to a weapon against which there was no defense. The punishment threat is based on devastating retaliation. Since both sides possessed devastating weapons against which neither could defend, the basic deterrent threat had to be punishment. There was no alternative.

Multiple Independently Targetable Reentry Vehicles

Development of multiple independently targetable reentry vehicles by the United States in 1970 and by the Soviet Union in 1975 was an event of similar magnitude. By increasing the number of warheads that could be delivered by a single missile, MIRVs allowed both for rapid multiplication of the number of warheads in each arsenal and for a consequent increase in the number and kinds of targets at which each side could aim its weapons. Combined with great strides in inertial-guidance technology during the 1970s, MIRVs also potentially provided the capability to strike the other side's nuclear forces.

Many analysts believe MIRVing was the single most destabilizing event of the nuclear age because it allowed contemplation of attacking an enemy with nuclear weapons to destroy retaliatory ability. With confidence in this counterforce capability, one can begin to think about waging nuclear war and winning in the sense of surviving due to "offensive damage limitation" (destroying enemy weapons before they can be used). This is considered destabilizing because it creates circumstances in which it might be tempting to cross the nuclear threshold and start a nuclear war with a preemptive attack.

Missile Defenses

The inability to protect the homeland by denying enemies the ability to attack American soil became an alarming prospect once the possibility of nuclear attacks was raised, and multiple efforts have been undertaken ever since to devise a system capable of defeating such an attack before it reaches American soil. Conceptually, a missile defense is attractive because it adds the possibility of denial to the retaliatory threat as a means to deter a potential nuclear enemy.

Historically, the Achilles' heels of missile defenses have been workability and cost. It was never clear that the United States could design and deploy a defense against a concerted Soviet nuclear attack involving literally thousands of incoming warheads, and the cost of any system has always been very high. As a result, missile defenses never became part of the Cold War arsenal.

Missile defense is the one element of the Cold War debate over nuclear weapons that has survived that era. There has always been an element of the strategic debate that argued that it was immoral for the United States not to attempt to defend itself from nuclear attacks, and Pres. George W. Bush and many of his defense analysts subscribe to that school of thought. With no Soviet-style opponent on the horizon, the focus of missile defenses has been redirected to the problem created by small, generally rogue countries that may attain WMD capability along with missile delivery capacity. As a practical matter, this is a physically simplified problem, since the candidate states (e.g., North Korea or Iran) will likely be capable of developing only very small missile arsenals that would be easier (although by no means easy) to intercept than a Soviet-style launch. The advocacy of a ballistic missile defense (BMD) system remains controversial on both grounds of workability against even a small attack and on the likelihood of such an attack. John Pike, spokesman for the Federation of American Scientists, has described the Bush plan for BMD as "a weapon that does not work against a threat that does not exist."[3] This artifact of the Cold War will be debated later in the chapter.

Basic Concepts and Relationships

Theorists of nuclear strategy developed their own language and logic to describe their unique part of military strategy. Some of their terms and concepts are drawn, directly or indirectly, from more conventional military considerations, but others are unique to the field. This section begins by defining and exploring basic ideas, moves to relationships between concepts, and concludes with the "conventional wisdom" about how these ideas contributed to the maintenance of nuclear deterrence.

Definitions

The basic concern in developing nuclear strategy is finding the best means to convince potential adversaries not to use their nuclear forces, in other words, deterrence. Three basic concepts are included in this definition of the problem: plans for using nuclear force (declaratory strategy), potential targets for nuclear forces (employment strategy), and the required nature (capability) of nuclear forces to fulfill their defined roles.

A country's *declaratory strategy* is its stated plan for using nuclear weapons in the perceived imminence or actuality of nuclear war. In view of the potentially devastating consequences of a nuclear exchange and very real questions about whether a nuclear war could be controlled short of a disastrous all-out exchange, emphasis at this level has not focused on sustained use and application of nuclear force. Rather the evolving strategies focused on the onset of nuclear hostilities, and a dichotomy emerged between those theorists who prefer preemptive or retaliatory strategies. A preemptive (first-strike) strategy is the intention to use one's nuclear forces *before* having absorbed a nuclear attack by an adversary. A retaliatory (second-strike) strategy is the determination to employ nuclear weapons only in response to nuclear attack.

A country's declaratory strategy is determined partly by, and helps to shape, its targeting priorities. Nuclear strategists have developed an antiseptic way of designating nuclear targets by distinguishing between so-called countervalue and counterforce targets. *Countervalue* targets are those things people value, most notably their lives and the productive capabilities that directly support and sustain people, and that would be necessary for postwar recovery. Countervalue targets include population centers, industrial complexes, power-generating facilities, and civilian transportation and communications networks. *Counterforce* targets are those things that contribute directly to the ability to wage war. They include a state's strategic nuclear forces and significant conventional forces that could be employed in response to a nuclear attack.

The counterforce-countervalue distinction is neither entirely new nor completely meaningful. The debate about attacking civilian populations (countervalue) or military targets (counterforce) was a prominent part of the strategic bombing controversy in World War II concerning "area" versus "precision" bombing. The distinction has always been more rhetorical than real given the destructive capability of nuclear weapons. Many counterforce targets are in cities (countervalue targets), for instance, and cannot be attacked with nuclear weapons without producing extensive collateral damage. Put more succinctly, a nuclear attack against Wright-Patterson Air Force Base (a counterforce target) would largely decimate the city of Dayton, Ohio, where it is located (a countervalue target).

A concept closely related to targeting preference is *nuclear capability*, which refers to the amount and quality of a country's nuclear power, its means of delivering that power, and its nuclear force's vulnerability to interception or preemptive attack. The distinction is typically made, in ideal terms, between a first-strike capability and a second-strike capability.

A *first-strike capability* is the ability to attack and destroy another country's capability to retaliate. Thus true first-strike capability emphasizes the ability to destroy counterforce targets, and the term is often used synonymously for counterforce capability. A country possessing a first-strike capability can issue plausible denial threats and deprive an adversary of the retaliatory, punitive deterrent threat. A *second-strike capability* is the capacity to absorb any possible nuclear attack and to retaliate with sufficient force to inflict unacceptable damage on the attacker. Thus a second-strike capability implements the punitive deterrent threat. Second-strike targets tend to be countervalue targets, both to punish an aggressor and to guarantee that a potential aggressor knows it will suffer terribly for committing a nuclear transgression.

Attainment of first- or second-strike capabilities requires development of forces with different characteristics. The primary characteristics of a first-strike force are size and accuracy. A first-strike force should be numerically larger—at least in terms of warheads—than its adversary since it must be capable of destroying the adversary's retaliatory weapons to achieve its goal of winning the exchange and not being destroyed in retaliation. Accuracy is obviously critical against counterforce targets because any weapon system not destroyed can be used in retaliation. Since, by definition, first-strike capability requires the ability to disarm an opponent, anything that raises questions about eliminating retaliatory forces dilutes the capability.

Second-strike capability, on the other hand, emphasizes invulnerability (survivability) of forces and penetrability of those forces to their target as primary characteristics. *Invulnerability* means that a force can survive a preemptive attack, and *penetrability* means that the force can get through defensive barriers to reach and destroy its targets. Any enemy capability that degrades either characteristic (e.g., an enemy ability to destroy retaliatory systems before they can be launched or effective active defenses) dilutes second-strike capability.

Relationships between Concepts

Notions about capability, declaratory strategy, and targeting are related to one another in at least two distinct ways. First, the ideas, particularly ideas about capability, are related in the sense that they gain meaning in large measure from their comparison with the capabilities of a potential adversary. Second, within a state's calculation of nuclear strategy, the three concepts are interrelated: capability influences choice of strategy and vice versa, and capability and strategy influence target priorities.

Although forces can be and are designed primarily to endow them with first- or second-strike capability by emphasizing one set or the other of required characteristics, actual capability can be judged only by comparing it with an adversary's capabilities. A given amount and type of force can constitute a first-strike or second-strike capability, or it can be inadequate for either, depending on the forces it confronts. In contemporary terms, the United States effectively has a first-strike capability against virtually all other states in the world, obviously including those that do not possess nuclear weapons but also those that have or may develop small nuclear arsenals. In the event of the threat of war in which the United States could be attacked with nuclear weapons, it could, if it chose to do so, launch a preemptive strike and destroy the threatening country's weapons without facing certain retaliation. The exception among (barely) conceivable nuclear opponents is Russia, which retains a large enough arsenal to absorb an American attack and retaliate. Against Russia, the United States has a second-strike capability.

Capability and declaratory strategy are also highly interrelated and interdependent. One's capability largely dictates one's strategic choices, including selection of a firing strategy. The declaratory strategy a country wants to follow also influences the kind of force capability it develops. In turn these determinations will, or at least should, largely determine targeting priorities.

There are two capability-strategy-targeting combinations that conventional wisdom from the Cold War suggests a country might seek to follow. A country with a large, very accurate nuclear arsenal might decide to adopt a first-strike strategy against counterforce targets. Conversely, that same country might decide it wants to adopt such a strategy and thus try to develop weapons with the capability to carry out the strategy. Having a first-strike capability is crucial to adopting the strategy because the major motivation for adopting this combination is to be able to "win" a nuclear war in the sense of being able to avoid a nuclear retaliation after destroying the opponent's weapons. The United States is currently (and for the foreseeable future) the only country with the physical capability to adopt this combination of strategy and targeting philosophy based on capability. The doctrine of preemption that is part of the Bush Doctrine expressed in the 2002 *National Security Strategy of the United States* is compatible with such a philosophy, although the United States has not publicly extended the idea of preemption to encompass nuclear weapons.[4] As we will see in the next section, most strategists have historically argued that this combination is destabilizing because of the incentives it produces for potential nuclear war opponents.

The other combination is one that includes second-strike-capable nuclear weapons with an intention only to fire those weapons in retaliation after having absorbed an initial attack. Such an intention can be attached to either a counterforce or a countervalue targeting philosophy, although it is normally associated with a countervalue orientation, for two reasons. The first is that, by definition, a second-strike force lacks the accuracy to take out enemy forces preemptively; and since it plans only to respond to an initial attack, most of the valuable opposition counterforce targets—notably nuclear forces—will likely have been expended in the initial attack. At the same time, the major purpose of a second-strike strategy is to minimize the likelihood that nuclear war will occur at all. One way to do so is to make the retaliatory consequences of launching the attack as painful and gruesome for the initial attacker as possible to dissuade the potential attacker from starting the war in the first place. Promising to kill as many citizens as possible in retaliation makes those prospects maximally unappealing.

Other combinations make less sense. A country with the capacity to carry out a successful first strike might say it would only fire its weapons in response to an attack, but no potential opponent could possibly believe that such a state would willingly absorb an attack it could avoid through preemption. At the same time, a state lacking first-strike-capable weapons cannot plausibly argue that it could fire first and "win" an exchange because it would be vulnerable to retaliation.

In the contemporary world, the most interesting situation is among actual or potential nuclear states whose arsenals either are or might be incapable of either first- or second-strike capability. This condition applies to most Third World states (about which there are proliferation concerns that are discussed in the next section) because such states will almost certainly have very small arsenals that, in most cases, will be vulnerable to preemptive attack. For such states facing a first-strike-capable state like the United States, their options may be either to surrender and avoid decimation or to fire first and hope for the best, since the failure to do so may leave them disarmed—what is known in nuclear strategy terms as the "use-them-or-lose-them" problem.

At the military strategy level, the distinctions between declaratory strategy and development and deployment strategies that result in force capabilities are sometimes muddied because developmental strategies that could alter the relationship between two countries involve substantial lead times. In formulating declaratory strategy and providing guidance in development and deployment, planners must emphasize developmental efforts that will result in desirable relationships between adversaries. In American circles at least, desirability has largely been equated with stability, and stability has been equated with reducing incentives to start nuclear war.

Nuclear Stability

Regardless of the reasons for developing different types of nuclear forces and strategies, the primary purpose of nuclear weapons is to deter a potential adversary from using them. Since the ability to control a nuclear exchange is conjectural and the potential consequences of the inability to control such conflict are so awful, major emphasis has been placed on avoiding the onset of nuclear war (the so-called nuclear threshold or firebreak). As a consequence, anything that decreases the likelihood of nuclear war is said to be stabilizing, and anything that increases the likelihood is destabilizing. Capability-strategy combinations can be viewed in that light.

In isolation and from the viewpoint of the possessor, a first-strike capability appears advantageous and desirable at first glance. The capability gives the holder great power over actual or potential adversaries, and if properly deployed, it affords the luxury of adopting either a preemptive or a retaliatory employment strategy. True nuclear superiority thus has an obvious appeal.

Considered as part of the nuclear relationship between two states, however, introduction of one-sided or two-sided first-strike capability is generally considered to be destabilizing. The key de-stabilizing element is that it can lead both states to adopt a pre-emptive strategy. For the powerful state, preemption has the po-tential advantage of being able to disarm the opponent and hence engaging in true "damage limitation" (avoiding the destruction of absorbing an attack). The characteristics that make first-strike capability appealing to the possessor, however, are extremely un-appealing and even unacceptable to the state at which that ca-pability is directed. That state is placed in a position of absolute nuclear inferiority and is left with constricted strategic options already raised. Thus a nuclear attack against the powerful state may become more, rather than less, likely than would be the case in the absence of clear nuclear superiority. Preemption seems at-tractive to the side that knows it must strike first, if it is to strike at all, and thus avoid having its forces destroyed unused.

The result is an "itchy-finger" effect. If both sides are com-mitted to preemption, they must anticipate the imminence of nuclear attack and calculate accordingly in any crisis. Crises by their nature are situations in which information is imperfect, and faulty interpretation and miscalculation can result in the decision to initiate a nuclear attack unnecessarily. The situation becomes even more unstable if both sides have first-strike capa-bility since both sides are necessarily committed to preemption, but it also applies if one state lacks a major force capability.

A second-strike capability does not present the same difficul-ties if both states have enough confidence in their capability to adopt retaliatory strategies. When both parties in a nuclear rela-tionship have second-strike capabilities and retaliatory strategies, the incentives to initiate a nuclear exchange are minimized, and the system has maximum stability. The advantage of a retalia-tory strategy in a crisis is that it reduces the need to calculate an adversary's intentions to launch an attack. Since there is no need to anticipate *whether* such an attack is imminent but simply a need to respond after the attack occurs, there is no itchy finger to make a crisis situation even tenser. Furthermore, an adversary's knowledge that an attack ensures a devastating retaliation also dampens preemptive incentives.

For second-strike-capability/retaliatory strategy to provide maximum stability, two conditions following from the defini-tion of retaliatory forces must be met. First, a nation adopting a retaliatory strategy must be confident in the second-strike capability of its forces. Doubts about its ability to absorb an attack and retaliate effectively may result in a temptation to fire all or part of its force first, particularly the most vulnerable elements. In addition, the potential adversary must see the second-strike capability of retaliatory forces as credible. If one's retaliatory strategy is to deter, the adversary must believe both in the survivability of the retaliatory force and in one's willingness to deliver the retaliatory blow.

Second, an adversary must believe that one's declared retaliatory strategy is implemented by a force suitable for that purpose and that one will, in fact, follow the strategy. As pointed out earlier, a second-strike capability can become or can appear to become a first-strike force (e.g., by gaining counterforce capability and warhead superiority). A force that is not unambiguously second strike in character can appear as a first-strike force to an adversary. In a crisis, uncertainty about the characteristics of, and intentions for, a force could lead to miscalculations and a decision to initiate nuclear hostilities. This is a particular problem for the United States as it faces the possibility of nuclear weapons proliferation to countries capable only of developing very small, vulnerable arsenals. One response to this destabilizing situation is missile defense.

Current Strategic Issues

The way nuclear weapons fit into more-general thinking about military force has changed more than any other force element and problem since the end of the Cold War. During the Cold War, as weapons technologies blossomed and arsenals proliferated in size, nuclear strategy found its home as an extension of the central confrontation between East and West, as the least conventional form of a highly symmetrical World War III. The bridge between a nuclear and a nonnuclear war between the superpowers was planning for the use of nuclear weapons on the conventional battlefield in Europe, an idea about which there was always decidedly more enthusiasm in the United States (which would not automatically be part of the nuclear battlefield and aftermath) than in Europe (which would be part of that irradiated piece of land).

179

In the post–Cold War world, the role of nuclear weapons has moved from the symmetrical to the asymmetrical warfare problem. Since there is essentially no danger of war between the large, conventional forces of the Cold War order, the remaining problems in the system are between the United States and countries that cannot challenge the United States symmetrically. The existence of the huge American nuclear arsenal only accentuates the gap in capabilities and the suicidal nature of attempting to confront the United States conventionally.

In this atmosphere, concern with nuclear weapons has largely shifted to the question of how these weapons might be used to support asymmetrical, rather than symmetrical, warfare goals. Attention has been diverted from the "central battle" in Europe to how some much-weaker opponent might be able to use nuclear and other forms of WMD for the asymmetrical purpose of altering a battlefield on which the new holder of these weapons seeks to change the odds in its favor. Thus the basic concern moves away from deterring a nuclear confrontation that could largely decimate humanity to the problem of rogues with a few nuclear (or biological or chemical) weapons who might use such weapons in support of some terrorist or terrorist-related end. The nuclear issues of the early 2000s deal with the problem of nuclear (and other) proliferation and whether it is necessary or wise to erect ballistic missile defenses as a hedge against proliferated weapons.

These issues are by no means new. Indeed they are chestnuts pulled from the Cold War fire and given a new meaning in the contemporary environment. Debate over how many countries should have nuclear weapons and what is the impact of new weapons states goes back to the 1950s and 1960s when the number of states began to grow; it was a highly emotional debate then, as it is now. The problem of missile defense was anticipated before the first intercontinental-range missile was successfully tested, and the current discussion is the third major debate on the subject.

Proliferation of Weapons of Mass Destruction

The prospect of WMD proliferation is a highly charged issue that refuses to leave the public eye, for at least two reasons.

The first is the nature of WMDs: they are—in their nuclear, biological, and chemical (NBC) variants—hideous weapons that kill indiscriminately and are primarily useful in attacking non-combatants who are protected from such attacks under international conventions of war. Some, of course, are more *massive* in their effects than others: chemical and biological weapons do not kill anywhere near as many people as nuclear weapons, even if the ways they kill may be more grotesque than a nuclear attack. At any rate WMDs are somehow uncivilized and immoral weapons that raise fear and fright in the population (thereby making them, in some sense, ideal terrorist weapons). This question of morality was sometimes raised about general exchanges between the United States and the Soviet Union but was largely submerged as something like the cost of war. Outside that grander setting, WMDs appear more unacceptable.

The other reason for concern is about who the proliferators may be. Once again this is a familiar problem from the Cold War era in new dressing. Cold War nuclear strategists devised a construct known as the "$N + 1$" problem to describe proliferation, where "N" referred to the number of states already in possession of nuclear weapons, and "$+ 1$" referred to the additional problems to stability caused by additional members joining the "nuclear club." Implicit in the formulation was the presumption that as long as "N" was the membership, things were manageably stable but that new additions made things worse, so that proliferation should be avoided. Proliferators, on the other hand, did not think that additions were a problem until they had become part of "N."

The issue was made more difficult because most of the states that possessed nuclear weapons were part of the major European-based system, whereas most of the potential proliferators came from the developing world. The notion that developing-world countries with nuclear weapons would create more problems than European possessors added an implicitly racial cast to the concern that was never lost on those countries whose possession of these weapons was opposed.

Cast in this light, the current concern over proliferation is not so different than it was before. During the Cold War, lists of possible nuclear proliferators were drawn that do not look much different than the lists drawn today. What is principally different is the more explicitly moral tone in which the antiproliferation argument is cast (the "axis of evil" states); the extension of the debate to include, more explicitly, chemical and biological weapons; and the tying of the concern to international terrorism.

If avoiding WMDs is the grand strategic problem, what strategic options are available? Essentially, there are two strategic alternatives: either the prevention of proliferation or the control of WMD possessors against whom attempts to prevent proliferation fail. The first thrust can be thought of as front-end deterrence, the second as back-end deterrence.

The goal of *front-end deterrence* is to keep potential proliferators from exercising the option to gain a proscribed weapons capability. Some of the efforts to do this have been multilateral: the Nuclear Non-Proliferation Treaty (NPT), the Missile Technology Control Regime (MTCR), and the various conventions outlawing chemical and biological weapons. Because some states see an advantage (or need) to develop these weapons, such efforts do not always succeed, and efforts to dissuade states from proliferating must recognize why states gain these weapons in order to convince them of the error of their ways.

States may decide to gain WMDs for several reasons. One may be simple prestige—a country may gain regional or international prestige by virtue of weapons possession. Closely related is the ability to intimidate unfriendly neighbors who do not possess such weapons. Yet another reason is to deter a neighbor who possesses WMDs from using them against you (from a fear of retaliation). Finally—and most ominous—is the desire and willingness to use these weapons for military gain. It is the latter motivation that most worries policy makers; especially the prospect that an irresponsible government may provide WMDs to a terrorist or similar group that would have few qualms about using the capability against American targets.

How does one keep countries from deciding to acquire these weapons? One way is through positive persuasion, offering incentives and rewards for compliance. As part of the NPT process, for instance, the United States and others have been willing to provide nuclear fuel rods to countries that turn in their spent rods before weapons-grade plutonium can be extracted from them (this was part of the arrangement between the United States and North Korea in 1994). If persuasion fails, then coercion may be the remaining option, either in the form of threats to take action to prevent proliferation from occurring (e.g., the Israeli strike against the Osirik nuclear plant in Iraq in 1981) or punitive actions to prevent proliferation from occurring (one of the stated purposes of the US attack on Iraq in 2003).

A strategic dilemma arose in response to US actions in 2003 regarding Iraq and North Korea. When Saddam Hussein was suspected of trying to produce WMDs and refused to cooperate fully with UN inspections of his programs, the United States led an invasion, in part, to prevent the Iraqi government from bringing those programs to fruition. When North Korea, on the other hand, threatened to activate what was suspected to be an ongoing nuclear weapons program, the United States reacted in a much more constrained, nonthreatening manner. The two situations were not, of course, identical, but one lesson that may have been learned by other potential proliferating countries is that the way to protect oneself from direct US intervention may be to rush to produce a capability before the United States can act, rather than simply remaining in a developmental program status.

If nonproliferation efforts cannot always prevent states from gaining these weapons, then efforts must turn to *back-end deterrence* to ensure that the weapons are not used. This problem is roughly analogous to that of preventing nuclear war during the Cold War, and the tools available to carry it out are the familiar Cold War tools of denial and retaliatory threats against potential transgressors. These threats were effective against the Soviet Union (at least there was no nuclear war, although there could be other reasons it did not occur). But will the same efforts work against contemporary nuclear-armed foes?

Those who fear that deterrence threats will not work cite fundamental differences between the Soviet Union and contemporary opponents. Deterrence worked against the Soviets, they maintain, because the Soviets were rational opponents who understood and feared the consequences of nuclear war and thus were deterred by threats to their existence. But what of fanatical terrorists who might come into possession of a few of these weapons? Would, for instance, fanatics willing to kill themselves by strapping dynamite around themselves be any less willing to die detonating a nuclear bomb? If they did so, against whom would we carry out the retaliatory threat? Would the terrorists care if we threatened to retaliate against a country or group of people that provided sanctuary for them? In other words, can contemporary opponents be deterred by the traditional retaliatory threats that were the staple of nuclear deterrence during the Cold War?

Some analysts conclude they would not and that the only meaningful alternative is to be able to deny perpetrators success in their mission. Denial can take on the two forms already suggested for suppressing terrorism. Counterterrorism actions such as hunting down and capturing or destroying nuclear weapons before they can be built or delivered offer one part of the approach. The other approach is antiterrorist actions designed to prevent or reduce the effects of a terrorist WMD attack. A principal means to reduce those effects is the capability to intercept an incoming attack before it reaches its target. If that attack might be launched aboard ballistic missiles, the answer then shifts to ballistic missile defense.

Missile Defenses

As already noted, the idea of missile defenses has been around for a long time and has always enjoyed a certain level of support. The current Bush administration thrust for missile defenses is the third time a forceful advocacy has been made, albeit against different opponents. The advocacy of missile defenses has been a central part of the neoconservative agenda for ensuring US military superiority and guaranteeing that US initiatives are not frustrated by opposition threats to respond with attacks against the United States. The issue of missile defense has, however, been plagued by questions of effectiveness and contributions to security that remain part of the public debate.

The intuitive, emotional appeal of missile defenses is undeniable on that surface level. These arguments were, of course, more powerful during the Cold War than today, when an effective defense against a Soviet nuclear attack on the United States could prevent the incendiary murder of countless millions of American citizens. While no one argues that terrorists or rogue states possessing a few such weapons could wreak the physical havoc the Soviet Union could have, their supposed greater ruthlessness and irrationality make the mandate of providing a hedge to save innocent lives a strong one.

In the mid-1960s, the fear of a nuclear-armed China fueled a desire for missile defenses, and the result was the Sentinel and Safeguard systems. The Sentinel system, which was to be deployed around major US cities, was publicly rejected when it became known that the missile interceptors would themselves have nuclear warheads that most Americans did not want stationed near their homes. A limited Safeguard system was briefly deployed around the ICBM complex at Grand Forks, North Dakota, but was quickly decommissioned in 1973.

The more famous proposal was President Reagan's Strategic Defense Initiative. It was by far the most ambitious BMD system ever proposed, aiming to provide an absolute barrier against even a massive Soviet strike against the United States. Reagan's purpose was to render nuclear weapons "impotent and obsolete" and thereby contribute to his ultimate goal of nuclear disarmament. The SDI was such a complicated, extensive proposal that it never got beyond the stage of researching components during the George H. W. Bush administration and was allowed to die under President Clinton.

Missile defense advocacies never die, however. Although the SDI was abandoned on the dual grounds of cost and effectiveness, the flame of missile defense continues at a lower level of scrutiny and ambition in the current form of national missile defense (NMD). The current program, like Sentinel and Safeguard, calls for a limited antimissile capability that could intercept a small (or accidental) launch by a rogue state. This requirement lowers the performance expectation of the system considerably below that proposed for the SDI, thereby obviating some of the criticism about whether it would work (although that remains conjectural), but has raised questions about whether the threat is adequate to justify the expense.

There are important policy and strategy questions to be asked about missile defense. The policy question is the workability and effectiveness of the system at an acceptable cost. Clearly, the better such a system works and the lower its cost, the more desirable (or less objectionable) it is. But what if its effectiveness is unknown or undemonstrated, like the current system? How much expense can one justify for a system of which the effectiveness is debatable? Since public monies spent on one priority are unavailable for others, how much risk does missile defense reduce and at what cost in terms of responding to other risks? None of these are easy policy questions.

The strategy question is whether (or how) missile defenses contribute to the deterrence of WMDs against the United States. One of the Cold War objections to BMD was that it might create a sense of false security for the possessor (false in the sense that one would never know in advance if the system actually worked) and might cause them to act more improvidently than they would, knowing that the consequences of such rash action involved their own destruction. There is a strand of parallel thinking among neoconservatives who advocate the NMD because it frees the United States from threats to use WMDs against it if it carries out certain foreign policy acts. To cite a concrete example, would the United States feel less constrained in dealing with the North Korean nuclear program if it had a missile shield to deflect a possible North Korean nuclear attack than without such a shield? Is that constraint good or bad?

Whether the United States will actually deploy the NMD remains a matter of conjecture. The structure of the debate, set in the 1960s, has not and probably will not change. Advocates will maintain that it is immoral not to try to protect the country from the ravages of a nuclear attack. Opponents will counter that it is more immoral to promise a protection that turns out to be an illusion and that the danger of such an attack is so remote as not to justify the expense. Advocates will say such a system can and must be designed and made effective; opponents doubt this will ever be the case. Meanwhile, the strategic effects remain in limbo.

Conclusions

Nuclear war, especially the general kind of conflict that highlighted the Cold War, was a special case for strategists of that era. It was the only contingency for which strategy aimed largely, if not wholly, at the avoidance of employing military forces in pursuit of national ends. It was also arguably the least likely form of warfare in which the United States might have engaged, but its potential was also the most consequential had it occurred. Nuclear strategy was very important strategic business in the Cold War era.

The problem of nuclear strategy has lost some of its centrality and urgency since the end of the Cold War. Nuclear Armageddon remains a physical possibility, but the scenarios under which it could occur have become progressively less plausible. Instead the nuclear problem has become a component of the WMD problem and as such, a part of the problem of asymmetrical warfare. What remains of the nuclear debate is under what circumstances hostile minor states might acquire WMDs and under what circumstances they might actually employ them against the United States—essentially the problem of weapons proliferation. The other remaining strand involves what the United States can and should do to lessen the threat posed by the possession of WMDs—*and* ballistic means of delivery—to the country. That problem has come to be associated with ballistic missile defenses. Where these concerns fit into the broader assessment of risk and risk reduction for the United States remains a matter of strategic debate that will be addressed in the last chapter.

Notes

1. Quoted in Richard Rhodes, *The Making of the Atomic Bomb* (New York: Touchstone Books, 1988), 676.

2. Bernard Brodie (1910–1978) was a professor at the National War College during the 1940s and author of many books on warfare. See listings in bibliography.

3. John Pike, "Ballistic Missile Defense: Is the U.S. 'Rushing to Failure'?" *Arms Control Today*, April 1998, http://www.armscontrol.org/act/1998_04/pikap98.asp.

4. Bush Doctrine, *National Security Strategy of the United States* (Washington, DC: The White House, September 2002), http://www.whitehouse.gov/nsc/nss.pdf.

SECTION IV
INFLUENCES ON THE PROCESS

Chapter 10

Fog, Friction, Chance, Money, Politics, and Gadgets

The strategy process is, in its basic form, a straightforward and sequential decision-making exercise. The simplicity of the process masks the difficulty of the decisions and the dilemmas that bedevil strategists. Further complicating the proceedings are the ubiquitous and often perverse influences posed by a host of factors, most of which are far beyond the control of strategists. The number of these variable and often uncontrollable factors is almost limitless, ranging from such obvious influences as geography to more subtle influences such as cultural heritage.

This chapter briefly addresses several of the most important influences: the Clausewitzian notions of fog, friction, and chance; and other factors such as economics, politics (domestic and international), and technology. The next chapter carries the examination further by looking at one very special influence, military doctrine.

The Clausewitzian Trio

The spiritual godfather of modern military thought in the Western world is Carl von Clausewitz. A veteran of the Napoleonic Wars, the Prussian intellectual characterized the essence of war as a situation clouded by fog, disrupted by friction, and often controlled by chance. Since the posthumous publication of Clausewitz's major work in 1831, military establishments throughout the world have expended enormous efforts to clear away the fog of war, reduce the friction in war, and minimize the importance of chance on the outcome of conflict. At best their efforts have met with only marginal success. However, recent technological developments would seem to hold out the promise of perhaps lifting the fog of war. Paradoxically, these same developments may increase rather than alleviate the problem.

Fog of War

The fog of war was the Clausewitzian metaphor for the perpetually incomplete and all-too-often inaccurate information

191

about the true state of affairs in war—what really is happening. Attainment of perfect information about the enemy has been, continues to be, and almost certainly will continue to be a near impossibility. Not only is information not always available (often due to the clever actions of the enemy), but available information may be incomplete, inaccurate, and/or contradictory (again, often due to the purposeful actions of the enemy). Information warfare is a "growth industry" in military affairs, both in reducing and increasing the amount of fog in the equation.

Even when accurate data are available, the data are subject to misinterpretation when processed into intelligence. Intelligence officers and commanders are often predisposed to believe the worst case indicated or to take the opposite course and put the available information in the best possible light. Unwarranted pessimism or optimism can be equally disastrous. The former can waste valuable resources preparing for phantom threats. The latter can lead to inadequate preparations for threats that are all too real.

Technological developments in the second half of the twentieth century brought new prominence to fog-of-war issues. Sophisticated aerial and space-based reconnaissance and surveillance systems, combined with inputs from a myriad of other sources ranging from high-tech electronic sensors to low-tech human operatives, all transmitting information to their clients in "real time," would seem to offer the promise of near-perfect and near-real-time information. However, even if one assumes all of these systems work flawlessly, the result may be an overwhelming blizzard of unrefined and unanalyzed information, the impact of which today would be exactly the same as that of the Clausewitzian fog of war nearly two centuries ago. At the same time, networked and Internetted electronic information and communication systems have created opportunities to cause an adversary considerable grief and perhaps irreparable damage. Broadcasting or transmitting false or misleading information, inserting inaccurate information into computer databases, and other such nefarious information warfare activities combine to provide a potentially devastating twenty-first-century twist to Clausewitz's nineteenth-century notion. As noted earlier, the manipulation of information is one of the main objectives of the fourth generation warrior.

Friction in War

Friction in war is closely associated, perhaps intertwined, with the idea of the fog of war. Most basically described, the concept of friction is akin to the twentieth-century notion of Murphy's Law; that is, whatever can go wrong will go wrong and at the worst possible moment. What goes awry is rarely a calamity in itself. Rather the Clauswitzian notion of friction considers the small and seemingly insignificant events or incidents—a short delay here, some bad weather there—which collectively drag down the overall level of performance, play havoc with timetables, and eventually can result in the failure to achieve intended objectives. Ultimately, the combined effects of such frictions can result in defeat—much akin to the notion of "death by a thousand small cuts." "For want of a nail a shoe was lost, for want of a shoe a horse was lost," and so forth seems a fitting epigram for friction in war.[1] Clausewitz warned that in war even the simplest things are difficult to accomplish. Surely every reader of this volume has had the experience of dealing with large bureaucratic institutions—whether educational institutions or government bureaucracies—and the attendant difficulties in getting even the most trifling matters properly addressed. In war the same sort of exasperating problems are compounded by fear, noise, the fog of war, and the actions of an enemy doing everything possible to increase the friction encountered.

Clausewitz also suggested that friction is what separates real war from war on paper. In the modern world, it is what separates well-scrubbed, elegant, multicolored slide-show briefings about operational plans from the dirty, bloody, and terrifying reality of the battlefield. It is what separates carefully calculated weapon-system performance estimates based on sterile tests and mathematical extrapolations from actual performance under fire in the chaos of battle. Clausewitz went on to warn that strategists must "know friction in order to overcome it . . . and in order not to expect a standard of achievement in their operations which this very friction makes impossible."[2]

Chance in War

The third element of the Clausewitzian trio is chance—pure dumb luck. In the high-tech world of the twenty-first century, we sometimes lose sight of the fact that pure chance can play a major role in success or failure in war. The advent of sophisticated statistical-analysis techniques, predictive computer-driven models, and the like cloud the fact that these tools and models may be based on erroneous data, inaccurate conceptions, and questionable assumptions. It is quite a simple matter to be seduced by such sophisticated techniques. It is also a simple matter to be seduced by their often overconfident and underexperienced practitioners who attempt to "ladle the fog of war with precise measuring cups," a legendary (perhaps apocryphal) comment attributed to a general officer referring to the young "whiz kids" who took over the Pentagon when Robert S. McNamara became secretary of defense in 1961. In Vietnam the whiz kids learned that war is not an engineering project that can be reduced to precise calculations. The enemy is never an inanimate object. Rather enemies are often clever, sometimes brilliant, and always determined men and women capable of daring, boldness, and rashness. The environment itself is, of course, less than perfectly predictable. Clausewitz warned that war is bound up with chance, and thus guesswork and luck play a huge role. Throughout American military history, chance has often played a significant role in spite of careful and often brilliant planning. Perhaps the most famous appearance of Dame Fortune was at the Battle of Midway in 1942. While still recovering from the disaster at Pearl Harbor, the US Navy read Japanese coded messages and realized that the enemy was about to launch an assault on Midway Island where they figured to destroy the remnants of the US Pacific Fleet. All of the remaining American aircraft carriers in the Pacific were quickly positioned to ambush the Japanese fleet.

For their part the Japanese had developed an elaborate operational plan—including a major diversionary action in the Aleutian Islands—and had assembled an overwhelming naval force. Even though the Americans knew the Japanese plans, on paper it appeared the Japanese had a crushing superiority. In spite of superior intelligence by the US Navy and detailed planning by the Japanese, the outcome of the battle rested on the incredibly good luck of US dive-bombers in the timing of their arrival over the Japanese fleet. First, the US bombers were fortunate just to find the enemy ships. Second, they arrived just when many Japanese aircraft were refueling and rearming, and the rest were out of position from having just engaged an earlier torpedo-plane attack. Thus by pure happenstance, the dive-bombers were virtually unopposed in their attack, and the damage they inflicted was magnified by detonation of Japanese bombs and fuel scattered about on the decks of the carriers. Had the dive-bombers not found the Japanese fleet or had they arrived perhaps 10 minutes later, the entire course of the battle might have been reversed.

Strategy and the Clausewitzian Trio

The concepts of fog, friction, and chance are relatively clear. But what impact do they have on strategists? The implications, it seems, are at least threefold—the first two are in terms of admonitions, the third in terms of an opportunity.

First, the principal message of fog, friction, and chance is that strategy (particularly at the operational level and below) must be flexible. Plans that rely on flawless execution, rigid timetables, and strictly sequenced actions are overly susceptible to failure. In general, the more complex the plan, the more likely something will go awry. Further, although careful planning attempts to reduce the element of chance to a minimum, strategists must remember that chance—dumb luck (or bad luck)—always remains a potent factor in success or failure.

The second implication has to do with the perils of hubris. Modern science and the wonders it has wrought can easily lead to smug self-confidence that can casually dismiss 200-year-old admonitions about fog, friction, and chance. Such hubris is unwarranted in any activity in which clever adversaries, Mother Nature, and our own errors of omission and commission can quickly combine in a frustratingly effective alliance that plays havoc with our carefully detailed plans. The clearest example is overestimation of our own capabilities and underestimation of the problems we confront; at this writing, postwar-Iraq may be an instance of this phenomenon.

The third message is that the more one can increase the fog and friction encountered by the enemy, the more likely it is that the enemy will meet defeat. Flexible plans with alternative objectives, counterintelligence, disinformation, deception, concealment, and campaigns to disrupt enemy command, control, and communication capabilities can all increase the enemy's friction problems and play a major role in its defeat, sometimes long before any blood is shed. Such actions not only can lead to serious errors by the enemy on the battlefield, but can also cause confusion and uncertainty that lower morale, sap aggressiveness, create tentativeness, and undermine initiative.

Economic Influences on Strategy

Economic factors are perhaps the most obvious influences on the strategy process. These influences can be viewed from two perspectives: first, the problems economic limitations present when making decisions within the process at the military strategy level, particularly in the development of forces, and second, the opportunities presented by economic influences at the operational strategy level.

As military forces have grown in size and the implements of war have become more complex, a large economic and industrial base has become more and more important to modern military forces planning for engagement in symmetrical warfare. Neither the village smithy nor cottage industries can produce the automatic weapons, artillery, tanks, ships, planes, munitions, and other equipment required for modern mechanized warfare. This has been particularly true since the Industrial Revolution and has been reemphasized in the age of electronics, dominating every aspect of modern, high-tech warfare. As a result the development and deployment (not to mention employment) of modern military forces put a considerable strain on any state's economic system. The economic strain has been compounded by the rapid growth of government spending on nonmilitary services, particularly in the liberal democracies.

As demands on government resources have grown in the liberal democracies, the military portion of the economic pie has shrunk relative to nonmilitary portions of the budget. This does not mean that military budgets have been reduced in absolute terms. In fact, US military budgets have grown rather consistently in absolute terms. The point here is that even though the US economy is much larger and more vigorous than it has been in times past, fewer of the government's economic resources

196

are available for military purposes. For example, in 1962 American military expenditures comprised just over 49 percent of total federal outlays. In 2001, military expenditures accounted for only 16.4 percent of federal outlays.[3] However, these trends have been at least temporarily reversed since the terror attacks of September 2001, as noted in the introduction.

The funding situation is further complicated by the soaring costs of developing and operating modern military establishments. This is particularly evident in the United States. Per capita personnel costs soared following the demise of conscription in the early 1970s. Weapon systems costs skyrocketed as they became more sophisticated, which led to heated debates during the 1980s between those who favored the expanded capabilities of fewer but more-sophisticated and expensive weapons and those who favored larger numbers of less-expensive and less-capable weapons. The verdict was to put the best possible technology into the fielded forces, even at the expense of numbers.

War in the modern world is always a "come-as-you-are" affair. At the same time, the foreshortened horizon for technology development requires continuous efforts to prepare the wherewithal required for the next war. Economic constraints play a major role in balancing this tug-of-war between current readiness and future capabilities. Regardless of their size, military budgets are finite, and thus there is always a tension between current readiness for war (appropriate stockpiles of weapons, munitions, etc.) and preparing for future conflicts (e.g., development and purchase of new weapon systems). Thus strategists are faced with another risk-management problem, this time based on the harsh realities of economics. In the simplest terms, it is a question of balancing current readiness (the risk of being unprepared today) against future capability (the risk of being unprepared tomorrow). Strategists can only strike the "correct" balance by assessing the current versus future risk of war.

The prospect of confronting asymmetrical warfare further complicates these economic calculations. Most asymmetrical strategies represent "warfare on the cheap"—manpower intensive but not resource intensive because asymmetrical warriors generally lack resources—but confronting that opponent with sophisticated military organizations may be disproportionately expensive. Will future asymmetrical strategists devise ways to bleed their symmetrical opponents into expending economic resources at politically unacceptable levels?

All of the foregoing factors influence military strategy decisions; that is, development, deployment, and broad plans for the employment of forces. However, these same factors may present opportunities at the operational level of strategy, opportunities to attack enemy "economic" targets that might provide dramatic and decisive effects on the battlefield. Much, of course, depends on the enemy's economic vulnerabilities and the nature of the war.

Although the crucial importance of economic factors has been reemphasized in the late twentieth century, it is certainly not a product of modern times nor is it a new idea to wage war by attacking an enemy's economy. The time-honored concept of a naval blockade is an attack on an enemy's economic system that attempts to destroy his commerce, cut off his imported materials and products essential to war-making capacity, and starve his populace into submission. Strategic bombing, which among other things attempts to destroy the vital centers of enemy industrial production, is a newer version of economic warfare. In a sense, naval blockade and strategic bombing have the same purposes, with bombing taking a more direct approach in the hope of achieving its purposes more rapidly. These efforts are most effective, of course, against opponents with an economic base that can be attacked.

Some forms of interdiction operations can also be considered economic warfare. Attacks on munitions stockpiles, transportation systems, and supplies en route to forces in the field are, in a sense, attacks on the enemy's economic system, its output, and its distribution system. The success of such attacks depends on a thorough knowledge and understanding of the enemy's economic vulnerabilities and the effect of those vulnerabilities on an adversary's combat capability within a useful period of time.

In a broader sense, economic warfare can be waged during peacetime—perhaps reducing the possibility of a shooting war, perhaps deciding the outcomes of a shooting war before the shooting starts. To a large degree, the Cold War struggle for influence and control that raged between the United States and the Soviet Union was economic warfare waged for control of the world's natural resources and trading lanes. Note, however, that economic struggles can also precipitate shooting wars. At least part of the reason for the Japanese attack on US forces in 1941 was Japan's perceived need to extend its economic power throughout the Pacific Basin combined with US embargoes on raw materials crucial to the Japanese.

Political Influences on Strategy

Politics, both domestic and international, are always potent influences on strategy decisions. War is a political act waged to achieve political objectives. Political requirements may clash with military aspirations, a fact well illustrated in Korea, Vietnam, Iraq, and every other conflict since World War II, much to the displeasure and consternation of many military professionals. All nuclear-era wars have been limited conflicts waged to achieve constrained political objectives using tightly circumscribed means. US military officers—reared, educated, and trained in an American tradition of total wars waged to destroy well-defined evils—found it difficult to adjust to a world in which wars would be waged for limited purposes. This resulted in considerable strain between the military leadership and their civilian masters. Among the results of this strain was the so-called "Weinberger Doctrine" of 1984. The doctrine promulgated six requirements or preconditions that should be met before going to war, proposals designed to prevent a repeat of the frustrations suffered in both Korea and Vietnam:

1. Vital national interests had to be at risk.
2. Fight with the intention to win.
3. Employ decisive force in pursuit of clear political and military objectives.
4. Reassess whether or not force is necessary and appropriate.
5. Reasonable expectation of congressional and public support.
6. Force used as a last resort.[4]

If anything, the Weinberger Doctrine strained civil-military relations further. While many in the military viewed the guidelines as the best defense against repeating the frustrations of

Korea and Vietnam, others—including many civilian and political leaders—viewed the doctrine as an act of military defiance, an attempt by the military to curb political choice, and a challenge to the concept of civilian control of the military.

The Weinberger Doctrine remains today as little more than a testament to the often frustrating experiences of major military powers fighting limited wars. It reminds us that war is only part of a broader political intercourse and that among the Western democracies, wars are conducted in accordance with the perceptions and directions of civilian political leaders.

Throughout the American experience, military leaders have rarely, if ever, been given free rein by their political masters. In point of fact, civilian leaders have often imposed themselves on military affairs to an extent that military leaders found disturbing long before the nuclear age. Pres. James K. Polk's hands-on approach to the Mexican War was perhaps the most flagrant example and a precedent for the close control experienced by the military in the Vietnam War. In the Civil War, Pres. Abraham Lincoln played musical chairs with his generals, and even in World War II, political decisions determined the broad course of military events as the Allies chipped away at the Axis empires.

On a less grandiose scale, decisions on weapon systems procurement, force structure, and even force basing continue to be controlled as much by the calculations of politicians facing reelection as on military practicality. If anything, the interest of political leaders in the details of military affairs has increased. Many political leaders are much attuned to the notion that war is too important to be left to the generals. Further, the advent of near-instantaneous worldwide communications has allowed them to control events to a level of detail unheard of in the past. The ability of a president to talk to nearly anyone in the field—even to a soldier in a rice paddy 10,000 miles away—offers an almost irresistible temptation to control directly and to bypass normal command and control structures.

The result is a political leadership (executive and legislative) that has a direct impact at every level of strategy. Political and military objectives are set, force structures designed and procured, and troops sent into combat, all under the close scrutiny and sometimes closer control of civilians. Perhaps worse for strategists in terms of long-range plans, the cast in control shifts with the changes in political fortune. But whichever way the political winds are blowing, strategists can be assured that politics will have a major impact on strategy decisions.

Impact of Technology on Strategy

For much of the past century, the US military was in head-long pursuit of technological solutions to its war-fighting problems. As the pace of scientific progress in all fields accelerated in the second half of the twentieth century, evermore sophisticated gadgetry and its presumed battlefield advantages became prime objects of American force development strategy. This effort to substitute American wizardry for American blood has met with enough success that, to a large degree, technological force multipliers are now the preferred currency of the American military realm.

Perhaps the largest technological impact on operational strategies in the twentieth century was made by taking war into the air and then into space. As a result, war became a "come-as-you-are" affair with disastrous consequences for the unprepared. Air- and space-based systems eventually set the stage for the introduction of the global positioning system (GPS) and the advent of precision-guided munitions. Some of the most important combined effects of all these technological advances have been far more efficient weapons delivery that, in turn, caused far fewer friendly casualties and far less collateral damage.

While these are all favorable trends resulting from the application of technological advances to battlefield problems, it appears that many Americans have come to expect their wars to be much more efficiently prosecuted and far less painful to endure than past wars. Such heightened expectations were well illustrated during the second Iraqi war when US columns advancing at breakneck speed toward Baghdad were forced to halt for several days because of a blinding sandstorm and the need to consolidate and secure extended lines of supply and communication. When this happened, pundits from the television news media, covering every facet of the war 24 hours a day, began speaking of bogging down in an Iraqi "quagmire," the same term used to describe the seemingly interminable war in Vietnam three decades earlier.

There is no question that the pursuit of high-tech weaponry has produced capabilities undreamed of only a few decades ago. But a note of caution is in order for strategists. Although modern technology has often proven important to success on the battlefield, its value can be overstated, its risks understated, and its opportunity costs obscured or ignored. If we examine the relationship of technology and warfare with a skeptic's calculating eye, we find several factors that should at least provide a cautionary note to the pursuit of high-tech solutions.

First, possession of superior technology does not guarantee effective use of that technology. The history of modern warfare is replete with examples of squandered technological advantages. In World War II, for example, the Germans failed to capitalize on their advantages in jet and rocket technologies. Had they concentrated their efforts on the production of jet-powered interceptors, the Allied strategic bombing offensive might have been in jeopardy. In the same light, had the Germans targeted the V-1 and V-2 weapons against embarkation ports in Great Britain, they might have seriously disrupted the logistical effort required to sustain the Allies on the Continent. Instead, the Germans concentrated on jet-powered attack bombers and rockets used as "vengeance" weapons against British cities.

Second, given enough time and resources, technology can be equaled by an enemy. Technological advances are based on physical laws, and thus, in effect, there are no real permanent technological secrets, just temporary technological advantages. Even without the scientific, economic, and industrial infrastructures to produce equal technology, opponents can often obtain sophisticated weaponry from allies, supporters, or arms merchants. The important point is that technological advantage is a relative thing. If an enemy develops or acquires equivalent technology, the advantage disappears, and force multipliers no longer multiply.

Third, technology can also be countered. It is particularly frustrating that some countermeasures are simple and inexpensive as well as effective. For example, chaff—simple strips of tinfoil—was first used to counter radar in World War II. It remains an effective counter. Technology can also be countered through the use of clever strategy and tactics. The United States went to war in Southeast Asia relying on sophisticated weapons that could deliver large amounts of fire and steel on almost any target. The enemy countered by using guerrilla tactics that provided few lucrative targets.

Fourth, technology may not perform as well as expected. Fortunately, we have experienced combat infrequently. But this blessing often means that many of the high-tech gadgets on which we have come to depend are untested in the rigors of combat. In spite of our best efforts, neither simulations, exercises, nor maneuvers can replicate the chaos, complexity, and terror of the modern battlefield. We often find it difficult to anticipate the counteractions of a clever and dedicated enemy. The result is that we can be frequently confronted in war by unexpected circumstances that seriously hinder the effective employment of our weapon systems, reducing or nullifying our technological advantage.

The message for strategists in all of this is important and basic. Other things being equal, superior technology on the battlefield offers significant advantages. However, this truth must be tempered with the notion that militarily significant technological advantage can be a fragile, perishable, and elusive commodity.

Conclusions

Strategy making is not an abstract form of building research designs and models that can be applied deductively to the world. Rather strategists must contend with an untidy world with numerous influences, only some of which can be controlled some of the time. After looking at the contributions of worldviews and doctrine in chapter 11, the discussion turns to the dilemmas posed by this untidy reality.

Notes

1. Iona and Peter Opie, eds., *The Oxford Nursery Rhyme Book* (New York: Oxford University Press, 1955), 116.

2. Carl von Clausewitz, *On War*, ed. and trans. Michael Howard and Peter Paret (Princeton, NJ: Princeton University Press, 1976), 120.

3. Congressional Budget Office, Washington, DC, http://www.cbo.gov.

4. Caspar Weinberger, "The Uses of Military Power" (speech, National Press Club, Washington, DC, 28 November 1984).

Chapter 11

Worldviews and Doctrine

Of the nearly endless list of outside influences that impinge upon decision makers in the strategy process, it is quite likely that the disparate worldviews held by soldiers, sailors, and airmen (a subject briefly introduced in chap. 7) have the most powerful and pervasive influence. Codified in service doctrine, these worldviews have had a significant impact on decisions at the military strategy level in terms of force structure and at the operational level in terms of campaign planning and execution.

Unfortunately, these different worldviews have often been at odds with one another with dysfunctional results. Spurred by such problems in the Vietnam War, as well as subsequent operations in Lebanon and Grenada, the US Congress passed and Pres. Ronald Reagan signed into law in 1986 landmark military reform legislation, the Goldwater-Nichols Department of Defense Reorganization Act. Among the many provisions of this far-reaching legislation was an attempt to force the individual services to think and act in a joint, mutually reinforcing manner. Further, the new law required the development of joint doctrine, which would be superimposed on the individual doctrines produced by the military services. It also required joint professional education and experience in joint billets before an officer could be promoted to the senior ranks.

Although there was much consternation among the services, the law has been implemented fully and has generally yielded very positive results and trends. However, the disparate worldviews of soldiers, sailors, and airmen remain. The reason for this is obvious—the vastly different natures of the environments in which the military services operate, which cannot be changed by congressional fiat. The Goldwater-Nichols initiatives to increase cooperation among the services will likely smooth the rough edges of competing worldviews, but they will remain and will certainly continue to have a major impact on strategists and the strategy process. It is important to understand that the authors are not passing judgment on the different worldviews.

They believe there are no right or wrong worldviews; rather there are simply different worldviews, the appropriateness of which must be determined for the situation at hand.

The Ground Force Worldview*

Ground forces are confined to and constrained by the harsh realities of geography, topography, flora, and fauna, all of which limit their speed and maneuverability. Every hill, river, and forest is an obstacle that must be overcome. Equally important, the problem of the surface warrior is often immediate because the enemy is both right in front of him and shooting at him. Combat for the man on the ground is very much an "up close and personal" affair. Although very impersonal, long-range artillery is an important part of the ground force arsenal; so is the bayonet, a very personal and very short-range weapon.

As a result, the surface warrior's worldview tends to be sharply constrained and focused on the immediate problem. For example, it is now clear that the commanders of the cross-channel invasion of northwest Europe in June 1944 were far more worried about their immediate problem, the initial lodgment on the shores of France, than about the subsequent breakout from the lodgment area and the drive toward the borders of Germany. Although the Normandy beaches offered many favorable conditions for the amphibious assault and subsequent force buildup, tall, thick hedgerows every few yards dominated the countryside behind the beaches, a situation that clearly favored the defending forces. This was just about the worst imaginable terrain for the breakout operations. In that event it became a yard-by-yard slugging match that continued from 6 June until 25 July 1944 when the breakout finally took place at Saint-Lô. One can argue whether or not picking the Normandy beaches for the D-day landings was wise, given the hedgerow-dominated countryside just inland. However, it is clear that the planners and commanders of Operation Overlord (a group dominated by surface warriors) were worried much more about the immediate problem

---

*Much of the discussion that follows is based on the groundbreaking work of Col John M. Collins, USA, retired, as published in *Grand Strategy: Principles and Practices* (Annapolis: Naval Institute Press, 1973).

of amphibious assault on the beaches and much less about the problems that loomed for subsequent operations.[1]

The same concentration on the immediate problem was again obvious in US Army doctrine in the 1970s. Focused on Europe with Warsaw Pact forces that considerably outnumbered NATO forces, the Army doctrine of "active defense" concentrated on "winning the first battle" in the hope that doing so would stop or at least blunt any enemy advance into western Europe. It was not until the late 1970s that the Army developed "AirLand Battle" doctrine that broadened the focus to include echeloned Warsaw Pact forces still days distant from the battles they would eventually fight.

With so much emphasis on the immediate problem—the enemy shooting at them—it should come as no surprise that ground warriors often take a very traditional view that the enemy's military is itself the enemy's center of gravity. They tend to subscribe to the "continental school" of strategy, believing that lasting victory can be achieved only by defeating and destroying the enemy's armed forces, occupying the enemy's territory by putting "boots on the ground," and thereby controlling the enemy's population. In short, for adherents of the continental school, the immediate problem for the soldier—the enemy army—is also the ultimate problem and the source of the adversary's ability to resist. Within this school of strategy, ground warfare is the "main event," and all other forces operate in support of ground forces.

The Naval Worldview

The traditional naval viewpoint is much different. As it is with the ground warrior, worldviews of sailors conform to the nature of the operating environment. Because the seas are so vast and present far fewer barriers, the sailor's worldview is much less constrained than that of the soldier. Only the shorelines of the great oceans constrain naval forces, and the range of naval airpower has significantly eased that constraint. Naval forces have an almost unrestricted ability to maneuver on a featureless battlefield that covers some 70 percent of the planet.

The broad worldview that results from these environmental factors also provides a very long-range perspective, for at least four reasons. First, the primary naval combat problem is often not immediate. The fact that contending navies are often widely separated has traditionally made the hunt for the enemy fleet a principal problem. Second, the creation of naval forces from the keel up requires an extremely long lead time. Third, sailors are the stewards of extremely expensive war-fighting assets, assets so expensive that they can be accurately regarded as national assets rather than just weapons or weapon systems. Fourth, most naval assets tend to stay in service much longer than air or land force assets. However, the fact that these enormous investments in gray steel can be lost in a matter of minutes heightens concerns considerably. The consequence of these formidable truths was best summed up in Winston Churchill's statement that at the battle of Jutland in 1916, Adm John R. Jellicoe could have lost the war in a single afternoon.[2]

Although less constrained compared to that of ground forces, the naval worldview remains limited because naval forces are still constrained. The world's shorelines define limits beyond which ships simply cannot sail. Unlike the broad oceans, narrow waters and sea-lane choke points also constrain naval forces. Thus it has been through the ages that great naval powers sought control of the vital maritime choke points such as the Strait of Malacca, Strait of Gibraltar, the Dardanelles, and the like.

Because of all these factors, the maritime school of strategy tends to look well beyond the adversary's deployed naval forces. Although sea control requires the neutralization of the enemy's fleet, gaining such control is only an intermediate objective that provides the basis for decisive, war-winning action. Control of the high seas and narrow choke points provides the naval preconditions required to disrupt an adversary's commerce, blockade its ports, cripple its economy, and thus destroy the enemy's economic basis for war making. Control of the seas provides the means to project power ashore at a place and time of choice and thereby control events on shore. The American campaign against Japan in World War II, particularly Admiral Nimitz' drive across the central Pacific, was a classic application of the maritime school of strategy.

The Airman's Worldview

Airmen have the least constrained worldview because they do not face the sorts of geographic limitations encountered by either soldiers or sailors. The all-enveloping air environment provides a superhighway from everywhere to anywhere. As a result airmen have a global worldview and think in terms of war as a whole rather than in terms of specific battles. Therefore, in classical airpower strategy, defeat of the enemy's airpower became an overwhelmingly important but nevertheless intermediate objective. Control of the air made it possible to launch direct aerial attacks against an enemy's industrial capability to produce the wherewithal of modern warfare. The resulting destruction of the enemy's "vital centers" could, the airpower theorists believed, bring an enemy to its knees in the minimum of time with the minimum of costs in terms of both blood and treasure. The strategic bombing campaigns against both Germany and Japan during World War II were examples of the classical airpower theory put into practice, with somewhat mixed results in both cases.

Both soldiers and sailors have centuries of historical evidence to bolster their theories of victory. From the beginning of the airpower era, they looked with some scorn and much dismay at airmen whom they considered to be brash, inexperienced upstarts. They scorned the idea of quick, clean victory in war and were dismayed that airmen put so much effort into attacking panacea targets far from the front lines rather than providing direct support to surface forces. Airmen, on the other hand, have a relatively short and checkered history at war and have much less evidence upon which to base their theory of victory. Part of the problem has been that, for most of the airpower era, their visionary reach far exceeded their technological grasp. The dawn of the nuclear era and the development of bombers with intercontinental range seemed to bring their visions to fruition; but it was not until late in the twentieth century, with the development of precision munitions, that airpower fully came of age.

Worldviews and Military Doctrine

Worldviews are important because they are codified in the doctrines of the land, sea, and air military services. Military doctrine has a number of definitions—some official, some unofficial—that often differ significantly by country and military service. Official definitions tend to be written in the military equivalent of "legalese," which often obscures doctrine's significance. Perhaps the best working definition—one that is accurate, concise, and yet retains the vitality befitting doctrine's potential importance—is also one of the simplest. *Military doctrine is what is believed about the best way to conduct military affairs.*

When properly formulated, doctrine is based on the best evidence available and tempered by mature, reasoned judgment. The principal source of doctrine is experience, and thus, in a sense, doctrine is a compilation and interpretation of concepts, actions, and such that have generally been successful in the past. Unfortunately, not all past experiences are relevant to the present (not to mention the future), and there is no guarantee that what is relevant today will remain relevant in the future. Hence, doctrine is a constantly maturing and evolving thing. Those "lessons" from the past that endure over an extensive period of time are not only generalized into doctrinal beliefs but have also been raised to higher levels of abstraction to become the so-called principles of war—doctrinal beliefs that are axiomatic.

By far the most important use of doctrine is to teach succeeding generations in a particular military organization the "revealed truth" about their service and their theory of victory. Doctrine should also form a storehouse of analyzed experience and military wisdom that provides the knowledge base for entering strategy debates and making strategy decisions. T. E. Lawrence (Lawrence of Arabia) succinctly stated the importance of this function when he commented that with 2,000 years of examples, there was no excuse for not fighting a war well.[3]

Unfortunately, the development and use of doctrine are problematic for several reasons. First, an objective analysis of experience is particularly difficult. The Vietnam War is a classic case in point because of the passions of service parochialism, political orientation, and the inability to delve into the records of the enemy. At this writing, 30 years after the fall of Saigon to the army of North Vietnam, there remains considerable debate about whether or not the United States succeeded in Vietnam (US forces were no longer in Vietnam when the final North Vietnamese offensive began) and the relative contributions of the various services to success or failure. Desert Storm has also been difficult to analyze, as both air and ground forces believe they have rightful claims to the lion's share of credit for the coalition victory. In this case both groups have strong cases to argue. Doctrine may not be properly formulated because it is overly influenced by the questionable predilections of the "senior officer present," a traditional problem that is all too common. Doctrine may not be properly formulated because there is a paucity of evidence available. This was always the case during the Cold War when dealing with the possibility of nuclear warfare. Thankfully, there had never been a nuclear war (at least not one in which both sides had nuclear weapons), and thus there was no empirical evidence about how a nuclear war could best be prosecuted.

Perhaps the most common doctrinal problem is the tendency to let doctrine stagnate. Changing circumstances (e.g., technological developments) must be evaluated because they can modify beliefs about important experiential lessons. The concept of unescorted, high-altitude, daylight precision bombing in World War II was largely driven by the idea that high-flying bombers would be very difficult to see from the ground and thus very difficult to intercept on the way to their targets. Further, US airmen also believed that even if intercepted, their heavily armed bombers flying in tight defensive formations could fight the way to their targets without suffering serious attrition. Such had been the American experience in exercises during the 1920s and early 1930s—before the invention and introduction of radar. Radar rendered those critical assumptions moot, and after attempting to fight their way to targets in German-occupied Europe and enduring staggering losses, the RAF Bomber Command went to night bombing raids to elude German fighters. Undeterred by the British experience, the US bomber forces tried their luck with their defensive formations and bombers bristling with machine guns. They suffered the same sorts of staggering losses. Fortunately, by early 1944, newly developed long-range fighters made it possible to escort the bomber formations all the way to their targets in Germany, which solved much of the heavy attrition problem.

Finally, doctrine can become irrelevant if the assumptions that support it are no longer valid, and some of the assumptions may never be explicitly stated. The development of US airpower doctrine provides a pertinent example. Based on the ideas of many of the early airpower theorists, but particularly those of Gen William "Billy" Mitchell and faculty members at the Air Corps Tactical School, the Army Air Corps went into World War II with a doctrine based on the belief that strategic bombing would (and should) be decisive in war. The World War II experience and the availability of nuclear weapons and long-range aircraft in the postwar era further ingrained this notion. Military budgets, force structures, equipment procurement, and training were all based on the central doctrinal belief in the deterrent and war-fighting decisiveness of strategic bombardment. Even the tactical air forces became mini-strategic forces in the late 1950s and early 1960s. However, crisis came in 1965 when the United States entered the Vietnam War and the bombing of North Vietnam began. American strategic airpower doctrine was found to be bankrupt in Vietnam because its underlying (yet unstated) assumptions were untrue in that situation. Strategic bombing doctrine assumed that all US wars would be unlimited wars fought to destroy the enemy and that America's enemies would be modern, industrialized states fighting modern, mechanized wars. Both assumptions were crucial to the validity of strategic bombing doctrine.[4] They were reasonable assumptions in the 1920s and 1930s but invalid during the 1960s when facing limited warfare in the Third World. The results were frustration, ineffective bombing, wasted blood, and ill-spent treasure.

As noted above, military worldviews differ widely and often lead to conflicts between soldiers, sailors, airmen, and marines at both the military and operational levels of strategy. At the level of military strategy, conflicts revolve around what kind and what size forces will be developed and deployed; questions which all revolve around budget allocations, with each service touting the importance and relevance of its own worldview. At the operational level of strategy, issues revolve around how a conflict will actually be prosecuted, and in those tense situations, tempers can easily flare. For example, during the first Iraqi war (Desert Storm), while coalition airpower struck deep into Iraq at political, economic, command and control, and other such targets, ground force commanders fumed, believing that targets important to them were being ignored. At one point a US Army general and a US Air Force general nearly came to blows over the issue.

Evolving Worldviews

The long and strongly held differences in worldviews outlined above have caused considerable difficulties in formulating strategy at several levels over the years. Looking to the future, this situation could either be ameliorated by the further development of a joint worldview, or it could be exacerbated by the robust development of new worldviews, the most likely being for special operations, space warfare, and information warfare.

Rather than evolving in a Darwinian sense, a *joint worldview* was dictated by the Goldwater-Nichols legislation mentioned earlier in this chapter. In addition to producing officers with joint experience—and thus a greater understanding of the sister services and their worldviews—the legislation also called for the development of joint doctrine; that is, a joint worldview that would supersede the traditional worldviews of ground, sea, and air and space forces. As a result, the production of joint doctrine has become a thriving cottage industry within the military. Whether or not the homogenization of service doctrines will ultimately produce a better or more useful worldview and doctrine remains to be seen. If successful, the joint worldview could significantly ease the fractious disputes between the military services at the levels of military and operational strategy.

The ascendancy of new worldviews could significantly complicate strategists' tasks, particularly at the military strategy level. Funding for the development of forces, especially new kinds of forces, is always contentious. This has already been seen in the world of *special operations*, the clandestine and unorthodox military operations designed to strengthen friends and defeat foes. For decades the special operators were viewed as necessary nuisances by traditional military organizations. However, it became more and more apparent during the Cold War that much of that conflict would likely be waged in the shadow world of the special operator rather than in conventional or nuclear confrontations between the superpowers. As a result Congress gave the special operations forces a special status, with their own "fenced" budget and designated advocates in the Pentagon. Since then, special operations forces have assumed larger and more important roles, including direct support of conventional forces.

The importance of special operations forces was very apparent in the war against the Taliban government of Afghanistan, where special operators worked directly with the friendly forces of the Northern Alliance. Although the facts are not fully revealed at this writing, it appears that the role of special operations forces behind enemy lines in the second Iraqi war (Operation Iraqi Freedom), both before and during the ground invasion, had a significant impact on the rapid disintegration of the Iraqi armed forces.

Doctrinal issues regarding *space warfare* could also complicate strategists' tasks. Over the past 25 years, space operations have become very important to many modern military forces, but always in a supporting role, such as providing intelligence, positioning information, communication links, and the like. At this writing (2006), space has been militarized but has not been weaponized. To this point, wars are not fought in or from that harshest of all environments. But space could be weaponized, and the "shooting" war could quickly extend to space and from space. The development and deployment of such capabilities would certainly complicate strategists' tasks at several levels.

The third complicating new worldview is *information warfare*. The idea of information warfare is, at once, very old and very new. Information, or the lack of it, has always been critically important to the successful (or unsuccessful) conduct of military operations. Military commanders have wanted to see over the next hill since the earliest days of organized warfare. Opposing forces have always done their best to ensure the enemy could not see over that hill, or that the view over the hill was distorted—intelligence operations spawned counterintelligence operations. As Winston Churchill was fond of noting, "In wartime, truth is so precious that she must often be attended to by a bodyguard of lies."[5]

In the modern age, radio transmissions and telephone lines became invaluable to a military's ability to share information and direct operations. Radio transmission interception and tapping into telephone lines quickly became important ways to gather information about an adversary. Aircraft ranging overhead could provide priceless reconnaissance beyond the next hill (and many other hills as well), and preventing reconnaissance aircraft from plying their trade or camouflaging what such aircraft might see became very important in the airpower age. The space age multiplied and broadened the opportunities

214

and methods to see over the next hill. All of that is essentially "old hat," building new sophistication into the age-old needs to gather and distribute information.

The new power and potentially revolutionary part of information warfare arrived with the advent of the digital computer and has been multiplied unimaginably by the advent of the Internet and other computer networks. Digital computers, of course, quickly became enormously rapid processors and storehouses of information. The Internet and World Wide Web of computer communications channels made vast amounts of information mobile at the speed ultrafast computers could process it and then distribute that information at the speed of light. Virtually every form of civilian industry and commerce has come to depend on computers and computer networks to control and monitor everything from company finances to inventory, as have governments become dependent upon computers and computer networks to conduct most of the ordinary business of the state. The military has, of course, also grown heavily dependent on networked computers for everything from mundane daily routines to critical logistics flows and battlefield operations. Further, embedded computers populate nearly every sophisticated weapon system.

One reaction to all of this activity has been the preliminary development of an idea that has been called "net-centric warfare," a concept that in theory would fully exploit the capabilities to net together in real time virtually all sources of information and all the users of that information. Full development of this concept has the promise of electronically overcoming traditional organizational and structural barriers and may thus provide the means for the most efficient and effective military operations.

As one would expect, however, the near-total dependence on computers and computer networks has brought with it serious vulnerabilities and risks, all of them multiplied by the concept of net-centric warfare. Dependence on computers and computer networks provides a portal through which adversaries may be able to electronically gain access to vital information. Such access allows intruders to do several things. First, just having access to the information may meet the intruder's needs in the sense of intelligence and counterintelligence operations. Second, the intruder can corrupt the information, perhaps in ways virtually undetectable, so

215

that certain systems (commercial or military) that depend on the information do not function optimally. Third, the intruder can insert information that will cause systems or systems of systems to fail catastrophically. Fourth, the intruder can insert information that will shut down or cause havoc in critical systems at a particular time, under certain conditions, or upon command. Such capabilities could threaten the sudden collapse of essential public services, the sudden collapse of the target's economic system, or the sudden collapse of the target's military defenses. This is the modern face of information warfare.

As a result of such dire possibilities, elaborate security schemes are required to fend off such would-be intruders bent on electronically rendering disaster on the unsuspecting target. Unfortunately, elaborate security procedures exact a tax from those they protect: a tax levied in time, manpower, and money required to establish and maintain the procedures and safeguards; plus a tax in decreased operating efficiency caused by the procedures and safeguards themselves. Further, experience so far has shown that even amateur "hackers" are incredibly clever and inventive at breaking into computer systems and networks that were ostensibly secure. One must also wonder if there are others who have penetrated systems and planted electronic "bombs" with such skill that their handiwork remains unknown, dormant, and awaiting orders to do its destructive work.

Where this cat-and-mouse game will end or if it will end is uncertain. It is clear, however, that in modern states, modern economies, and modern military establishments, the dependence on computers, computer networks, and the flow of electronic data over those networks continues to grow. With that growth came the promise of increased efficiencies and effectiveness in governing, in economic affairs, and in military operations. On the other side of the coin, strategists need to understand that the risks attached to such dependence have also grown apace in both number and potential consequences.

Conclusions

The ways that soldiers, sailors, and airmen (perhaps spacemen) view war and their part in it varies because of a number of things, including the environments in which they operate and

216

the consequent constraints and priorities those environments impose or create. In turn those preferences are reflected in very different doctrinal preferences that can come into conflict when devising strategies at all levels, as land, sea, air, and space assets are blended together in the face of a common foe.

The face of war, however, is undergoing change, as suggested in the last sections, and these changes will require further alterations of service and joint doctrines. For instance, in a world where the United States faces few potential enemies that mirror our forces, what is the role of a large capital ship or main battle tank or heavy bomber in combating cyberwar? Are air forces becoming dependent on special forces to locate and target elusive asymmetrical opponents who cannot be adequately surveilled by aircraft or satellites? Will space be weaponized in addition to being militarized? Will fully integrated computer systems and networks prove to be a boon to military forces or an Achilles' heel? These and many other questions will affect the evolution of doctrine and its translation into strategy.

Notes

1. Russell F. Weigley, *Eisenhower's Lieutenants: The Campaign of France and Germany 1944–1945* (Bloomington, IN: Indiana University Press, 1981), 35.

2. As quoted in Geoffrey Bennett, *The Battle of Jutland* (London: David and Charles, Ltd., 1980), 41–42.

3. Quoted in J. A. English, "Kindergarten Soldier: The Military Thought of Lawrence of Arabia," *Military Affairs* 51, no. 1 (January 1987): 10.

4. Briefly, the argument is that modern, industrialized states provide the ideal targets for strategic bombing. An enemy fighting a modern, mechanized war makes those industrial targets important. Given the destruction involved, it would seem the only time one would engage in heavy bombing of industrial areas would be in an all-out, total war.

5. Sir Winston Churchill (remarks, conference with Franklin D. Roosevelt and Joseph Stalin, Tehran, Iran, 30 November 1943), http://www.loc.gov/exhibits/Churchill/wc-unity.html.

SECTION V
CONTINUING DILEMMAS

Chapter 12

The Dilemmas of Conventional War

Previous chapters have described the decision process involved in making strategy, how the decisions are related one to another, and the numerous influences that twist, constrain, and alter an otherwise straightforward process. This chapter and the two that follow examine several continuing dilemmas facing strategists in the conventional, asymmetrical, and nuclear arenas. The authors have alluded to many of these dilemmas previously, and thus the discussion in this section serves as a summary from the perspective of the strategy decision process and the likely nature of future conflicts.

As noted earlier and explored further in the next chapter, the overwhelming superiority of US conventional forces creates a paradox of sorts. American forces are so powerful that only the foolhardy will confront them on conventional terms in the future. In that case the only way to fight the US military may be to change the rules of engagement and engage in what is increasingly called asymmetrical warfare, the subject of the next chapter.

For Whom and What Do We Prepare?

Until the end of the Cold War, this continuing dilemma centered much more on the "what" portion of the question than on the "whom." During those years, which in retrospect seem so simple and calm, the "who" was assumed to be the Soviet Union in worst-case scenarios or, in lesser cases, Soviet allies or so-called client states. The "what" question, on the other hand, caused the headaches. If the "who" were the Soviets, the United States faced the possibility of its national survival being directly at risk in the nuclear regime and the survival of its closest and most important European allies being at stake in a highly mechanized, fast-moving, major conventional war. If the "who" were a Soviet ally or client state, the stakes would likely be a great deal less, but the "what" could range from lesser degrees of conventional mechanized warfare all the way to insurgency and terrorism.

The Soviets, of course, no longer exist. In the nearly half-century duel of the titans, only the United States was left standing, a military colossus without peer. Many (most notably the neoconservatives) try to promote China as a potential peer competitor, but to do so in anything less than a far-distant time frame is a difficult-to-sustain argument. The bottom line is that since the demise of the Soviet Union and the end of the Cold War, the United States has not had what the *Quadrennial Defense Review* called a peer competitor, and the military threat to the survival of the United States no longer exists except in the abstract (Russia does still possess a significant nuclear arsenal). However, this is not to say that there could be no serious threats to the United States.

It is very clear that several states and some nonstate actors have the military wherewithal to cause significant damage to the United States. The detonation of a few nuclear weapons carefully placed to cause the maximum amount of damage would be a disaster of biblical proportions, but it would not threaten the survival of a state as large, as economically strong, as socially cohesive, and as militarily capable as the United States. The likelihood of such a state-sponsored nuclear attack is very low because nuclear deterrence for the most part still prevails, even in the new world order. It is obvious to all that if such an attack could cause a "disaster of biblical proportions" in the United States, the retribution exacted by the United States would certainly involve the rapid extinction of the offending state in a fiery cataclysm that only the most fanatic martyrs would ever contemplate. The United States continues to hold all the trump cards in the nuclear realm, unless the attacker is immune to nuclear retribution, as might be the case should a nonstate actor come into possession of one or a few nuclear weapons. This subject is revisited below.

The disparity in conventional military power between the United States and everyone else was well demonstrated in a stunning performance against the Iraqi armed forces, both in 1991 and again in 2003. In 1991 many analysts regarded the Iraqi armed forces to be among the most capable and best equipped outside of NATO and the Warsaw Pact. Their swift and abject defeat stunned nearly everyone, including the Russians who had supplied and mentored the Iraqi military for several decades. In 2003 the confrontation was no contest from the beginning. But even though much was expected of the US military against the overmatched Iraqis, their swift march to Baghdad again surprised many, including the Iraqi forces that apparently collapsed in confusion and terror. With such a spectacularly demonstrated disparity in conventional-force capabilities, it is difficult to imagine any state or nonstate actor attempting to wage offensive conventional, symmetrical warfare against US forces.

However, the requirement for the US military establishment to maintain its conventional-war capability still exists for at least three reasons. The first and most obvious reason is to act as a deterrent. The idea that others will not dare to wage conventional war against the United States is very comforting but is predicated on the continued size, technological sophistication, and operational expertise of the US military in the art of conventional warfare. The second reason is that the United States may again be called upon to aid others with conventional forces, as happened in Kuwait, Bosnia, and Kosovo. The third reason is that the administration of George W. Bush proclaimed a national security strategy that specifically includes the possibility of waging preemptive war. One reason for such preemptory action was alluded to above—undeterrable entities (nonstate actors, so-called rogue states, etc.) armed with some quantity of weapons of mass destruction. The presumption is that preemptive actions by the United States would most likely be nonnuclear (at least in the beginning) and probably would involve the large-scale use of conventional forces (although the use of unconventional forces is also quite probable). Thus publicly declared policy has put conventional warfare "back in play," so to speak.

The controversial doctrine of preemptive conventional warfare assumes that the United States will seize the initiative in such "wars of choice." Many basic truths and associated requirements cascade from this original assumption. First, US forces are likely to be called upon to engage quickly almost anywhere on the globe. Second, effective preemption with conventional forces requires deploying preemptive forces to the critical area with great speed and engaging enemy forces before they can react effectively. This is generally not a problem for air forces and may not be a significant problem for naval forces, including Marine Corps forces afloat. However, it can be a very significant problem if US Army ground forces are initially required for effective preemption.

If ground forces are to be used early in a preemptive operation, they must be able to deploy very quickly, meaning that they must be much "lighter" than they were at the end of the twentieth century in order to facilitate air transportation to the scene of the conflict. However, lighter forces make soldiers very nervous because they would be forced to rely on air and naval forces for their heavy firepower. On the other hand, many would argue that building a lighter Army would unilaterally abrogate much of the combat power of the Army and thus narrow the conventional warfare advantage between the United States and everyone else. Further, lighter Army forces quickly begin to look much like the Marine Corps, which can lead to serious political and, in turn, funding problems, a situation that both the Army and the Marine Corps would consider to be politically perilous.

The only effective alternative to lighter Army forces is to effectively preposition Army heavy equipment so that it can be "mated" with troops deployed by air to the region. This alternative assumes that (1) the United States will know long in advance all of those locations where it might be called upon to wage a preemptive operation, (2) the United States will be allowed by a foreign government to conveniently preposition heavy equipment nearby, and (3) the mating of equipment and troops can be done with enough speed to effectively preempt.

Preemption will also place great strains on air mobility assets. Rapid movement to preempt will virtually always require air transport of ground forces as well as supporting assets for airpower, logistics support, and the like. Evacuation of casualties and some categories of noncombatants may also be done largely with airpower. This situation will remain until port facilities become available in the theater of operations and until ground transportation facilities and ground lines of communication are established and secured.

Operations Tempo and the All-Volunteer Force

During the period extending from 1989 through this writing in 2006, the tempo of operations for the US military was at a very high level. The number of large expeditionary operations during that short period was unprecedented. They began with operations in Panama in 1989, followed quickly by deployments of major combat and support forces to Saudi Arabia, Turkey, and elsewhere in the area for Operation Desert Shield, followed by Desert Storm. On the heels of success against Iraq came, in succession, deployments to Somalia, Bosnia, Kosovo, Afghanistan, and again to Iraq. And of course, there were a good number of smaller operations (e.g., Haiti) plus the usual humanitarian relief efforts in every corner of the globe.

Although they appear to be discrete operations, many of these operations required the continuing presence of US forces long after the news media and the attention of the American public had shifted elsewhere. For example, the first Iraqi war never effectively ended. Following the cease-fire and evacuation of Iraqi troops from Kuwait, US and British aircrews, supported by large logistical and command and control contingents, continued to fly combat missions inside Iraq to enforce the "no-fly zones" imposed by the victorious coalition (Operations Southern and Northern Watch). Bombing missions to destroy Iraqi air defense sites occurred frequently, occasioned by radars from those sites "lighting up" coalition aircraft and by intermittent launchings of Iraqi air defense missiles. These missions continued until the start of the second Iraqi war in 2003. Following that quick military victory, nearly 150,000 US troops remained to enforce the peace and begin rebuilding Iraq amid sporadic guerrilla-style attacks that threatened to require an even larger force.

US troops have also remained in Afghanistan long after the fall of the Taliban government—and as in Iraq, sporadic fighting continued involving remnants of the Taliban and the al-Qaeda terrorist group. Beyond those operations, US forces remain engaged in supporting peacekeeping, nation building, and counterdrug operations in the Balkans, Latin America, and in various other spots throughout the world.

The Bush national security strategy of preemption leads any reasonable observer to believe that a high operations tempo for US military forces is likely to continue. The question that naturally arises from all of this activity concerns its effect on the all-volunteer military. With frequent deployments overseas, often in harm's way, what will be the likely impact on enlistments? What will be the impact on the future leadership of the military? Will recruiting cadets for the military academies and ROTC[1] suffer in terms of numbers, or quality, or both? Will retention of experienced officers and skilled enlisted personnel suffer and thus compound any recruiting problems?

The first impact may be felt in the reserve components—the reserve forces and the National Guard. During the past decade, the military has activated reserve component units with great regularity and sent them overseas to perform combat or combat-support operations. Since the end of the war in Vietnam, more and more of the combat capability and critical combat-support capabilities have been transferred to the reserve components for a variety of reasons.[2] For example, in terms of airpower, more than 50 percent of all tanker aircraft and transport aircraft are in the reserve elements, not to mention more than 35 percent of all fighter and attack aircraft.

After pondering this issue, the question that invariably comes to mind concerns a return to conscription—the draft—which the United States suspended in 1973. Would such a radical step be possible politically? If so, would it make sense militarily, particularly for a military that is used to fight wars of choice rather than wars of necessity? Other than maintaining sufficient numbers, would conscription offer any real advantages or would the drawbacks of short-term conscripts outweigh any possible advantages?

What Roles for Allies?

The disparity in military capabilities between the United States and virtually everyone else continues to grow. The issue of disparity revolves not so much around numbers but much more around technological capabilities and the professionalism born of experience. The technology issue is particularly difficult. First, the US military would very much like for its allies to use similar equipment and systems that can work together easily with its own systems. In the extremely busy modern battlespace, systems that cannot work together seamlessly can present serious physical hazards to friend and foe alike. Further, the difficulties encountered trying to integrate such systems into an overall war-fighting scheme can far outweigh the military benefits of their use—the political benefits of their use being an entirely different question.

Although US forces would like to have their allies use compatible equipment, it is also true that they will probably never have much of the "top-of-the-line" US military technology. Some technology is so valuable that it cannot be passed on to even the closest of allies—stealth technology being a good case in point at this writing. It is highly unlikely that any other country will be offered the opportunity to purchase an F-117 stealth fighter-bomber or a B-2 long-range, heavy stealth bomber for the foreseeable future. The other side of the coin is that even when top-of-the-line equipment can be purchased, many allies cannot afford (or will not afford) enough of it to make a real difference. The result is that allies and potential allies are likely to have military forces that, at least in terms of technology, are second rate and/or may not be compatible and easily integrated into combined operations with US forces.

If that is true, and "becoming more true" with each passing year, what roles should America's allies play? How can a "coalition of the willing" capitalize on the diverse capabilities of its members? This is a question both important and vexing today and will become more so in the future.

However, the more important question may be, what allies? As the United States is perceived to assume more and more the position and attitude of a hegemonic power, others, including many long-standing allies, may begin to form other groups in attempts to provide some degree of counterbalance to what they perceive to be a potentially dangerous situation.[3] Indeed, this sort of behavior may have already manifested itself in such things as the French refusal to permit overflight rights to US warplanes en route from the United Kingdom to Libya during Operation El Dorado Canyon in April 1986, while Spain, Italy, and Greece refused the use of their bases. In that instance, 18 US F-111 warplanes were forced to fly a long and arduous route south from RAF Lakenheath in Great Britain then east over the Strait of Gibraltar into the Mediterranean and on to Libya. After their bombing runs, they returned by the same route—in total a 14-hour flight including eight aerial-refueling operations. The refusal of many states, particularly important allies such as France and Germany, to join the United States in the second Iraqi war may have also been early manifestations of this balancing behavior.

Given the disparity in terms of military power between the United States and everyone else and the discussion above about how difficult it can be to weave allies into a combined military operation, some may wonder why strategists should worry about allies and balancing behaviors. There is a difference, however, between the difficulties that arise when trying to integrate allies into combined operations and those that former allies might cause in an opposition role. Certainly the French overflight refusal and the refusal of Spain, Italy, and Greece to provide basing support in 1986 points out the difficulties even passive opposition can create. Thus the question in the future may be, does the United States have any allies of substance? The doctrine of preemption combined with a penchant for unilateral action may also raise the question, how many allies can the United States afford to alienate?

Dealing with 24-Hour News

Once known as "the CNN effect," the rise of multiple 24-hour television news channels whose coverage spans the globe creates significant problems for political and military leaders at several levels in the strategy process. As early as the Vietnam War—long before the advent of round-the-clock live news coverage—it became obvious how much impact pictures of war can have when played on a home television screen. In some cases such graphic news coverage can cause a groundswell of support for military operations. Such was certainly the case for the news coverage of the 9/11 terrorist attacks in 2001. Earlier, pictures of starving women and children in Somalia mobilized support for humanitarian operations that later came to such a very sad end. No sooner had aid been dispatched to Somalia than pictures of atrocities in the Bosnian civil war dominated the nightly news, preparing the American public to support US operations in Bosnia and later in Kosovo.

Conversely, news reporting can mobilize public opinion against military operations. Gory pictures of the body of a dead US soldier being dragged through the streets of Mogadishu were key in the ignominious withdrawal of US forces from Somalia. Reporting (and pictures) about the slaughter of the Iraqi army by coalition airpower on the so-called highway of death in 1991 played an important role in stopping the first Iraqi war long before all of the military objectives were achieved, most importantly before the destruction of the elite Republican Guard divisions.

The military took two very different approaches to news coverage in the first and second Iraqi wars. In the first war, most of the hard news was dispensed via daily briefings that were well conducted but obviously told the story the military wanted to tell. Reporters were allowed to talk with troops in the field only in the presence of a "handler" and generally were not permitted to visit the front lines during active operations. News personnel chaffed at being kept away from the front lines, unable to report the real war because they could see only the aftermath left by the rapidly advancing coalition forces.

In the second Iraqi war, news personnel went through extensive training designed to keep them safe and out of the way of the combat soldiers. Those who successfully completed the training were "embedded" in ground force units and were allowed to do live broadcasts on the go via satellite retransmission. This experiment gave a unique close-up look at the troops operating in the field, complete with the noise, confusion, and frustrations inherent in combat operations. Unfortunately, daily news briefings from the coalition headquarters in Qatar were very frustrating because they were heavily scripted to "stay on message." One member of the press became so frustrated that he asked one of the briefing officers (a general officer) why the press should attend the briefings since so little hard information was made available.

There may be no good compromise between the needs of the press in a free and open society and the operational needs of the military. Regardless of whether or not there is a good compromise, the government and its military must deal effectively with the voracious appetite of the press for every scrap of information around the clock. How well they deal with the press can have a significant impact on the success or failure of the ongoing operation.

Conclusions

The face of conventional, symmetrical warfare has changed greatly since the end of the Cold War. The implosion of the

229

Soviet bloc has left the United States with no credible conventional opponent, a situation unlikely to change in the near future. Partly as a result, the role of conventional forces has shifted, at least implicitly, to priorities such as support for the Bush policy of preemption. That thrust, in turn, has raised significant questions about the stress it creates for existing US forces and the degree to which unilateral preemption may alienate American friends and allies. The future of the policy of preemption is controversial and problematical and so, too, may be conventional forces wedded to that policy.

Notes

1. The Reserve Officer Training Corps (ROTC) at college campuses across the country supplies the largest portion of the officers for the US military.

2. The most obvious reason is to save money—on paper, reserve component units cost much less to maintain than do active duty units. As to other reasons, following the Vietnam War, Gen Creighton Abrams, Army chief of staff, restructured much of the Army by putting key combat-support elements in the reserve components. This action ensured that no large-scale deployments could take place without mobilizing the reserve forces—an action traditionally viewed as politically dangerous and strategically precipitous.

3. See the works of Kenneth N. Waltz, in particular *Theory of International Politics* (New York: McGraw-Hill, 1979).

Chapter 13

Asymmetrical Warfare Dilemmas

Whether Americans like it or not (and most who have thought about the subject probably do not), asymmetrical warfare in its various forms has become a, possibly *the*, central military problem facing US policy makers and strategists. It is a problem largely of their own making and one they have implicitly committed to perpetuating. The enabling cornerstone of the Bush Doctrine, after all, is the existence and continuation of a superior conventional US military force. The intended purpose is to assure a maximum ability to influence the world in ways supportive of US interests such as the promotion of democracy. The unintended consequence is to create an environment in which the only way a conceivable foe can challenge the United States is by employing asymmetrical strategies.

Probably just the tip of the asymmetrical iceberg has surfaced. As the survey in chapter 8 suggested, mutations of standard insurgent warfare—the form of asymmetrical warfare most familiar from the Vietnam experience and before—are arriving on the scene. They borrow from the conceptual core of insurgent warfare (e.g., virtually all of them feature ambush as a primary tactic) and adapt those principles to their particular terrain (e.g., deserts rather than jungles) and purposes (e.g., criminal insurgency rather than the struggle for political control of government). Because of the highly motivating need to avoid extinction at the hands of heavily armed symmetrical warriors, there is no reason to believe these strategies will not continue to evolve, reinforcing strategic elements that work and dumping those that do not.

Another reason that asymmetrical strategies are likely to present a primary problem is geographic. Most of the violence (and potential for violence) today is in the developing world: Asia, Africa, and parts of Latin America. In those places vulnerable to the conditions in which violence is likely to occur, its overwhelming form is internal war for one purpose or another, and internal war tends to be particularly desperate and bloody. Moreover, most of the places where fighting will occur are remote, mountainous jungles (southern and Southeast Asia, sub-Saharan Africa, northern South America, and Central America) or rugged and dry mountains (central Asia). These areas are not well suited for the European-style warfare, born on the northern European plain, from which so much of symmetrical warfare is derived. Mechanized maneuver warfare, for instance, is impossible to conduct in mountains where there are no roads; and even though innovations like air cavalry allow troops to be moved to otherwise inaccessible terrain, it is not a very efficient way to make war against an illusive enemy who does not stand and fight.

Asymmetrical warfare is also a style with which the United States has never been particularly comfortable and against which it has not been spectacularly successful. In its early history, the United States had some success in asymmetrical warfare. The campaigns of Francis Marion (the "Swamp Fox") in South Carolina were classic applications of insurgent tactics of which modern asymmetrical warriors would approve. By adopting tactics such as ambush and hiding behind trees rather than marching across fields in linear formation to be slaughtered by better trained and equipped British troops, Marion and his followers earned the kind of scorn from their symmetrical opponents that is now heaped upon opponents adopting the same tactics against the United States today. The British, for their part, never devised a successful strategy to deal with this form of warfare—a point worth remembering. In World War II in Asia, Americans fought as and led guerrilla elements in places like Burma and the Philippines with great success.

The first major dilemma that the United States faces dealing with asymmetrical warfare opponents is a historic lack of success in devising and implementing effective counter-asymmetrical-warfare strategies. The US military has been much more effective operating as asymmetrical warriors than at trying to defeat others carrying out asymmetrical strategies.

The reader may balk at this assertion and argue that the United States has never been defeated by asymmetrical warriors and has generally prevailed on the battlefield regardless of the nature of the opposition. To paraphrase a North Vietnamese colonel talking to his American counterpart, Col Harry

Summers, at a reunion 20 years after the war was over, such an argument is true and irrelevant.[1] One of the ways that symmetrical warriors bend the rules to achieve their ends is by changing the definition of victory. One example, as mentioned in chapter 8, is to prevail by not losing. In Vietnam, for instance, the United States constantly prevailed in battle, and any comparison such as casualties would indicate a thorough American victory. The problem was that the definitions of victory were derived from the criteria of symmetrical warfare. The Vietnamese definition of victory was outlasting the foe until it tired of the contest and left. It worked for their ancestors against Kublai Khan in the eleventh century, and it worked against the Americans in the twentieth century. One cannot help but wonder if it will work again against the Americans in Iraq in the twenty-first century.

Why has the United States (which is certainly not alone in suffering from this problem) not devised successful ways of dealing with what may become the most frequent military problem faced in the foreseeable future? Put another way, what is there about the approach to this problem that impedes the ability to deal successfully with asymmetrical approaches?

There are at least two categories of answers to the question. The first is conceptual. Asymmetrical warfare is not the mode of fighting that US strategists have encountered through much of their historical experience, and it is thus a style of warfare to which they have not devoted anywhere near the intellectual energy as toward more symmetrical warfare problems. Dealing with asymmetrical warfare requires thinking "outside the box," which is rarely a rewarded forte within military organizations.

Part of the conceptual problem is generally underestimating the challenge posed by the asymmetrical warrior. Asymmetrical warfare is somehow not quite "military" in the traditional sense—it is not equipment or firepower intensive, its warriors usually do not wear proper uniforms (if they wear uniforms at all), they often do not adhere to a conventional rank structure, and they either ignore or are ignorant of rules and conventions of war, for instance. Moreover, Americans tend to view the differences between themselves and asymmetrical opponents as *deficiencies* on their enemies' parts that make them less worthy and less formidable opponents. When conceived in this way, it is a short intellectual step to dismissing the problem as unimportant or unworthy of serious thought.

Part of the problem is institutional as well. Reflecting its historical experience and intellectual preferences, the US military is organized to fight conventional, symmetrical wars, and it is highly resistant to changing that organization. Each of the services has some resources devoted to asymmetrical problems, and the Special Operations Command (SOCOM) is in charge of the United States' unconventional capability; but the capabilities that exist have, by and large, been forced on the services (the only reason SOCOM exists is because the Congress insisted on it being an independent command) and are thought of by the "mainstream" elements in the services as a regrettable appendage. The performance of special operations forces in Afghanistan and Iraq improved their prestige greatly but not to the point that the joint chiefs are disassembling infantry units and converting them to special operations.

The anti-asymmetrical-warfare bias is reflected especially strongly at the leadership levels of the services. Chiefs of staff of the services (or equivalent titles) come from the conventional warfare specialties that have been designed for symmetrical warfare, and since those who have risen to flag rank have done so through the symmetrical warfare specialties, they are unlikely to abandon them once they become leaders. The exception to this statement is the term of Gen Henry "Hugh" Shelton, a career special forces officer, as chairman of the Joint Chiefs of Staff, but the only reason he was eligible for the job was the creation of SOCOM, which allowed him to gain the fourth star necessary to achieve that office. Another special operations veteran, Gen Peter J. Schoomaker, was appointed chief of staff of the Army in 2003.

This introduction has featured two themes in the dilemma of dealing with asymmetrical warfare. The first theme has been that asymmetrical warfare is now a part of the major strategic challenge facing the United States, and it is a problem that is likely to endure. The second theme is that the United States, along with other developed countries whose militaries are grounded in symmetrical warfare, is not particularly well equipped physically and intellectually to deal with the challenges posed by adaptable asymmetrical warriors who will likely continue to change the nature of the problem as time and experience dictate. The task in the remaining pages is to define the problem and to start to think about its solutions.

Nature of the Problem

Asymmetrical warfare is not only different from conventional warfare in the military manner in which it is conducted; it is also different in terms of the problems for which it is carried out, of how those who carry it out think and act, and in terms of the often more-intimate relationship between political and military matters that exists in asymmetrical campaigns. Asymmetrical warfare is not only militarily unconventional; it is also intellectually unconventional as well. That makes it harder to understand its underlying dynamics, which the transposition of how to think about these things will not clarify. Americans have trouble getting inside the mind of the asymmetrical warrior because it is hard for them to rise above thinking solipsistically.

For most Americans, their first real encounter with an asymmetrical foe was in Vietnam. Granted, this war was not as unconventional in political purpose as some subsequent asymmetrical wars have been (it was fought for control of government, a conventional purpose). Nevertheless, the intensely political nature of the war as a contest about realizing Vietnamese nationalist goals clearly exceeded Americans' ability to think about the uses of force, notably the willingness to endure casualties and other forms of privation far in excess of any they would have been willing to endure in a similar situation.

This problem has not been overcome in more recent experiences. Internal conflict within the United States is not entirely absent, but it almost never reaches the height of desperation that is typical in developing-world internal wars. Americans have difficulty truly appreciating the depth of animosity that Bosnian Serbs, Croats, and Muslims or Muslim Kosovars and Serbs have toward one another. The idea of hatred that could fuel the genocide in Rwanda is beyond Americans' conceptualization, and they have consistently underestimated the depths of tribal/clan/religious animosities among population groups in central Asia (notably Afghanistan and Iraq).

235

Most of the situations that result in asymmetrical warfare are deep-seated with long historical bases of which Americans are likely to be only partially aware, and the tendency is to oversimplify and "conventionalize" them. In Afghanistan, for instance, the United States took the leadership in convening a *loya jirga* (a kind of interclan summit meeting) in 2002. The purpose of invoking this historical institution was to move forward the process of smoothing animosities among groups and thus paving the way for a movement toward democracy. *Loya jirgas* have historically served the function of working through differences among groups, but those differences are deep (especially after a long war such as the one that had recently ended); they tend to take many months, even years to complete their agendas. The ground rules set by the United States provided for a month-long session. The problems were deeper than those faced by a congressional conference committee trying to resolve differences in the wording of a piece of legislation. Americans simply lack the feel for the depth of political division and desperation that is frequently present in developing-world countries (or occasionally between countries) and which can lead to these brutal conflicts because there is essentially nothing in their own experiences that would lead them to do the same kinds of things. Assuming implicitly that if one would not act in a certain way means that no one should and that simply calming the situation will make the problem go away is the height of solipsism.

The first step in dealing with asymmetrical wars is to understand why they are occurring and thus what, if anything, can be done to solve the problems they represent. Thinking everyone should (and does) think and react the way one does is the sin of solipsism, and it is a sin that can lead to wrong decisions. Osama bin Laden had, after all, been proclaiming for a decade before the attacks of 11 September 2001 that the United States would be punished if it did not quit "desecrating the holy lands" of Saudi Arabia. He made no secret of this demand, but US intelligence analysts found it so outlandish that they did not take it seriously. When President Bush prematurely announced that "major combat" was over in Iraq, he did not include an asterisk in his announcement that said that low-level resistance by those Iraqi elements most harmed by the outcome would continue to be aimed at Americans (an entirely predictable outcome), but given the nature of the complex situation in that country, such a resistance should not have come as a great surprise to anyone.

It is virtually a given that the initial brush the United States has with asymmetrical warfare conditions will be one where strategists less than fully understand the dynamics of the situation. This is partly true because these events occur at places toward which Americans historically have not devoted much attention: how many Niger specialists were there in Washington to review whether that government was likely offering to sell nuclear materials to Iraq in 2002? Moreover, Americans are likely to have difficulty understanding motivations with which they cannot identify: mass amputation of hands and feet to facilitate an illegal diamond trade (Sierra Leone) is not something with which most Americans can identify.

The problem of understanding has both policy and strategy implications. The major implication for policy makers is to be certain that they have a firm enough grasp of the situation to determine whether sufficient US interests are involved to justify US involvement, whether that involvement will actually help solve the problem, and whether US forces will be able to extricate themselves with some positive sense of accomplishment. The implication for strategists is whether they adequately can grasp the politico-military situation to devise military means that will reinforce rather than detract from the underlying political problems.

These problems are likely to become increasingly difficult as these situations become increasingly asymmetrical. It is one thing to understand a Vietnam situation in which the opposition employed unconventional strategies to accomplish conventional purposes. Moving through the progression of asymmetrical warfare from new internal war to fourth generation warfare to terrorism and even beyond, both the purposes and the means are likely to become more and more unconventional and asymmetrical. But how?

With no pretense of being inclusive or exhaustive, there are at least five fairly predictable problems that will arise in the future. Undoubtedly there will be more.

First, the political and military aspects of these conflicts will continue to merge, and distinctions between military and civilian assets and targets will continue to dissolve. This has been true in all the forms of asymmetrical warfare examined herein, beginning with traditional insurgency, and there is no reason to believe it will abate. For one thing, merging the civilian and military aspects of society provides cover for the asymmetrical warrior from symmetrical forces that continue to abide by conventional distinctions between civilian and military targeting (the laws of war). It is further true because these situations are marked by the nonexistence of a common center of gravity toward which both or all sides seek to appeal. No place is likely to be immune from conflict in the future. Decrying as an atrocity the human tragedy that results from extending the battlefield to society as a whole may be morally satisfying, but doing so should not obscure the fact that society as a whole is now part of the war zone.

Second, the opposition in these conflicts will increasingly consist of nonstate actors often acting out of nonstate purposes. The bands of "fighters" so common to African conflicts will often be joined by private terrorist organizations housed in states with varying degrees of state approval, and their purposes will often be to rid the state of some evil or to rid the state of its ability to suppress their felonious behavior. These nonstate actors will often have sufficient support among some faction or region in the country that they will be difficult to track down and capture or destroy, as Osama bin Laden and Saddam Hussein have proven to be.

Third, the opposition posed by these asymmetrical foes will almost certainly be protracted, although the tempo and intensity of that opposition will likely vary greatly from situation to situation. These groups will almost always represent the aspirations or fears of some group within a country (or across countries) that provides them with support and some level of succor that makes them as difficult to root out and destroy as a well-established traditional insurgency has proven to be in the past. The very asymmetry in the situation that forces these groups not to act according to established rules may also militate toward a very low, sporadic level of violence, depending on the relative balance of forces. As the United States has discovered in Iraq, however, even the most smashing symmetrical victory does not mean that the resistance has collapsed or that the war is over.

Fourth, these conflicts will often occur in the most fractured, failed states where the conditions arise for people to engage in acts of desperation like suicidal terrorism. The practical effects of this situation are that the purposes and means will likely be more incomprehensible than they would be in more stable, Westernized countries. It also means that the problem of ending the violence will include a generous amount of nation building with uncertain results and questionable support at home (see below). No one should enter one of these conflicts thinking it will be quick or easy to resolve.

Fifth, the situations are likely to become even more asymmetrical and thus incomprehensible. It is often said that military establishments engage in planning for the last war, and such preparations could be disastrous in the future. Once again the Iraqi resistance may represent one such permutation that is illustrious of the future. Faced with a symmetrical foe against which it had no chance, did the Hussein leadership simply order its best fighters to blend into the population and then conduct apparently random, unpredictable attacks (terrorist style) against American occupying forces, hoping that the American public would tire of the trickle of body bags returning and thus end the occupation? Getting one step ahead (rather than behind) asymmetrical change is a major strategic priority.

Countering Asymmetrical Wars

Faced with the reality of involvement in an asymmetrical warfare situation, the first question that must be asked is, what is the desired outcome? It is not as easy a question to answer as it might appear on the surface because different end states require different qualities of involvement with varying degrees of certainty and experience.

Broadly speaking, there are two categories of outcomes. The first is stopping whatever physical problems that have caused US forces to become involved in the first place. In the case of insurgency, this may entail the physical defeat of whichever side the United States opposes (e.g., aiding in the overthrow of the Taliban in Afghanistan), stopping the atrocities in a new internal war or fourth generation war (imposing order in Sierra Leone), or uprooting a terrorist network by stripping away its state sponsorship (the outcome of helping to overthrow the Taliban). The more traditional military goal of toppling a government deemed unacceptable (the Saddam Hussein regime) that fights asymmetrically falls into this category as well.

This first task, which one of the authors has elsewhere referred to as *conflict suppression*, is a sequential process that generally consists of three activities, of descending military content.[2] The first step is *peace imposition*, and it consists of military actions, normally by combat troops, to remove whatever military barriers there are to creating a peace or whatever other postmilitary state one seeks (military barriers to replacing a government, for instance).

Once the postmilitary job has been completed, the task then moves to *peace enforcement*, which consists of action necessary to assure that the situation does not revert to its former unacceptable condition. This task begins with the enforcement of physical order, including the suppression of elements that seek reversion and assuring the population that the peace being enforced is preferable to the previous status quo. Peace enforcement introduces political skills of persuasion to the mix but remains basically a military task of maintaining order; it is a task for which military police are well suited.

If the situation stabilizes adequately, the task moves on to *peacekeeping*, the maintenance of a peaceful condition that the target population has come to prefer to the prior condition in which they existed and where the desire to revert is largely absent. Once this condition is reached, the task of the peacekeeper is simply to facilitate desired change—a task normally conducted by lightly (defensively) armed observers and monitors. A litmus test of whether a situation has moved from peace enforcement to peacekeeping is what would likely occur if the force is removed and is a reflection of the level of acceptance of the change that has been imposed. The perceived need for continued peace enforcement suggests a likelihood of reversion; true peacekeepers expect to leave behind a transformed, self-sustaining condition.

Conflict suppression activities do not solve the underlying conditions that cause countries to interfere in the internal affairs of others. Rather conflict suppression can be thought of as the equivalent of treating the symptoms of a disease or illness;

it may staunch the bleeding that has been the outward manifestation of the problem, but it is not sufficient to recreate the
"health" of the "patient."

At that, the problem of conflict suppression raises some interesting strategic questions that relate to the evolution of a
situation from peace imposition to stable peace at the end of
the peacekeeping. How does one move the process along? The
experience of the 1990s suggests that peace imposition is best
accomplished by convincing the target population of the futility
of resistance, and the tactic that evolved was physical intimidation of the population. In Somalia this tactic was not applied,
and the Somalis did not fear the United Nations Operation in
Somalia (UNISOM) forces adequately not to attack them. The
same was true when true peacekeepers (lightly armed) were
sent into a war zone in Bosnia as part of the United Nations
Protection Force (UNPROFOR), and the result was that the war-
ring factions abused them. Missions in Haiti and subsequently
in the Balkans were much more heavily armed and equipped,
and the population did not attack the peace enforcers.

Intimidation is a tactic, not a solution, however; if the situation
does not stabilize to the point that active coercion is no longer
needed to keep the population at bay, then intimidation must
give way to some other method. For the United States, one of
the boundaries on physical involvement in asymmetrical situations inherited from the 1990s is the perceived need to limit US
casualties. The reason is clear. Although the American public has consistently shown a willingness to endure casualties
when they consider the cause worthy and progress being made
toward achievement, the goal of asymmetrical opponents will
be to negate both of those perceptions. Inflicting casualties on
US forces may achieve both goals by raising questions about
why the intended subjects of US assistance would respond in
such a clearly unappreciative manner.

How does one respond to low-level, asymmetrical resistance?
One answer is aggressive military action—a continuation of
peace imposition—scouring the countryside, for instance, for
pockets of resistance and, with any luck, rooting them out. The
advantage of this approach is that it is proactive and militarily
satisfying if successful. The disadvantages are that it virtually
assures additional casualties and may prove frustrating if the

opposition adopts evasive tactics inherited from traditional insurgency doctrine (which it almost certainly will). Early aggressive patrolling in Iraq, after the "major fighting" was declared over, illustrates this situation.

The other method of response is to avoid pressures to "bring the troops home" by reducing the number of casualties, and the means of doing so is to withdraw those forces from harm's way to the greatest extent possible. Pulling the forces out of hostile hinterlands controlled by opposition forces and creating a de facto political partition has been effectively (if not officially) done in Bosnia (there are still enclaves where UN peacekeepers do not patrol) and in Afghanistan, where large parts of the countryside have reverted to control by traditional factions. Even the Taliban has returned as a factor. The advantage of such an approach is that it does not create a test of the often paper-thin support for these operations by raising the casualties issue. The disadvantage, of course, is that it does not solve the original problem and, to some extent, tacitly concedes failure.

Moving beyond conflict suppression toward an environment in which peacekeeping occurs requires changing the underlying sources of violence that give rise to one or another form of asymmetrical violence. That activity is *nation building*—the complex of actions undertaken to transform the target society from one that produces the various forms of asymmetrical warrior to one where the motivation to become this kind of warrior is eradicated.

Nation building is aimed at attacking and "curing" the underlying disease which causes the symptoms that are the objective of conflict suppression. If one starts from the presumption that the conditions that gave rise to some form of asymmetrical warfare situation must be addressed if the problem is not to recur, then the curative is the removal of those underlying conditions.

The problems will not always be the same, and like the forms of asymmetrical warfare, they will also likely evolve and change over time. In traditional insurgency, these underlying conditions usually were tied to governmental corruption, inefficiency, or favoritism directed toward some groups and withheld from others who formed the opposition. In Vietnam, for instance, the Americans argued long and unsuccessfully with their South Vietnamese counterparts that fundamental land reform was necessary to win the hearts and minds of the Vietnamese peasants who formed the backbone of Vietcong support. In the new internal wars, state political failure combined with economic and often social misery form the backdrop for bitter conflicts over small rewards. A sense of misery and hopelessness form much of the seedbed within which terrorists and fourth generation warriors breed as well. In some cases these same kinds of conditions may be present in countries against which international action occurs, as in Iraq.

Recognizing that, nation building becomes necessary, and implementing a successful nation-building program is far more difficult than conflict suppression. After the Somali debacle, techniques for stopping the fighting then enforcing the peace were gradually developed for internal war situations where there was little organized internal opposition and where most of the population came to prefer the stability provided by foreign occupiers to the violence and instability in their absence. The difficulty, of course, is that merely stopping the fighting does not address or solve the real problems that caused the violence in the first place.

Nation building, on the other hand, is difficult. There is no general, accepted blueprint of how to do it, either theoretically derived or based in successful experience. The closest equivalent is the reconstruction and transformation of Germany and Japan after World War II, but it is not a very exact analogy. Germany and Japan were highly advanced countries before the war, not highly underdeveloped states with severe internal problems like those in most places where contemporary nation building occurs. Moreover, each case of nation building is likely to be distinct because of national differences where it is attempted: nation building in Bosnia, for instance, may not provide many useful guidelines for building postwar Iraq.

That is not all. The process of nation building is likely to be long, expensive, and potentially frustrating, and experience to date suggests that none of these factors has been adequately appreciated in advance of mounting the effort. A long process involves an extended occupation in one form or another, and the longer occupations last, the less popular they are likely to become. If the goal is to create (or restore) a condition wherein economic success is possible, the rebuilding (or building) process is likely to be very expensive (usually by some multiple of prewar estimates) and not very popular with the American public when its dimensions are known and compared with domestic priorities. And, at the bottom line, the whole thing could fail or, at the least, not accomplish all it sets out to accomplish, a source of potential frustration.

Having said these negative things, the development of a workable nation-building strategy is absolutely necessary for continued US involvement in asymmetrical warfare situations. Such a strategy must meet two criteria: there must be a clear demonstration that the plan is well thought out and that it will likely work, and there must be an equally clear public commitment to enduring the sacrifices that implementing such a strategy entail. The alternatives to meeting these criteria are equally obvious: either a continued string of successful conflict suppressions followed by unsuccessful nation building and a reversion of situations to their former status (or worse), or abstention from involvement in asymmetrical warfare situations. The dilemma, of course, is that strategies have been developed for accomplishing the interim goal (conflict suppression) but not for the ultimate goal (nation building).

The purpose here is not to lay out a comprehensive nation-building strategy. To do so would be entirely pretentious and beyond the scope of this work. Instead, this section briefly lays out the elements such a strategy must include and what its military elements might be.

A successful nation-building strategy will have at least four dimensions, depending on where you place specific activities. The first is political and contains several tasks: the restoration of order, the reinstatement or development of political order to allow continuation of that order, and the identification and installation of a legitimate indigenous set of political actors. None is easy.

The restoration of order is the first and most fundamental task. Until people feel safe and secure, no other progress is possible. The problem is that most of the kinds of places where nation building must occur either lack a reliable constabulary or security force to carry out this task, or that force was part of the problem. In the interim, properly trained military forces (military police, for instance) must carry out this task while indigenous or internationally recruited police are enlisted and trained. Development or restoration of a criminal justice system (courts, judges, etc.) in which the people have faith is part of this aspect of the problem.

If order is to be retained and strengthened, then political institutions—democratic, if the United States is involved—must be developed as well. In many cases, there will be no developed institutions, the institutions will lack legitimacy (not be accepted as fair), or there will be no democratic traditions on which to base institutional development. For the institutions to become accepted, there must be the active participation of representatives of the population in their development, a clear problem in multiethnic or otherwise divided countries where the tradition has been for one group to rule at the expense of others.

At the same time, rule must be gradually turned over to the representatives of the people themselves. The major problem here is that the identification of personnel acceptable to the people as a whole—a representative government—may be easier to say than to accomplish in fractured societies. Outsiders are unlikely to know or fully appreciate the subtleties of local politics. Finding the right leadership is difficult, and the problem is made more difficult if outsiders choose that leadership, making it subject to being charged as a puppet of the interveners.

The other dimensions can be mentioned in passing because they share the complexities of the political dimension. The economic problem begins with the restoration or development of basic infrastructure that has probably been destroyed or subjected to sabotage during the fighting: power and water must be restored; streets, bridges, and airport runways repaired or rebuilt; jobs created or restored; and the like. Doing these things takes time and money, and it hardly ever happens as fast or as cheaply as anticipated. Until the infrastructure is restored, the subsequent tasks of creating sufficient economic prosperity to give the population economic hope (a key element in "draining the swamp") cannot even begin.

The other dimensions are social and psychological. Intergroup conflict along religious, ethnic, or some similar internal division is the normal condition in states that require nation building. Normally intergroup violence and atrocity have been part of the problem, and healing the wounds created is a necessary, but very difficult, part of the national reconciliation that must occur if these states are to emerge from the process as stable members of the international system. A much less discussed dimension is psychological. Since these wars are often accompanied by acts of atrocity against family members and others, there is almost inevitably a surplus of medical and psychological problems in large segments of the population (especially children) that the countries cannot surmount themselves, either because they have deficient health care systems or because those systems have been victims of the fighting.

Conclusions

The experience of the United States in Iraq serves as testimony of the difficulties posed by the practitioners of asymmetrical warfare. The low-level but persistent campaign of ambush and assassination of US fighting forces and their Iraqi supporters following the defeat of the Saddam Hussein regime is just the latest form in the evolution of resistance by an inferior force faced with overwhelmingly negative odds. Whether they will succeed or whether the coalition will be able to crush their resistance remains an unanswered question that only time will resolve.

The problems caused by asymmetrical warfare are arguably the most important strategic challenge for the United States in the early twenty-first century. Terrorism, one of the forms of asymmetrical warfare discussed in chapter 8, has already been elevated to that status in the wake of 9/11; and the apparently largely unanticipated Iraqi variant, a hybrid of Vietnam-style insurgency (certainly in its intentions toward the United States) and fourth generation warfare, should focus analytical attention on other forms of asymmetrical warfare as well.

This challenge is particularly important if the United States wants to maintain its position as the most powerful country in the world militarily, as the Bush Doctrine and its neoconservative champions trumpet. At the level of symmetrical warfare capability, that status is unchallenged. That condition will only change if other countries greatly increase their physical commitment to defense or the United States greatly reduces its commitment, and neither of these contingencies is likely.

What is likely is that potential opponents of the United States will continue to devise methods to *negate* the effect of overwhelming US force, thereby reducing its relevance and the ability of the

United States to apply that force effectively in the service of its interests. In that case the strategic challenge for the United States is to avoid the diluting impact on US sway that effective asymmetrical warfare strategies can impose. What is needed is an effective *counter-asymmetrical-warfare strategy.* That does not now exist.

What is the role of strategists in this enterprise? Beyond the rhetorical injunction to understand better and prescribe strategic and tactical advice, there are two broad challenges. The first is a better strategic sense of anticipation of what the asymmetrical warrior will do in the future to frustrate the United States. Such an effort must begin with a better sense of the past and present. The US military devoted much of the post-Vietnam era to understanding the problem of insurgency and counterinsurgency, and developed sophisticated precepts for counterinsurgency actions against traditional insurgents. Some of that doctrine is clearly relevant to aspects of contemporary asymmetrical warfare and may even form the core of an effective counter-asymmetrical-warfare strategy.

But asymmetrical warfare situations have gone beyond the experiences that have been reduced to doctrine. The campaign in Iraq, for instance, bears some resemblance to the campaign by which Hezbollah forced Israel to withdraw from southern Lebanon in 2000, but there is little direct evidence that US strategists have studied that event or incorporated its lessons learned into their own strategy. What is needed is closer study of which asymmetrical techniques are successful and unsuccessful. Then assume that potential opponents are doing the same thing and that the successful techniques will recur in future actions. Potential adversaries of the United States are almost certainly doing this kind of analysis and planning; US strategists can only "get ahead of the curve" if they do the same thing. The alternative is to be unprepared and surprised at the next application of asymmetrical means against Americans.

Anticipation of future asymmetrical contingencies serves the second strategic challenge as well. That challenge is an improved ability of strategists to advise political authorities both of what can and cannot be accomplished against the asymmetrical warrior and what the costs of these campaigns is likely to be. Although the record will remain clouded for some time, it appears that the United States did not anticipate either that there would be a postconquest Iraqi resistance or what form it might take. Should that have been the case, or should strategists have been able to warn leaders about possible consequences in advance? The decisions may not have been altered, and maybe that advice was offered and rejected (a distinct possibility, given the political focus on overthrowing Saddam Hussein); it is not known at this point. It would, however, certainly have been a valuable contribution both to the original decision about whether to proceed with the invasion and, if that decision still would have been positive, how to plan for what to do upon arriving there.

Your authors have argued that there has been the tendency within the military and political establishments to underestimate the problems posed by the asymmetrical warrior. Such an assumption should have been permanently consigned to the intellectual slag heap of strategy after the Vietnam experience, but it has not been. As long as US forces think the problem of asymmetrical warfare is a simple task against an inferior foe ("any good soldier can defeat a guerrilla"), the ingenious asymmetrical warrior will exploit that conceit to their disadvantage. Are not Americans smarter than that?

Notes

1. Harry G. Summers Jr., *On Strategy: A Critical Analysis of the Vietnam War* (Novato, CA: Presidio Press, 1995).

2. Donald M. Snow, *When America Fights: The Uses of U.S. Military Forces* (Washington, DC: Congressional Quarterly Press, 2000).

Chapter 14

Threats, Interests, and Risks

This text concludes by returning to the relationship between policy and strategy and the implications of that relationship for strategists. Strategy does not, of course, exist in a vacuum but is the response to external conditions and domestic preferences for ordering or reordering those conditions. When the situation potentially involves the use or threat of force as a greater or lesser part of the intended response, military strategists are engaged in the process.

In the area of national security, that is the focus; the main thrust of policy is threats to the state and its interests. Policy makers and strategists come at this aspect of politics from somewhat different but intersecting perspectives. The role of policy makers is to assess the international climate, to determine what threatens US interests in that environment, and to place priorities on which interests are the most important—something like the hierarchy of survival, vital, major, and peripheral interests described in chapter 3. Once those interests are prioritized, the next task is to determine which of those interests are threatened, the severity of the threat, and the consequences of failing to reduce the gap between interests and threats. The problem at this point, in other words, involves risk and its management. The major role of policy makers is to determine which risks will be addressed, to what degree they will be addressed, and how many and what kinds of resources will be allocated to the particular set of threat-based risks there are in the environment.

Military strategists perform as advisers up to this point. Once threats have been identified, they help to define the nature of the threat, the consequent risks, and the extent, if any, to which the military instrument may be relevant. Assuming the threat or actual use of military force may be potentially involved, strategists enter the loop by laying out various options for achieving the goals of the state: what role can military force in various forms of application accomplish or not accomplish in the pursuit of negating or reducing the risk-creating threat? Once policy decisions have been reached and resources have been allocated, strategists turn their attention to devising and implementing the plans that result from the process.

Note what strategists do and do not do. First and foremost, they are *not* charged with the identification and ordering of national priorities, which is a political decision firmly within the realm of the policy maker. Strategists may have strong feelings, opinions, and even expertise in analyzing the international environment that the policy makers analyze and decide about, but they move beyond their role as strategists when entering the priority-ordering process. Likewise, the role of strategists is narrow or nonexistent regarding the allocation of resources in support of national policies. At the point of determining which threats to allocate resources to nullify and in what amounts, the role is limited to suggesting if a particular resource allocation is adequate to pursue a particular strategy successfully, which is largely a technical judgment. Their role is nonexistent when it comes to suggesting what resources should be spent on different priorities, which is the heart of the political process.

None of this suggests that strategists have no legitimate voice in setting national priorities and determining how to achieve those goals. Everyone has political values and ideas about what the country should and should not do in general and in specific situations. The point is that when one moves from analyzing and recommending at one level rather than another, one is performing a different role.

These distinctions are important in an international environment where there is less than consensus about what the nature of the threat is, what the role of the United States can and should be, and what actions will effectively promote realization of its goals in the world. As observed in previous chapters, the environment has changed markedly since the end of the Cold War, and the relative simplicity and concreteness in which grand national strategy is fashioned and applied down the operational chain has become more complicated than it used to be. With that change, the bond and agreement that formerly marked the relationship between policy makers and strategists have been strained as well. The world in which policy and strategy exist is a lot more ambiguous and difficult than it was two decades ago.

Strategy during the Cold War

Although it certainly did not appear so to strategists at the time, the policy and strategy environments of the Cold War were remarkably orderly and concrete. There was certainly agreement on the core of the grand national strategic problem; essentially everyone agreed that Soviet-centered communist expansion posed the greatest threat to American and allied interests—including national survival after nuclear-tipped missiles entered arsenals. As a result, there was something like consensus at both the policy and strategy levels about the core of the solution. Any disagreement existed only at the peripheries in terms of where to apply the policy and strategy. Those disagreements, however, were never totally resolved and have moved front and center since the end of the Cold War.

At the heart of the policy consensus was the containment of communism. First articulated in the latter 1940s, this policy asserted that it was in the interest of the United States to resist the expansion of communism to states where it did not already exist—in other words, to contain communist expansion. Moreover, those places most menaced by this prospect were the places most important to the United States, principally Western Europe and Northeast Asia, whose continued independence from communism was deemed vital. Thus American interests and threats to those interests basically coincided, providing reasonably clear guidance to strategists, whose task was the implementation of that policy. The gravity of the threat meant there was little opposition to making resources available for peacetime defense (at least after Korea), a situation unprecedented in previous American experience.

The strategic problem was how to frustrate presumed Soviet aggressive intentions. As the Cold War began in the second half of the 1940s, the problem centered around the risk of an invasion of Western Europe by a Red Army that did not demobilize after World War II. The North Korean invasion of South Korea raised the prospect of a military threat in Northeast Asia, a problem made worse by the triumph of the Chinese Communists in their civil war in 1949. Soviet possession of nuclear weapons added to the strategic dilemma.

The strategy for managing the threat and reducing the risk it produced became a series of planning cases already discussed earlier. The worst case was a Soviet nuclear attack on the US homeland, and it was "solved" by an evolving policy of nuclear deterrence based on maintaining forces that could guarantee a devastating response should the Soviets launch such an attack. That policy was supposed to convince the Soviets of the futility and suicidal nature of their attack and thus dissuade them from launching it in the first place.

In Western Europe, the major planning problem was a massive conventional thrust by Soviet (and, after 1956, accompanying Warsaw Pact) forces westward with the intent of overrunning and subjugating the countries of the NATO alliance. The strategic response was a NATO deployment intended to convince the Soviets they would be repelled short of their goals by NATO conventional forces; a somewhat implicit part of the US-NATO counterthreat was the possibility of escalation to theater nuclear war to assist in slowing and stopping the invading forces. This latter prospect caused some disagreements within the alliance since many Europeans realized a nuclear defense of their territories could leave them as devastated as the invading Soviets might.

There was little disagreement that these were the major strategic problems flowing from the imperatives of containment and that both needed to be addressed to reduce risks to tolerable levels. Any operational disagreement centered on which deserved the most resources since the forces needed to deter nuclear war and those needed to fight a conventional war in Europe (or Northeast Asia) were almost entirely discreet. In times of resource shortage, funding one might mean not funding the other completely.

There was, of course, a third planning contingency and case on which there was less consensus, and that was the problem of Third World conflicts or what is now called asymmetrical wars. This was a problem that did not truly emerge until the 1950s when countries in the Afro-Asiatic world in particular began to achieve their independence from colonial rule. Many of the newly independent countries, nominally pro-Western at birth (since they gained independence from and generally adopted the political systems of Western democratic countries), were also unstable, providing an opportunity for the Soviets—and the Chinese—to spread their communist gospel more globally. When containment was formulated, this problem did not exist and was not addressed. When the competition between communism and anticommunism became universal, the question was whether containment also applied to the so-called Sino-Soviet periphery and beyond. George F. Keenan, the father of containment, argued it did not; to policy makers concerned with the spread of communism anywhere, this answer was not acceptable because the failure to extend the containment line meant ceding increasing amounts of the globe to a communist rule that might eventually threaten the overall global political and military balance.

The result was a policy and strategy debate about these Third World conflicts that is worth mentioning because it is mirrored in the contemporary debate. At the policy level was the question of where and to what extent US interests were sufficiently affected to justify (or not justify) US involvement in generally internal conflicts where one side was supported by the West and the other by communists (see discussion in chap. 8). In most cases there were insufficient intrinsic interests for the United States to become involved in most places in the Third World, where its interest levels were major at most, more likely peripheral. As a result, the only way to upgrade the level of interest to a sufficient level for any kind of US involvement was as part of the Cold War competition. Almost no one argued that allowing countries to go communist was a good thing; on the other hand, there was disagreement over what the United States should be prepared to do to avoid that outcome. The options were always to do nothing, to provide materiel support for anticommunist forces without committing US forces (essentially the Nixon Doctrine), or US military participation at one level or another.

The strategic question was how to use US forces effectively in support of thwarting communist expansion. The initial response was the "lesser-included case," the idea that preparing for the most stressful case—a Soviet invasion of Western Europe—also meant that other, less militarily stressful situations were covered as well. Thinking of unconventional warfare in conventional terms had the dual advantages of avoiding the siphoning of physical resources away from the "central battle" in Europe and of avoiding a major emphasis on a style of warfare that the US military felt uncomfortable with anyway. This approach to the problem was largely discredited during the Vietnam conflict, and the result was the concerted attempt to develop expertise and force capability in the area of counterinsurgency warfare after Vietnam.

The great consensus about Cold War policy and strategy turns out to have been less complete than most tend to remember it in the area of unconventional warfare in the Third World. There was consensus on the central problem of Soviet- (and Chinese-) American confrontation and how to devise policies and strategies to deal with the risks those problems created, and the thrust of thought on military strategy congealed around these problems. The result is a legacy that has some resemblance to an albatross: a way of thinking and, to a large extent, a force structure defined and refined to deal with a strategy and policy problem that no longer exists. What is left is the problem for which the least agreement was developed.

Contemporary Strategy

The strategic case on which there was the least consensus during the Cold War is now the central concern. The parallel is paradoxical. At the policy level, there is a conceptual similarity between the anticommunism that was at the core of policy and strategy during the Cold War and, since 9/11, the "war" on terrorism, which has replaced communism as the central focus of US concern. The Soviets, however, were a concrete policy problem with a highly conventional strategic response. Suppressing terrorism presents a highly amorphous opponent that must be confronted in highly unconventional ways. The admixture of the conventional identification of the problem (policy) and the highly unconventional nature of the response (strategy) creates much of the dilemma.

The central problem then and now reflects some of the disagreement that was never entirely resolved regarding Third World insurgencies during the Cold War on at least three dimensions: the question of resolving the importance of interests in specific situations, a policy disagreement on the extent and nature of American activism to deal with the problem, and the development of an appropriate strategy to implement the policy decisions. Each dimension merits some consideration.

The central political and, hence, policy question arises from the fact that US interests and threats to them do not, by and large, coincide. This is the difficulty previously identified as the interest-threat mismatch, and it contrasts sharply with the Cold War. Then, the United States' most important interests were highly and directly threatened, and risk reduction flowed from that co-incidence: strategists needed to protect the American homeland from nuclear attack and Western Europe and Northeast Asia from attack, to cite the two most obvious examples.

Threats to important US interests are not as evident today. Evidence of this problem is illustrated by the debate about whether the United States should intervene in new internal wars in places like Liberia. Were Liberia the source of, say, some vital resource necessary for American well-being, the answer would be obvious and positive. But the fate of Liberia does not have a direct bearing on any vital US interest beyond the promotion of a peaceful world order, and that leads to ambivalence.

The notable exception to the interest-threat mismatch is ter-rorism, of course, but it is a threat that is hard to counter because its source is difficult to specify. Threats traditionally have been assigned to concrete political entities like states, but the source of the terrorism threat is more elusive and thus dif-ficult to counter. If, as its chroniclers contend, non-state-based fourth generation warfare is the future of war, this problem will recur in the future.

The interest-threat mismatch also leads to a policy disagree-ment about where the United States should and should not be willing to use force in the future. Since there are no concrete and enduring enemies against whom to prepare, the outcome of this debate (if there ever is one) has great bearing on the problems of strategists. On one side of the policy debate are those with an ex-pansive agenda for employing American military strength in the name of countering terrorism and promoting American ideals like democracy. Whether this neoconservative position will survive the experience in Iraq is currently an open question. The other side of the debate counsels a more restrictive view. Traditional realists argue that US force should only be used when clearly vital inter-ests are at stake, while multilateralist internationalists contend that realism should be extended to encompass humanitarian disasters as well. Neither position offers detailed guidance about contingencies and problems strategists must contend with or for which they must prepare.

If specific guidance in terms of concrete potential adversaries is missing or incomplete, one strategic mandate is clear: the problem of counter-asymmetrical-warfare strategy. The experience of the United States and its adversaries over the past quarter century or so is absolutely clear on this point: if one has to fight the Americans, do not fight them on their terms. That is the clear lesson of the first Persian Gulf War and the Afghanistan campaign of 2001. On the other hand, changing the rules—fighting asymmetrically—may offer a chance. The American withdrawal from Vietnam, the experience in Somalia, and possibly the long-term outcome in Iraq all point in this direction. Knowing this, it is clear that the development of a coherent and effective strategy to deal with countering the asymmetrical warrior should be among the highest strategic priorities for the United States, a position such strategy has never occupied in the past.

Conclusions

It goes without saying that the contemporary international environment represents a strategically challenging time, but it is probably an observation that most students of strategy would have made about their own times throughout history. It is certainly true that different times create different challenges, threats, and risks to be countered; what differentiates the times are the constellations of strategy and policy problems one encounters. In that sense, the current strategic environment is indeed unique.

What makes today different for the United States is its unique position in the international system. Through much of its history, the United States was a medium power whose importance began to expand in the early twentieth century. After World War II, US importance—and the responsibilities it brought—had expanded to the point that it was one of the two most important powers in the world, a superpower.

With the implosion of the Soviet Union, the United States is the only surviving superpower, a position in the world system that some analysts argue is akin to that of the Roman Empire. This status means the United States is the only country in the world with truly global interests and the means to pursue those interests. Regardless of the place or the situation, what the United States considers its interests to be matters. Those who fall under the shadow of US interests may not always like that fact, but they cannot avoid recognizing it.

This superiority extends to the military realm of strategists. It is both a matter of fact and policy that the United States is committed to retaining a military position second to no other country. As argued, this superiority is largely defined in terms of traditional, symmetrical capabilities, as those are defined in the contemporary scene. A consequence is that whenever military activity is proposed anywhere in the world, the question of US participation will be raised. Peacekeeping operations, such as those in African countries (e.g., Liberia) are a prime example.

Another consequence, which has been a featured part of arguments set forth here, is that no potential adversary of the United States is likely to be willing (or able) to confront the United States in a traditional military manner. As a result, the problem for a potential foe is how to negate the firepower and technological superiority that is at the heart of US military superiority, and it is the heart of the US strategic problem to devise ways to blunt the effects of that negation: counter-asymmetrical-warfare strategy.

As argued, this will be an evolving problem where opponents of the United States borrow from other's successes and failures in dealing militarily with the Americans. What are the lessons of the Iraqi resistance to US occupation, for instance, for future asymmetrical warriors? At the same time, what can the US military learn from that same experience as it prepares for other contingencies that may bear some resemblance to the threat in the Middle East but which may also be different, depending on the nature of the adversary and the physical setting in which it is preparing to fight? These are the most interesting strategic questions faced.

Bibliography and Suggested Readings

Arms Export Control Act. Public Law 90-629. *US Code.* Vol. 22, secs. 2751–99.

Bennett, Geoffrey. *The Battle of Jutland.* London: David and Charles, Ltd., 1980.

Brodie, Bernard. *The Atomic Bomb and American Security.* New Haven, CT: Yale University Press, 1945.

—————. *National Security Policy and Economic Stability.* New Haven, CT: Yale University Press, Institute of International Studies, 1950.

—————. *Strategy and National Interests: Reflections for the Future.* New York: National Strategy Information Center, 1971.

—————. *War and Politics.* New York: Macmillan, 1973.

Bush Doctrine, *National Security Strategy of the United States.* Washington, DC: The White House, September 2002. http://www.whitehouse.gov/nsc/nss/pdf.

Churchill, Sir Winston. Remarks. Conference with Franklin D. Roosevelt and Joseph Stalin, Teheran, Iran, 30 November 1943. http://www.loc.gov/exhibits/Churchill/wc-unity.html.

Clausewitz, Carl von. *On War.* Edited and translated by Michael Howard and Peter Paret. Princeton, NJ: Princeton University Press, 1976.

Collins, John M. *Grand Strategy: Principles and Practices.* Annapolis, MD: Naval Institute Press, 1973.

Drew, Col Dennis M., and Dr. Donald M. Snow. *Making Strategy: An Introduction to National Security Processes and Problems.* Maxwell AFB, AL: Air University Press, 1988.

English, J. A. "Kindergarten Soldier: The Military Thought of Lawrence of Arabia." *Military Affairs,* January 1987, 10.

Johnson, Pres. Lyndon B. Remarks. Texas Electric Cooperatives, Inc. dinner meeting, Austin, TX, 4 May 1965.

Keegan, Sir John. "In This War of Civilization, the West Will Prevail." *London Daily Telegraph,* 8 October 2001. http://www.telegraph.co.uk/opinion/main.jhtml?xml=%2Fopinion%2F2001%2F10%2F08%2Fdo01.xml.

Kennan, George F. *Measures Short of War: The George F. Kennan Lectures at the NWC 1946–47.* Edited by Giles D. Harlow and George C. Maerz. Washington, DC: National Defense University Press, 1991.

Liddell Hart, B. H. *Strategy*. New York: Meridian Printing, 1991.

Lind, William S.; Col Keith Nightengale, USA; Capt John F. Schmitt, USMC; Col Joseph W. Sutton, USA; and Lt Col Gary I. Wilson, USMCR. "The Changing Face of War: Into the Fourth Generation." *Marine Corps Gazette*, October 1989, 22–26.

Nixon, Pres. Richard M. "The Nixon Doctrine—'United States Foreign Policy for the 1970s: A New Strategy for Peace.'" Report presented to Congress 18 February 1970. http://www.presidency.ucsb.edu/ws/print.php?pid=2835.

Nuechterlein, Donald E. *America Recommitted: United States National Interests in a Restructured World*. Lexington, KY: University Press of Kentucky, 1991.

———. *A Cold War Odyssey*. Lexington, KY: University Press of Kentucky, 1997.

———. "National Interests and National Strategy." In *Understanding U.S. Strategy: A. Reader*, edited by Terry L. Heyns. Washington, DC: National Defense University, 1983.

Opie, Iona and Peter, eds. *The Oxford Nursery Rhyme Book*. New York: Oxford University Press, 1955.

Ramonet, Ignacio. "Servile States." Le Monde diplomatique, English ed., October 2002. http://mondediplo.com/2002/10/01servile.

Rhodes, Richard. *The Making of the Atomic Bomb*. New York: Touchstone Books, 1988.

Snow, Donald M. *UnCivil Wars: International Security and the New Internal Conflicts*. New York: St. Martin's, 1996.

———. *When America Fights: The Uses of U.S. Military Forces*. Washington, DC: Congressional Quarterly Press, 2000.

Snow, Donald M., and Dennis M. Drew. *From Lexington to Desert Storm: War and Politics in the American Experience*. Rev. ed. Armonk, NY: M. E. Sharpe, 2000.

Summers, Harry G., Jr. *On Strategy: A Critical Analysis of the Vietnam War*. Novato, CA: Presidio Press, 1982.

Van Creveld, Martin. *The Transformation of War*. New York: Free Press, 1991.

Vance, Cyrus, secretary of state. "US Foreign Policy: Our Broader Strategy," 27 March 1980, Department of State, Current Policy no. 153. Reprinted in *Case Study: National Security*

Policy under Carter, Department of National Security Affairs. Maxwell AFB, AL: Air War College, 1980–1981.

Waltz, Kenneth N. *Theory of International Politics*. New York: McGraw-Hill, 1979.

War Powers Resolution of 1973. Public Law 93-148. 93rd Cong., H. J. Res. 542, 7 November 1973. *US Code*. Vol. 50, secs. 1541–48.

Weigley, Russell F. *Eisenhower's Lieutenants: The Campaign of France and Germany 1944–1945*. Bloomington, IN: Indiana University Press, 1981.

Weinberger, Caspar. "The Uses of Military Power." Speech, National Press Club, Washington, DC, 28 November 1984.

Wylie, J. C. *Military Strategy: A General Theory of Power Control*. Annapolis, MD: Naval Institute Press, 1989.

Index

aerial bombardment, 166–68

Afghanistan, 23, 35, 47, 105, 107, 149, 159–60, 162, 164, 214, 225, 234–36, 239, 242, 256

Air Force, 21, 212

AirLand Battle, 207

airmen, 118–20, 126, 205, 208–9, 211–12, 216; worldview, 208

airpower, 9–10, 21, 47, 104, 124, 168, 207, 209, 214, 224, 226, 229; doctrine, 211–12

allies, Allies, 7, 14, 19, 57, 60, 72, 106, 112, 116–18, 136, 139, 144, 200, 202, 221, 226–28, 230

all-volunteer force, all-volunteer military, 224–25

al-Qaeda, 35, 47, 65, 107, 150, 159–60, 225

anti-asymmetrical-warfare, 234

anticolonialism, 132

anticommunist, 253

antiterrorism, 161–62

area bombing, 118, 173

Arms Export Control Act, 80, 99

Army, 21, 104, 207, 212, 224

artillery, 6, 23, 121, 138, 196, 206

asymmetrical warfare, 46, 65–67, 130–32, 135, 139–43, 150, 152–56, 158, 160–64, 180, 187, 197, 221, 231–39, 242, 244, 246–48, 256; strategies, 131, 197, 247

atomic bomb, 168, 187

Axis, 14, 41, 116–17, 182, 200

Ba'ath Party, 17

Baghdad, 16, 57, 67, 201, 223

Balkans, 113, 147, 225, 241

ballistic missile defense (BMD), 172, 184–87

Barbarossa complex, 71

Battle at Blenheim, 6

battlefield, 3, 5, 7, 11–15, 23–26, 62–64, 68, 109, 116, 127, 129, 138, 151–52, 179–80, 193, 196, 198, 201–3, 207, 215, 232, 238; strategy (tactics), 23–26, 116

Battle of Midway, 194

"benign hegemony," xiv

blockade, 117, 125, 198, 208

Bosnia, 23, 41, 107, 148, 164, 223, 225, 228, 241–43

Bush Doctrine, 41, 43, 51, 64, 84, 163, 176, 187, 231, 246

Bush, George H. W., 64

Bush, George W., 45, 68, 87, 165, 171, 185, 223; administration, 45, 68–69, 87–88, 149, 184–85, 223

Cable News Network (CNN), 96, 98, 145, 228

capability-based planning, 61

Carter Doctrine, 35, 84

Carter, Jimmy, 35, 99

casualties, 4, 9, 23, 64–65, 68, 117, 129, 137, 148, 153, 201, 224, 233, 235, 241–42

cease-fire, 124, 225

center of gravity (COG), 126–29, 140–41, 144, 147, 207, 238

Central Intelligence Agency (CIA), 85, 88–90

Chaing Kai-shek, 134

Chairman of the Joint Chiefs of Staff (CJCS), 85, 88, 234

chance (in warfare), 65, 78, 131, 154, 158, 191, 193–95, 239, 256

chief executive officer (CEO), 81

China, Chinese, 15, 64, 82, 134, 144–45, 185, 222, 251, 253–54

Civil War, 7–9, 71, 115, 126, 128–29, 133–35, 145, 200, 228, 251

Clausewitz, Carl von, 9, 54, 191–95

Clausewitzian trio, 191–95

Clinton, Bill, 41, 64, 68, 86–88, 90, 107, 185

CNN effect, 228

coalition of the willing, 227

Cold War, 10–12, 15–18, 20–21, 34, 38–42, 51, 56, 59–61, 67–68, 70–71, 84, 103, 105–7, 109, 111–13, 131, 133, 144–45, 165, 167, 171–72, 175, 179–81, 183–84, 186–87, 198, 211, 213, 221–22, 229, 250–51, 253–55

communism, communist, 15, 31, 39–40, 51, 61, 73, 251, 253–54

component campaigns, 121–22, 125

computer networks, 215–17

Confederacy, 126–27

Congress, 26, 44–45, 64, 78–84, 90–92, 96, 99, 121, 205, 213, 234
conservative bias (news media), 55, 60–61, 69, 96
Constitution, 79–80, 82, 90
containment policy, 15, 31, 36, 39–40, 60, 67, 251–53
continental school of strategy, 207
contingencies, 14, 19–20, 60, 62, 113, 246–47, 256–57
conventional war, 130, 140, 144, 180, 221, 223, 252
counter-asymmetrical-warfare, 163–64, 232, 247, 256–57
counterforce, 171, 173–76, 179
counterinsurgency, 142–43
counterintelligence, 138, 195, 214–15
counterterrorism, 161–62, 184
countervalue, 173–74, 176
Cuban missile crisis, 20, 85
cumulative strategies, 122–23
cyberspace, 3

decision making, 116; exercise, 87, 119; process, 14, 26, 107
declaratory strategy, 172–75, 177
Democratic People's Republic of Korea (DPRK), 58
Department of Agriculture, 18, 78
Department of Defense (DOD), 85, 87–88, 205
Department of Homeland Security, 61
deployment of forces, 20–21, 37, 65, 95, 103, 105–6, 110–13, 167, 177, 196, 198, 214, 252
Deputies Committee (DC), 33, 51, 85–87, 125, 187, 203, 248
Desert One, 19, 48
Desert Storm, See Operations
détente, 40
deterrence, deterring, 15, 20–21, 34, 59, 112, 166–68, 170, 172, 180, 182–84, 186, 222, 252
development of forces, 20, 23, 103, 105–6, 108–10, 112–13, 174, 177, 196–98, 201, 213–15
dilemmas, 107, 112–13, 191, 203, 219, 221, 231
diplomatic, 19, 31, 42, 44, 46, 48, 86
direct strategies, 124
Director of Central Intelligence (DCI), 85, 88–89

doctrine, 25, 35, 41, 43, 51, 64, 84, 99, 135, 139, 141, 163, 166, 176, 187, 191, 199–200, 203, 205, 207, 209–13, 217, 223, 228, 231, 242, 246–47, 253; joint doctrine, 205, 213
"draining the swamp," 47, 245

economic warfare, 196–98
Eisenhower, Dwight D., 12
11 September 2001 (9/11), 11, 37, 41–42, 47, 86, 90, 104–5, 146, 150, 152, 156, 228, 236, 246, 254
embedded journalists, 229
employment of forces, 3, 12, 20–22, 74, 79, 103–6, 110–13
ethnic cleansing, 123, 145, 147
executive branch, 77–79, 81, 86, 91
Executive Committee (ExComm), 85
expeditionary forces, 20, 106, 116

fifth column, 67
fighters, 23, 47, 122, 148, 211, 238–39
firebombing, 128
firepower, 5, 46, 63, 65–66, 109, 127, 138, 141, 154, 224, 233, 257
First Amendment, 97
first-strike capability, 173–75, 177–78
fog of war, 191–94
force deployment, 37, 103, 105–6, 110; strategy, 110
force development, 103, 105–6, 108, 110, 201; strategy, 108, 201
force employment strategy, 20, 42, 64, 103–8, 112, 172, 177
foreign policy, 31, 44, 49, 51, 55, 57, 68, 78, 84–86, 88, 93, 95, 99, 186
forward-deployed forces, 111
fourth generation warfare, 65, 131–32, 143, 147–52, 154–55, 158, 164, 237, 246, 255
Frederick the Great, 6–7, 12–13
French Revolution, 4, 7
friction in war, 39, 116, 191, 193, 195–96

Gadhafi, Mu'ammar, 159
Geneva conventions, 154
genocide, 145, 235
Germany, 18, 110, 118–19, 169, 206, 209, 211, 217, 227, 243; Schweinfurt, 118
global positioning system (GPS), 201
globalization, 41, 43, 49–50

Goldwater-Nichols Defense Reorganization Act of 1986, 88, 121, 205, 213
grand national strategy, 14, 17–24, 26, 31, 36, 38–39, 41, 50, 53, 55–57, 59, 67, 77, 92, 95, 98, 103, 206, 250
grand strategy actors, 77
Grant, Ulysses S., 115
gross domestic product (GDP), 45
ground forces, 106, 119–21, 206–8, 210, 224; worldview, 206
guerrilla, 12, 110, 125, 133–35, 138–39, 141–42, 163, 203, 232, 248
Gulf War, 19, 35, 57, 63–65, 80, 109, 124, 256

Haiti, 41, 145, 148, 159, 225, 241
heavy forces, 21, 110, 224
hegemonic power, 227
Hezbollah, 66, 159, 247
high technology, 11–12, 43, 63–64, 109
hijacking, 160
Ho Chi Minh, 16, 133, 135
Homeland Security Council, 86
homeland security, homeland defense, 21, 36–37, 61, 86, 103–6, 132, 160
hostage taking, 160
humanitarian relief, 225
Hussein, Saddam, 16–17, 35, 47, 54, 57, 74, 95, 113, 164, 183, 238, 240, 246, 248
hydrogen bomb, 167, 169
hyperpower, xiii

Inchon, 15
indirect strategies, 124
Industrial Revolution, 8–9, 115, 196
information warfare, 192, 213–16
inside-out approach, 124
instruments of national power, 3, 17, 19, 31, 42, 50
insurgencies, 132–33, 135–36, 138, 140, 143–47, 254; infrastructure, 135, 137–39, 142; warfare, 131–35, 139–43, 231
intelligence, 42, 57–59, 85, 88–90, 92, 136, 140, 142–43, 156, 162, 165, 192, 194, 214–15, 236
intercontinental ballistic missile (ICBM), 10, 167, 185
interest groups, 92–94
internationalist, xiii
Internet, 215

intifada, 66
Iran-Contra affair, 89
Iraq, Iraqi, 11, 16–19, 23, 35, 42, 45–48, 54, 57, 61, 63–64, 67, 80, 95, 97, 107, 113–14, 123–24, 130, 132, 134, 149, 153, 162–64, 183, 199, 201, 212, 222–25, 228–29, 233–39, 242–43, 246–48, 255–57
Irish Republican Army (IRA), 157
Israeli Defense Force (IDF), 158

Japan, Japanese, 71, 75, 123, 126, 128–29, 166, 194–95, 199; Hiroshima and Nagasaki, 166–68
joint campaigns, 118, 121–22; doctrine, 205, 213; worldview, 213
Joint Chiefs of Staff (JCS), 26, 85, 234
jointness, 119–20

Kennan, George F., 40, 51
Kennedy, John F., 85, 169
Khomeini, Ruhollah, 89
kidnapping, 160
Kissinger, Henry, 87
Korea, 15, 18, 23, 36, 58, 61, 67, 70, 74, 107, 110, 171, 182–83, 199–200, 251. See also North Korea (DPRK)
Kosovo, 23, 39, 41, 64, 107, 117, 123, 145, 148, 164, 223, 225, 228
Kuwait, 16, 223, 225

land forces, 115
Latin America, 84, 135, 225, 231
law enforcement, 156, 162
Lee, Robert E., 115
legislative branch, 90
Liddell Hart, Sir Basil, 54
linear warfare, 5
Linebacker II, 22
low intensity conflict (LIC), xv
loya jirga, 236

Maginot Line, 22
major interests, 34–35, 37–38, 50, 67, 249
Mao Tse-tung, 134
Marine Corps, 164, 224
maritime choke points, 208
McNamara, Robert S., 194
media (news), 83, 92, 95–98, 113, 130, 151, 201, 225
Middle East, 17, 59, 106, 113, 257

military budget, 26, 39, 54, 68–69, 88, 196, 212–13
military operations other than war (MOOTW), xiv
military strategy, 14, 19–24, 26, 31, 53, 74, 95, 103, 107–8, 112–13, 116, 122, 130, 156, 166, 170, 172, 177, 196, 198, 200, 205, 212–13, 254; coordination of, 108, 112
missile defenses, 167, 171, 180, 184–87
Missile Technology Control Regime (MTCR), 182
Mitchell, Billy, 212
modern warfare, 4, 7, 45, 108, 115, 118, 130, 150, 167, 196, 202, 209, 216
money, 48, 54, 91, 94, 127, 191, 216, 230, 245
Monroe Doctrine, 84
multiple independently targetable reentry vehicle (MIRV), 167
muskets, 5, 8, 150
Muslims, 145, 235

Nader, Ralph, 93
narco-insurgency, 144–45
nation building, 47, 149, 225, 239, 242–45
National Economic Council (NEC), 86
National Guard, 226
National Intelligence Estimates (NIE), 88
national interest matrix, 33
National Liberation Front, 133
national missile defense (NMD), 185–86
national security, 3, 14–15, 17–18, 20, 22, 24, 26, 37, 41, 51, 54–57, 59, 68–69, 75, 77–79, 83–93, 95–99, 115, 156, 176, 187, 223, 225, 249
National Security Act of 1947, 77, 79, 85
National Security Adviser (NSA), 85, 89
National Security Council (NSC), 26, 77–78, 81, 85–89, 187
national security objectives, 14–15, 17, 20, 22, 24, 115
national security policy, 55–57, 59, 75, 77–78, 83, 85–87, 90–91, 93, 99, 156
nationalism, 7, 132
NATO, xv, 34, 60, 71, 106, 117, 207, 222, 252
naval aviation, 121
naval forces, 43, 104, 115, 119–21, 207–8, 224

naval warfare, 121, 198
naval worldview, 207–8
Navy, 104, 128, 194
neoconservative, 41, 164, 184, 246, 255
net-centric warfare, 215
new internal wars (NIW), 144–45, 148, 163, 243, 255; warfare, 131–32, 237
new world order, 113, 222
Nicaragua, 34–36, 107
Nixon Doctrine, 84, 99, 253
Nixon, Richard M., 82
nonmilitary considerations, 8
nonstate actors, 31, 152–53, 155, 222–23, 238
Northern Alliance, 47, 214
Northern Ireland, 87, 157
North Korea (DPRK), 15, 58, 61, 171, 182–83
nuclear, biological, and chemical (NBC) proliferation, 181
nuclear confrontation, 10, 15, 165, 180
nuclear deterrence, 15, 112, 166–68, 172, 184, 222, 252
nuclearization, 59, 113
Nuclear Non-Proliferation Treaty (NPT), 182
nuclear strategy, 165, 167, 172, 174, 177, 179, 187; confrontation, 10, 15, 165, 180; deterrence, 15, 112, 166–68, 172, 184, 222, 252; containment, 15, 31, 36, 39–40, 60, 67, 251–53; stability, 177
nuclear war, 10, 15, 34, 66, 112, 140, 165–67, 170–72, 175–77, 179, 181, 183, 186–87, 211, 252; warfare, 130, 169, 211
nuclear weapons, 10, 15, 21, 34, 58–59, 105, 110, 130, 165–68, 170–73, 175–77, 179–81, 183–85, 211–12, 222, 251
Nuechterlein, Donald, 32–34, 36, 51

objective(s), 3, 10, 12–17, 20, 22–23, 25, 36, 39, 54, 56, 116, 121, 125, 140–41, 146–47, 157, 208–10, 242
operational strategy, 14, 22–24, 26, 69, 110, 115–16, 118, 120, 122, 125, 130, 195–96, 198, 212–13
Operations, Desert Storm, 151, 164, 210, 212, 225; El Dorado Canyon, 227; Iraqi Freedom, 214; Overlord, 206

operations tempo, ops tempo, 149, 224–25

orchestrating campaigns, 22–23, 115–16, 122, 125–26

Osama bin Laden, 157, 236, 238

outside-in approach, 124–25

Pacific, 16, 70, 110, 123, 128, 194, 199, 208

Palestinians, 43, 87, 158

parallel strategies, 123

peace dividend, 12, 68

peace enforcement, 240

peacekeeping, 65, 107, 145–46, 149, 225, 240–42; operations (PKO), 257

People's Republic of China, 82

peripheral interests, 34, 38, 67, 249

Persian Gulf War, 19, 35, 57, 63–65, 80, 109, 124, 256

Policy Coordination Committees (PCC), 85

political action committee (PAC), 92–93

political influences, 199

politico-military concepts, 13, 21–23

politics, 4, 7, 18, 25, 31–32, 53–54, 57, 107, 133, 144–45, 157, 164, 191, 199, 201, 230, 245, 249

post–Cold War world, 18, 107, 113, 180

Powell, Colin, 87

precision bombing, 173, 211

preemptive, 41, 84, 171–75, 177–78, 223–24

Principals Committee (PC), 85

proliferation, 4, 9, 176, 179–83, 187; NBC, 181; nuclear, vii; WMD, 165, 167, 180

Prussians, 6, 9, 54, 191

Quadrennial Defense Review, 41, 222

Reagan, Ronald, 38, 88–90, 185, 205

regime change, 17, 35, 47, 54

Reserve Officer Training Corps (ROTC), 230

retaliatory force, 21, 105, 112, 171–74, 176–79; raid, 159; threat, 183–84

revolutionary, 131–32, 134–35, 146, 215

revolution in military affairs (RMA), 62–65

Rice, Condoleezza, 89

rogue states, 184, 223

Roosevelt, Franklin D., 165, 217

Royal Air Force (RAF), 118, 211, 227

Rumsfeld, Donald, 87

Russian worldview (contrasted to US), 70–72

Rwanda, 145, 147, 149, 235

Saddam Hussein, See Hussein, Saddam

Schoomaker, Peter J., 234

sea control, 106, 119, 122, 208

second-strike capability, 173–76, 178–79

Sentinel and Safeguard systems, 185

sequential strategies, 122–23

shadow government, 136–37

Somalia, 41, 64, 107, 145, 148, 225, 228, 241, 256; Mogadishu, 64

Soviet Union, Soviets, 10–11, 15–16, 21, 33–35, 38–41, 49, 51, 59–60, 62, 71–73, 84, 90, 106–7, 109, 111–12, 116–17, 133, 144–45, 159, 169–71, 181, 183–85, 198, 221–22, 230, 251–54, 257

space-based systems, 4, 120, 192, 201

space power, 119

space warfare, 213–14

special forces, 47, 213–14, 217, 234

special operations, 213–14, 234

Special Operations Command (SOCOM), 234

State Department, 51, 84, 86–87, 99

stealth bomber, 227

Strategic Air Command (SAC), 21

strategic culture, 55, 69–71, 73

Strategic Defense Initiative (SDI), 91, 185

strategy, asymmetrical warfare, 131, 197, 247; battlefield (tactics), 23–26, 116; continental school of, 207; counterinsurgent warfare, 143; cumulative, 122–23; declaratory, 172–75, 177; direct, 124; graduated and parallel, 123; grand national, 14, 17–24, 26, 31, 36, 38–39, 41, 50, 53, 55–57, 59, 67, 77, 92, 95, 98, 103, 206, 250; indirect, 124; military, 14, 19–24, 26, 31, 53, 74, 95, 103, 107–8, 112–13, 116, 122, 130, 156, 166, 170, 172, 177, 196, 198, 200, 205, 212–13, 254; nuclear, 165, 167, 172, 174, 177, 179, 187; operational, 14, 22–24, 26, 69, 110, 115–16, 118, 120, 122, 125, 130, 195–96, 198, 212–13; sequential, 122–23

strategy dilemmas, 107, 112–13, 191, 203, 219, 221, 231
strategy making, 3, 7, 9, 18, 48, 50, 53, 55–56, 60, 77, 203, 210, 221
strategy process, 3–4, 7, 9, 13–14, 16–17, 20–21, 24–27, 31, 50, 55, 57, 70, 98, 103, 106–7, 191, 196, 205, 221, 228
Sun Tzu, 134, 153
superpower, 11, 15, 18, 38, 41, 50, 107, 112–13, 144, 256–57
surveillance, 4, 192
survivability, 174, 179
survival interests, 34, 56, 251
sustainment, 110

Taliban, 47, 105, 107, 159, 214, 225, 239, 242
technology, 4–5, 11, 25, 62–64, 73, 105–6, 109, 115, 121, 123–24, 127, 170, 182, 191, 197, 201–3, 226–27
terrorism, 33, 36–37, 49, 66, 68, 86, 131–32, 136–37, 143, 148–49, 152, 154–62, 164, 182, 184, 222, 237, 239, 246, 254–55; global war on, 41, 95, 146, 254; state-sanctioned, 159; state-sponsored, 159
terrorist(s), 12, 41, 47, 56, 61, 104–5, 107, 152, 154–59, 161–62, 180–82, 184, 225, 228, 238–39
Tet offensive, 97, 152
theater of operations, 22, 115, 122, 224
Third World, 59, 84, 107, 131–34, 144, 176, 212, 252–54
threat-based planning, 61
threat-based risks, 249
threats, 36, 39, 58, 61, 107, 170, 174, 183–84, 186, 192, 222, 249–51, 255–56
Treasury Department, 86
Truman, Harry S., 166
Turner, Stansfield, 89
24-hour news, 145, 228

unconventional warfare, 131, 253–54
unilateralism, xiii
United Nations Operation in Somalia (UNISOM), 241
United Nations Protection Force (UN-PROFOR), 241

US Air Force, 21, 212
US Army, 21, 104, 207, 212, 224
US Marine Corps, 164, 224
US Navy, 128, 194

Vietcong, 11, 23, 37, 62, 129, 133, 136, 152–53, 243
Vietminh, 16, 132–33, 136
Vietnam, 10–11, 15–16, 22–24, 37–38, 49, 62–63, 66, 70, 74, 91, 97, 107, 110, 123, 127, 129, 131–36, 151–53, 163, 194, 199–201, 205, 210, 212, 226, 228, 230–31, 233, 235, 237, 242, 248, 254, 256
vital interests, 15, 31–37, 39, 43, 50, 53, 56, 112, 145, 199, 249, 251, 255

warhead, 169, 179
War of 1812, 70, 103
war on terrorism, 41, 95, 146, 254
War Powers Act of 1973, 44
Warsaw Pact, 106, 207, 222, 252
watchdogging, 91, 96
weapons of mass destruction (WMD), 10, 47, 57, 95, 160, 171, 182, 184, 187, 223; proliferation, 165, 167, 180
Weinberger Doctrine, 199–200
Western Europe, 21, 34, 49, 59–60, 111–12, 207, 251–53, 255
White House, 51, 81, 83, 86–87, 89, 97–98, 161, 187
worldviews, 118–19, 126, 203, 205–7, 209, 212–13; airman's, 208; and military doctrine, 209; ground force, 206; joint, 213; naval, 207–8; Russian, 70–72
World War II, 10, 14–15, 22–23, 31, 36, 40, 44, 67–68, 71, 84, 89, 104, 107, 116–17, 119, 121–23, 126, 167–69, 173, 199–200, 202, 208–9, 211–12, 232, 243, 251, 256
World Wide Web (WWW), 105, 215
worst-case analysis, 112
worst-case scenarios, 221

Yamamoto, Isoroku, 71, 75
Yugoslavia, 64, 145